LIFE WITH
FATHER
AND MOTHER

With acknowledgments to the editors of *The New Yorker,* *Harper's Magazine, The Ladies' Home Journal, The Saturday* *Review of Literature, The New Republic,* and the *Literary Re-* *view* of the *New York Evening Post,* in which periodicals some of the chapters in this collection first appeared.

CONTENTS

—

GOD AND MY FATHER

LIFE WITH FATHER

LIFE WITH MOTHER

Contents

GOD AND
MY FATHER

GOD AND MY FATHER

In my boyhood, I never had a doubt that the beliefs they taught me were true. The difficulty was to live up to them, and to love God. Most of the time I was too busy to think of such things: but then a problem of conduct would face me, or a duty I had forgotten, or my own private feelings at night after saying my prayers, and at such times religion would confront me like a Sphinx in the landscape. I would stand before it like a hypnotized bird before some great ageless serpent, unable to think of or feel any way of escape.

I believed in the Bible. Creation, to me, meant a Creator. And since there was someone so great and powerful that He had created us all, I felt I had better learn His wishes. They were supposed to be good. I wanted to live in harmony with Him—no battle of wills. Yet I also wished greatly to get away and live as I liked.

If I could have been sure that the Creator was my ally or friend, that would have been a great comfort, in those days. It would have not only saved me from worry, it would have set me free to go about my business with confidence, both in Him and myself. Or if I could have surrendered myself to His rather bleak guidance, that again might have been a relief to me. But—I couldn't do it. I didn't quite trust Him or love Him enough to do that.

I thought of God as a strangely emotional being. He was powerful; He was forgiving yet obdurate, full of wrath and affection. Both His wrath and affection were fitful, they came and they went, and I couldn't count on either to continue: although they both always did. In short God was much such a being as my father himself.

What was the relation between them, I wondered—these two puzzling deities?

MY FATHER'S RELIGION

My father's ideas of religion seemed straightforward and simple. He had noticed when he was a boy that there were buildings called churches; he had accepted them as a natural part of the surroundings in which he had been born. He would never have invented such things himself. Nevertheless they were here. As he grew up he regarded them as unquestioningly as he did banks. They were substantial old structures, they were respectable, decent, and venerable. They were frequented by the right sort of people. Well, that was enough.

On the other hand he never allowed churches—or banks—to dictate to him. He gave each the respect that was due to it from his point of view; but he also expected from each of them the respect he felt due to him.

As to creeds, he knew nothing about them, and cared nothing either; yet he seemed to know which sect he belonged with. It had to be a sect with the minimum of nonsense about it; no total immersion, no exhorters, no holy confession. He would have been a Unitarian, naturally, if he'd lived in Boston. Since he was a respectable New Yorker, he belonged in the Episcopal Church.

As to living a spiritual life, he never tackled that problem. Some men who accept spiritual beliefs try to live up to them daily: other men, who reject such beliefs, try sometimes to smash them. My father would have disagreed with both kinds entirely. He took a more distant attitude. It disgusted him when atheists attacked religion: he thought they were vulgar. But he also objected to have religion make demands upon him—he felt that religion too was vulgar, when it tried to stir up men's feelings. It had its own proper field of activity, and it was all right there, of course; but there was one place religion should let alone, and that was a man's soul. He especially loathed any talk of walking hand in hand with his Saviour. And if he had ever found the Holy Ghost trying to soften his heart, he would have regarded Its behavior as distinctly uncalled for; even ungentlemanly.

The only religious leader or prophet I can think of who might have suited my father was Confucius—though even Confucius would have struck him as addled. Confucius was an advocate of peace, and of finding the path; and he enjoined the Golden Rule on his followers long before Christ. My father would not have been his follower in any of these. Finding "the path"? Not even Confucius could have made him see what that meant. He was too busy for that, too hot-tempered for peace, and the Golden Rule he regarded as claptrap; how could things work both ways? Whatever he did unto others he was sure was all right, but that didn't mean that he would have allowed them to do the same things to him. He saw other men as disorderly troops, and himself as a general; and the Golden Rule was plainly too mushy to apply in such circumstances. He disciplined himself quite as firmly as he tried to discipline others, but it wasn't necessarily by any means the same kind of discipline. There was one saying of Confucius', however, with which he would have agreed: "Respect spiritual beings—if there are any—but keep aloof from them." My father would have regarded that principle as thoroughly sound.

When Confucius was asked about the rule to return good for evil, he said: "What then will you return for good? No: return good for good; for evil, return justice." If my father had been asked to return good for evil he would have been even more pithy—his response would have consisted of a hearty and full-throated "Bah!"

If he had been let alone, he would have brought up his sons in this spirit. But my mother's feelings and teachings were different, and this complicated things for us. Like my father, she had accepted religion without any doubtings, but she had accepted more of it. She was far more devout. And she loved best the kind of faith that comforted her and sweetened her thoughts. My father didn't object to this at all—it was all right enough—for a woman: but it led to her giving us instructions that battled with his.

They both insisted strongly, for example, on our going to church, but they didn't agree in their reasons. It was the right thing to do, Father said. "But why do we have to go, Father?" "Because I wish to bring you up properly. Men who neglect going to church are a lazy, disreputable lot." A few might be good fellows, he would admit, but they were the exceptions. As a rule, non-churchgoers were not solid, respectable citizens. All respectable citizens owed it to themselves to attend.

My mother put it differently to us. She said we owed it to God. Church to her was a place where you worshiped, and learned to be good. My father never dreamed of attending for any such reason. In his moral instructions to us he never once mentioned God. What he dwelt on was integrity. My mother once wrote in my plush-covered autograph album, "Fear God and keep His commandments"; but the motto that Father had written on the preceding page, over his bolder signature, was: "Do your duty and fear no one." And nobody could tell him his duty—he knew it without that, it seemed. It wasn't written down in any book, certainly not in the Bible, but it was a perfectly definite and indisputable thing nevertheless. It was a code, a tradition. It was to be upright and fearless and honorable, and to brush your clothes properly; and in general always to do the right thing in every department of life. The right thing to do for religion was to go to some good church on Sundays.

When Father went to church and sat in his pew, he felt he was doing enough. Any further spiritual work ought to be done by the clergy.

When hymns were sung he sometimes joined in mechanically, for the mere sake of singing; but usually he stood as silent as an eagle among canaries and doves, leaving others to abase themselves in sentiments that he didn't share. The hymns inculcated meekness and submission, and dependence on God; but

Father was quick to resent an injury, and he had no meekness in him.

> "Jesus, lover of my soul,
>   Let me to thy bosom fly,
> While the nearer waters roll,
>   While the tempest still is nigh."

How could Father sing that? He had no desire to fly to that bosom.

> "Hide me, O my Saviour, hide,
>   Till the storm of life be past;
> Safe into the haven guide,
>   Oh receive my soul at last . . .
> All my trust on thee is stayed;
>   All my help from thee I bring;
> Cover my defenseless head
>   With the shadow of thy wing."

But Father's head was far from defenseless, and he would have scorned to hide, or ask shelter. As he stood there, looking critically about him, high-spirited, resolute, I could imagine him marching with that same independence through space—a tiny speck masterfully dealing with death and infinity.

When our rector talked of imitating the saints, it seemed drivel to Father. What! imitate persons who gave their whole lives to religion, and took only a perfunctory interest in the affairs of this world? Father regarded himself as a more all-round man than the saints. They had neglected nine-tenths of their duties from his point of view—they had no business connections, no families, they hadn't even paid taxes. In a word, saints were freaks. If a freak spent an abnormal amount of time being religious, what of it?

The clergy were a kind of freaks also. A queer lot. Father liked Bishop Greer and a few others, but he hadn't much respect for the rest of them. He thought of most clergymen as any busy man of action thinks of philosophers, or of those scholars who discuss the fourth dimension, which is beyond human knowing. He regarded the self-alleged intimacy of our rector with that fourth dimension most sceptically. He himself neither was nor wished to be intimate with a thing of that sort. But this didn't mean that he doubted the existence of God. On the contrary, God and Father had somehow contrived to achieve a serene and harmonious relation that the clergy themselves might have envied.

How did Father think God felt towards my mother? Why, about the way he did. God probably knew she had faults, but He saw she was lovely and good; and—in spite of some mistaken ideas that she had about money—He doubtless looked on her most affectionately. Father didn't expect God to regard *him* affectionately—they stood up man to man—but naturally God loved my mother, as everyone must. At the gate of Heaven, if there was any misunderstanding about his own ticket, Father counted on Mother to get him in. That was her affair.

This idea runs far back, or down, into old human thoughts. "The unbelieving husband is sanctified by the wife." (First Corinthians, vii, 14.) Medical missionaries report that today, in some primitive tribes, a healthy woman will propose to swallow medicine in behalf of her sick husband. This plan seems to her husband quite reasonable. It seemed so—in religion—to Father.

As to his mental picture of God, I suppose that Father was vague, but in a general way he seemed to envisage a God in his own image. A God who had small use for emotionalism and who prized strength and dignity. A God who probably found the clergy as hard to bear as did Father himself. In short Father and God, as I said, usually saw eye to eye. They seldom met, or even sought a meeting, their spheres were so different; but they had perfect confidence in each other—at least at most moments. The only exceptions were when God seemed to be neglecting His job —Father's confidence in Him was then withdrawn, instantly. But I'll come to this later.

As to the nature of God's sphere, namely Heaven, compared to Father's, the earth, Heaven wasn't nearly so solid and substantial. Father had all the best of it. Life here on earth was trying, but it shouldn't be—it was all right intrinsically—he felt it was

only people's damned carelessness that upset things so much.
Heaven on the other hand had a more serious and fundamental
defect: the whole place was thin and peculiar. It didn't inspire
much confidence. Father saw glumly that the time would come
when he'd have to go there, but he didn't at all relish the prospect. He clung to his own battered realm.

Yet its faults and stupidities weighed on his spirit at times: all
the chuckle-headed talk and rascality in business and politics. He
was always getting indignant about them, and demanding that
they be stamped out; and when he saw them continually spreading everywhere, it was maddening. Nature too, though in general
sound and wholesome, had a treacherous streak. He hated and
resented decay, and failing powers. He hated to see little children
or animals suffer. His own aches and pains were an outrage; he
faced them with anger. And aside from these treacheries, there
was a spirit of rebellion in things. He would come in from a walk
over his fields—which to me had seemed pleasant—oppressed by
the balky disposition both of his fields and his farmer. He would
get up from an inspection of his account books with the same
irritation: there were always some bonds in his box that hadn't
behaved as they should. And twice a day, regularly, he would
have a collision, or bout, with the newspaper: it was hard to
see why God had made so many damned fools and democrats.

I would try to persuade him sometimes—in my argumentative
years—that it would be better for him to accept the world as it
was and adapt himself to it, since he could scarcely expect to
make the planet over, and change the whole earth single-handed.
Father listened to this talk with suspicion, as to an advocatus
diaboli. If he ever was tempted to give in, it was only in his weak
moments; a minute later he was again on the warpath, like a
materialistic Don Quixote.

There was one kind of depression that afflicted Mother which
Father was free from: he never once had any moments of feeling
"unworthy". This was a puzzle to Mother, and it made her look
at Father with a mixture of awe and annoyance. Other people
went to church to be made better, she told him. Why didn't he?

He replied in astonishment that he had no need to be better—he was all right as he was. Mother couldn't get over his taking this stand, but she never could get him to see what the matter was with it. It wasn't at all easy for Father to see that he had any faults; and if he did, it didn't even occur to him to ask God to forgive them. He forgave them himself. In his moments of prayer, when he and God tried to commune with each other, it wasn't his own shortcomings that were brought on the carpet, but God's.

He expected a good deal of God, apparently. Not that he wanted God's help, of course; or far less His guidance. No, but it seemed that God—like the rest of us—spoiled Father's plans. He, Father, was always trying to bring this or that good thing to pass, only to find that there were obstacles in the way. These of course roused his wrath. He would call God's attention to such things. They should not have been there. He didn't actually accuse God of gross inefficiency, but when he prayed his tone was loud and angry, like that of a dissatisfied guest in a carelessly managed hotel.

I never saw Father kneel in supplication on such occasions. On the contrary he usually talked with God lying in bed. My room was just above Father's, and he could easily be heard through the floor. On those rare nights when he failed to sleep well, the sound of damns would float up—at first deep and tragic and low, then more loud and exasperated. Fragments of thoughts and strong feelings came next, or meditations on current bothers. At the peak of these, God would be summoned. I would hear him call "Oh God?" over and over, with a rising inflection, as though he were demanding that God should present himself instantly, and sit in the fat green chair in the corner, and be duly admonished. Then when Father seemed to feel that God was listening, he would begin to expostulate. He would moan in a discouraged but strong voice: "Oh God, it's too much. Amen. . . I say it's too damned much. . . No, no, I can't stand it. Amen." After a pause, if he didn't feel better, he would seem to suspect that God might be trying to sneak back to Heaven without doing anything, and I would hear him shout warningly: "Oh God!

I *won't* stand it! Amen. Oh damnation! A-a-men." Sometimes he would ferociously bark a few extra Amens, and then, soothed and satisfied, peacefully go back to sleep. . . And one night in the country, when the caretaker of our house in town telephoned to Father that the rain was pouring in through a hole in the roof, I heard so much noise that I got out of bed and looked over the banisters, and saw Father standing alone in the hall, shaking his fist at the ceiling, and shouting in hot indignation to Heaven, "What next?"

But Father was patient with God after all. If he didn't forgive, he forgot. His wrath didn't last—he had other things to think of —and he was genial at heart. The very next Sunday after an outburst he would be back in church. Not perhaps as a worshiper or a devotee, but at least as a patron.

MY FATHER AND HIS PASTORS

A man who accepts a religion without being religious lets himself in for more hardships than one would suppose. My father persisted most manfully in going to church; and he usually entered its portals at peace with the world and settled himself down contentedly in his end seat: but somehow before very long his expression would darken, as his hopes of hearing a sensible service little by little were dashed; and he came out in an inflamed state of mind that could not have been good for him.

The Episcopal service in general he didn't criticize; it was stately and quiet; but the sermon, being different every Sunday, was a very bad gamble. And once in awhile there would be an impromptu prayer that he would take great offense at. Sometimes he disliked its subject or sentiments—if he chanced to be listening. Sometimes he decided it was too long, or its tone too lugubrious. I remember seeing him so restive during a prayer of that kind, that—although the entire congregation was kneeling in reverence —he suddenly gave a loud snort, sat up straight in his pew, and glared at the minister's back as though planning to kick it.

I glanced over at Mother. She had been sailing along devoutly, as best she could, in the full tide of prayer, with the lovely rapt look that would come at such times on her face; but she had also begun to watch Father out of one eye—for whenever a prayer was longer than usual she feared its effect on him—and now here he was sitting up and she had to stop praying and turn away from God to this obstinate, obstinate man. "Put your head down," she whispered fiercely; and then, when he wouldn't, she felt so furious at him, and so impotent, and so guilty for having such feelings, and so torn between her yearning to sink back again into the sweet peace of prayer and her hot determination to make the bad boy in Father behave, that she sent him a look like a flash of lightning, shooting out through quick tears; indignant to the very roots of her red hair, and as hurt as a child. This sank into him. He never would at any time kneel in church—she had given up struggling for that—but at last with a deep angry growl he once more bent stiffly down.

Toward the latter part of his life Father found a minister whose sermons he liked. This was the Reverend Mr. Henshaw of Rye, where we lived in the summer. Mr. Henshaw wasn't "one of these pious fellows," Father said, with approval—though why piety was so unsuited to the clergy he never explained. And some years before this, one summer on the Hudson near Tarrytown, there was a Mr. Wenke, an earnest young cleric, who also found favor. But this was mostly because one of the vestry, old Mr. John Rutland, was very strict with Mr. Wenke about the length of his sermons. Mr. Rutland had got it into his head that all sermons should end at twelve, sharp; and if he saw Mr. Wenke being carried away by his own eloquence, he would take out his watch and stare ominously, first at him, then at it. Pretty soon Mr. Wenke's roving eye would be caught and held by this sight. He would falter or sometimes almost choke in the midst of his flow, then lamely end his remarks, and get out of the pulpit.

In the city at this same later period Father went to St. Bartholomew's, and there too the various clergymen suited him, though not quite so well. He liked St. Bartholomew's. The church itself was comfortable, and the congregation were all the right sort. There was Mr. Edward J. Stuyvesant, who was president of three different coalmines, and Admiral Prentice who had commanded the Fleet, and old Mr. Johns of the *Times;* and bank directors and doctors and judges—solid men of affairs. The place was like a good club. And the sermon was like a strong editorial in a conservative newspaper. It did not nag at Father, it attacked the opposition instead; it gave all wrong-headed persons a sound trouncing, just the way Father would have.

Mother didn't enjoy these attacks. Denunciations upset her. She took almost all denouncing personally, as directed at her, and it made her feel so full of faults that she trembled inside, though she looked straight back up at the preacher, round-eyed and scared but defiant. She preferred something healing, and restful; some dear old tale from the Bible. But denunciations satisfied Father. He liked something vigorous. And in general he instinctively took to the Established Church pattern—a church managed like a department of a gentleman's Government. He liked such a church's strong tory flavor, and its recognition of castes. He liked its deference to sound able persons who knew how to run things, and its confidence in their integrity and right point of view. In effect, it put such men on their honor, without foolishly saying so. No other approach would have found a way into their hearts.

But nothing is perfect. After Father had made himself at home in this reliable temple, he discovered too late that even here a man wasn't safe. The rector began talking about the need for what he called a New Edifice. He said the church had a leak in the roof, and the neighborhood was changing to business, and that they had received a good offer for the property and had better move elsewhere. This gave Father an unsettled feeling. He wished to stay put. But the rector kept stirring things up until he at last got his way.

Committees were appointed, and active teams of workers were organized, who began to collect large subscriptions from every parishioner. Father paid no attention to all this. It was no plan of his. If they insisted on having better quarters, he would try to enjoy them, but aside from this effort the rest of it was not his affair. It was only when he was made to see that he too would have to subscribe, that Father became roused and startled. This had never occurred to him. He said he might have known it was just a damn scheme to get money.

He was still more upset when Mother told him what sum was expected of him. He had imagined that they would want fifty dollars, or even a hundred; and that was enough to depress him. But she said that since he had bought a good pew they would expect him to give several thousand. This was like an earthquake.

Father in fact took it as some wild cataclysm of nature, some unheard-of violent destruction of an honest citizen's peace. After roaring out that the rector and his Christian workers could all go to hell, he barricaded himself every evening in his cyclone cellar —the library—and declared he wouldn't see any callers. This lasted a week. Then when he had cooled down a little, Mother had a long talk with him, and told him who were on the committee—some men whom he liked. She said he would really have to subscribe. He'd at least have to see them.

He waited, fretful and uneasy, for the attack to begin. One night when Mother was sitting in her room, there were sounds of talk in the library. She hurried down the passageway, clutching her needle and mending, and listened at the door. Father was doing all the talking, it seemed. He was stating his sentiments in his usual round tones, strong and full. He got more and more shouty. Mother began to fear the committee mightn't like being scolded. But when she opened the door on a crack and peeked in, there was no one in there but Father. He was in his easy-chair, talking away, with his face all puckered up, and he was thumping his hand with a hammer-like beat on his newspaper. "In ordinary circumstances," he was saying to the imaginary committeemen, "in ordinary circumstances I should have expected to subscribe to this project. But during the past few years my investments" (thump, thump, on the newspaper) "have shown me heavy losses." Here he thought of the New Haven Railroad and groaned. "*Damned* heavy losses!" he roared, and flung the paper aside. "Who the devil's that? Oh, it's you, Vinnie. Come in, dear Vinnie. I'm lonely."

I don't recall how much he gave in the end, but I think it was a thousand dollars. The reason Mother thought that he would probably have to give more, was that our pew was way up in front; it was—so to speak—in a fine section. All our neighbors were prominent. There may have been plenty of ordinary Christians in other parts of the building, but I did not see them. Furthermore this pew, though a small one, had cost Father five thousand dollars, and parishioners were being asked to give as

much as the cost of their pews. Father had hated to invest all
that money in a mere place to sit, but he could sell out again
some day, and meanwhile he had a good pew. He rented the
one in Rye for a hundred and twenty dollars a year, but a
family that wanted a good pew at St. Bartholomew's in those
old days used to buy it. They went to the sexton or somebody,
and told him what size and so forth, and after awhile he would
negotiate a purchase for them from some other parishioner. Pews
were like seats on the stock exchange. Nobody speculated in pews,
of course, and they rarely changed hands; but they went up and
down in price, naturally, as the demand rose or fell; and after
Father had bought his—most unwillingly—from old Mr. Baggs,
he used to ask Mother periodically for the current quotation.
Mother disliked to get this. It obliged her to ask the sexton, who
was dignified, and who didn't like to quote pews; and another
objection was that after Father bought they went down in value.
When she came home with the news that the last sale had been
for thirty-two hundred, Father said she had led him into this
against his own better judgment, and now the bottom was drop-
ping out of the market and he never would get his money back.
"Old Baggs, *he* knew. He was a shrewd one," he declared. "Egad,
yes! He knew when to sell." And he swore that if that damned
pew ever went up again he would unload it on somebody.

When the church moved away from its old quarters, Father
wouldn't go with them. After having had to help build a New
Edifice which he had not wanted, he felt he'd had enough of
such experiences and needed a rest; and he stopped going to
church altogether, except in the country.

All during my childhood, before our St. Bartholomew period
started, we went to a more homelike church that was less rich
and fashionable. It was squeezed in between some old houses on
Fifth Avenue near Tyson's Market, and it had a choir of men
and boys in surplices, who sang mellow chants, and a narrow but
high vaulted roof that rang with the organ music, and stained
glass with deep colors; and best of all I thought was Mr. Dryden,
the sexton, who had extraordinarily long pointed whiskers that

waved in the air when he was in a hurry—a pair of thin curly streamers. He nearly always was in a hurry, and I liked attending this church.

Nowadays there is an office-building there, as tall as a dozen such churches, the air is full of gasoline and the avenue is shut in and darkened; and the powerful traffic throbs by with a tense, roaring hum. But when I was a boy the low houses were set back from broad sidewalks, there was fresh air and plenty of room, and window boxes of flowers; and a bit of green here and there, trees or ivy; and a wide field of sky.

I suppose that the reason we went to this church that I speak of, the Church of the Peace Everlasting, was because it stood near our home. Its name, at least so far as Father was concerned, was a mockery, for he suffered most cruelly there. Yet he went there for years. Yes, and he kept right on going without any question of changing. He disliked change more than he did suffering. In the end he burst out and bought his liberty along with Mr. Baggs' pew—so the latter was cheap after all: but he lost the best years of his life at the Peace Everlasting.

The clergyman there was the Reverend Dr. Owen Lloyd Garden. He was a plump, bustling man, very good-hearted and pleasant; though in spite of his good-heartedness and kindness I never felt at ease with him. He never seemed to speak to me personally, but to a thing called My Child. He was more at home speaking to a large audience than to a small boy, however. He had warm and sympathetic feelings toward people en masse. The congregation responded to this quality in him, and liked him; and he not only kept the pews filled but he sometimes attracted such crowds that Mr. Dryden would scurry by with his whiskers flying straight out behind him, putting chairs in the aisle.

Dr. Garden had come over to New York from England, but by descent he was Welsh. He had a broad red face, thick black hair, and a square blue-black beard. His robes were red, black and white. His strong English accent was a point in his favor, in an Episcopal church; it seemed to go well with the service. But owing we understood to his Welsh descent he was very emotional, and he used to plead with us at times in his sermons, in a sort of high mellow howl. My father disliked this. In the first place he heartily detested having anyone plead with him; in the second place Dr. Garden seldom could plead without crying. It wasn't put on at all; he was deeply moved by his own words. The atmosphere became tense and still when he leaned from his pulpit, and stretched out his arms yearningly to us, and sobbed, "Oh, my people." The whole church was hushed. At such moments Father would testily stir in his seat. "The damned Welshman, there he goes sniveling again," he would mutter.

This would horrify Mother. From her end of the pew she would signal him that he must stop. If he didn't notice, she would tell my small brothers to pass word along to me that I must make Father keep still. It was like expecting a boy to make the jungle behave. The most I felt up to was to get him to see Mother's signals, and that meant that I had to pull myself together and poke him. This was nervous work. He was a muscular, full-barreled man; there was nothing soft in him to poke; and he had a fiery way even of sitting still. It was like poking a stallion. When he became aware that he was being prodded, by my small, timid finger, he would turn fiercely upon me and I would hastily gesture toward Mother. Mother would whisper, "Clare! You mustn't!" and he would reply, "Bah!"

"Oh, Clare!"

"I know, Vinnie; but I can't stand that damned—"

"Sh—sh! Oh, hush!"

Another thing he detested was the picture Dr. Garden drew, sometimes, of a business-man sitting in his office at the close of his day. Dr. Garden didn't cry over this, to be sure, but he grew gentle and solemn—he spoke as though he himself were standing at that business-man's side, like an unseen Presence, a loving Good Influence, evoking the man's better self. He apparently had only the haziest ideas of a business office, but he drew on his imagination freely to fill in the picture. He would describe how this hard-headed man sat there, surrounded by ledgers, and how after studying them closely and harshly for hours he would chance to look out of his window at the light in God's sky, and then it would come to him that money and ledgers were dross. Whereat, as the gathering twilight spread over the city, this strange wax-work figure of a business-man would bow his head, and with streaming eyes resolve to devote his life to Far Higher Things.

"Oh damn," Father would burst out, so explosively that the man across the aisle jumped, and I would hear old Mrs. Tillotson, in the second pew behind, titter.

Aside from the wild untruth of such pictures of business, from Father's point of view the whole attitude involved was pernicious. Anyone dreamy enough to think of money as "dross" was bound to get himself in hot water; that went without saying; it was a sign both of ignorance of, and of disrespect for, finance. Father had more respect for finance than he had for the church. When he left the financial district behind him to visit the church, he felt as I suppose Moses felt coming down from the mountain. Moses found people blind to his mountain and worshiping a calf idiotically, and Father found Dr. Garden capering around something he called Higher Things. Well, let him caper if he wanted to—that was all he was good for. My father was a more charitable Moses who expected no better. But this flighty parson went further—he wanted Moses to join him! Betray finance for this stuff and nonsense! It was enough to make a man sick.

It was Father's custom to put one dollar in the contribution plate weekly, no more and no less. When Mr. Gregg brought the plate to our pew, Father would first pass it on to us, and we boys would each thump in a nickel, trying to produce a loud ringing sound, as though it were a quarter; and Mother would quietly slip in her offering in a tight little roll; more than she could afford to give, probably, and saved up God knows how. Then Father would hand the plate back to Mr. Gregg, who would patiently wait, while Father took out and unfolded a crisp new dollar bill, and drew it through his fingers so as to make a little crease in it, lengthwise, and laid it out flat on top of everything else, large or small.

This dollar was apt to become the subject of a debate, going home. Mother felt there were Sundays when such a sum was not enough. It bothered her dreadfully, after a sermon that had described some great need, to see Father, absolutely unmoved, put in only his dollar.

Father's first gun in reply was that a dollar was a good handsome sum, and that it would be better for Mother if she could learn this. He had a great deal to say on this point. His second gun, which he would then fire off at her with still more enjoyment, was that any money he gave to the church would be wasted —it would be spent by a pack of visionary enthusiasts in some crazy way. "Sending red-flannel weskits and moral pocket-handkerchiefs to the heathen," he quoted.

But after awhile Mother found a counter-argument which actually beat both of his: she made him feel that it was beneath his own dignity not to put in more, sometimes. Even then he didn't surrender; he compromised instead on this method: before starting for church, he put his usual dollar in his right-hand waistcoat pocket, but in the left-hand pocket he put a new five-dollar bill; and he stated that from now on he would make a handsome offer to Garden: let him preach a decent sermon for once and he would give him the five.

This made every sermon a sporting event, in our pew. When Dr. Garden entered the pulpit we boys watched with a thrill, as though he were a race-horse at the barrier, jockeying for a good start. He looked rather fat for a race-horse, but he was impressive and confident, and it was kind of awe-inspiring to see him go down every time to defeat. He always either robbed himself of the prize in the very first lap by getting off on the wrong foot— a wrong key of some sort—or else in spite of a blameless beginning he would fail later on: he would as it were run clear off the course that Father had in silence marked out for him, and gallop away steadily and unconsciously in some other direction. It gave a boy a sobering sense of the grimness of fate.

"I don't see what the matter was today," Mother would declare, going home. "You should have given more than a dollar today, Clare. It was a very nice sermon." But Father would

MY MOTHER'S DISCOVERY

In spite of his warlike behavior in our hours of worship, Father seemed to me one of the mainstays and chiefs of the church. On weekdays he was a layman, struggling violently with his environment—his business, his family, his home-life, the cook and the coffee—and in general with the natural heat of his feelings among all these antagonists. But on Sundays, after breakfast was over, and the coffee and its sins had departed, and Father had peacefully finished his morning cigar, he put on his shining high hat and he marched us to church; and there, on the end of our pew, was a silver plate with his name on it; and the organ music was rolling and solemn, and Father was a pillar of God.

I felt sure that he was a very good pillar too, and better than most. Better than Mr. Gregg, for instance, who was the church treasurer, and who was a devout but slouchy old Christian with an overdressed wife. And as good as Colonel Hamilton—well-groomed, military-looking, patrician—who seemed to a little Episcopalian like me the very essence of Christianity.

But these other pillars were vestrymen, and Father was not. They seemed to "belong" more than he did. Father didn't happen to want to be a vestryman, but he couldn't be anyhow. I don't recall how I became aware of it; but there was an obstacle.

And another thing, there was a mysterious rite called communion, with soft music in it, and a great deal of whispering and murmuring by Dr. Garden; amid which the congregation, a few at a time, left their pews, and crowded irregularly forward and knelt at the altar. Dr. Garden then said something to each of them, and gave each one a drink; a very small drink from a very large goblet of gold. When all of that group had had theirs, they walked back to their seats, and others passed forward and knelt.

I could see the soles of their shoes. Colonel Hamilton had his soles blacked, and they looked trim and elegant; but Mr. Gregg's were almost worn-out, and as stubby as mine.

This rite came after the regular service, it was a separate matter, and less than half of the congregation "stayed for communion." Mr. Gregg always stayed. Colonel Hamilton was more independent—he only stayed when he liked. Mother stayed as regularly as Mr. Gregg did. But Father not once.

There was some tension between Father and Mother about this, I felt; but they didn't discuss it before me. She never asked him to stay. She never even asked if he were going to. It was understood that he wasn't. He walked home ahead with us boys, feeling as lively as we did; and Mother arrived twenty minutes later for our one o'clock Sunday dinner. Once in a while she was half-an-hour later, and Father said "Damn."

The principal course at our Sunday dinners was a great roast of beef, surrounded by fat roasted potatoes and rich Yorkshire pudding. They were all piping hot, and when Father carved the beef it ran juices. We were not allowed to play with our toys on Sundays, and we had to wear our best clothes, but that dinner was some compensation. Afterward we read, or took walks. There were no week-ends out of town in those days, and golf was almost unknown to us. Father usually read Hume and Smollett's *History of England,* with his head nodding more and more over it, and his cigar going out. I think it must have been on one of those long afternoons, that Mother, when she thought I was old enough, explained about Father.

She said nobody could go to communion who had not been confirmed. Everybody was baptized, as a baby, to make him a Christian; that was the first step; but to be a full member of the church, one had to learn the creed and the catechism, and go up to the altar, and promise to do and believe everything that his godfathers had promised for him. And the bishop would then lay his hands on him, so he could go to communion.

She said she hoped I would be confirmed when I was thirteen or fourteen, but it must be of my own free will and choice, for it was a great step to take. Father hadn't taken it yet, she confided. She didn't say why.

I took Mother's prayer-book upstairs with me and looked up the baptism service, to see what my godfather had committed me to, with his promises. Mr. Currier was my only living godfather. He had gone pretty far. He had renounced the Devil and all his works, on my behalf, and the pomps and vanities of this wicked world, and the sinful lusts of the flesh. Mr. Currier was such a good old man he had probably thought nothing of it; but I wondered whether I would ever feel up to "renouncing" all that.

I asked Mother a great many questions about confirmation, and from what she said I saw that I'd have to be confirmed by and by. I couldn't get out of it. It wouldn't be fair to Mr. Currier for me to refuse, and leave him responsible to God for my sins all my life.

I looked over the catechism. It was long. It would be hard to learn all that by heart. I inquired whether Father knew the catechism. But Mother said not to ask questions.

My head at once felt full of questions, such as who Father's godfather was, and how much longer he'd wait, and whether he didn't ever get cross about Father's delay.

But it made Mother cry when I asked these. She said I would know by and by. She said Father had been very busy and had had to work very hard; and that she hoped he would be confirmed soon, when he had a little more time.

Mother evidently had her heart set on Father's learning the catechism and letting the bishop lay his hands on him; but Father didn't feel like it. And the rest of the story, as I heard it later, was this:

When Mother married Father she had naturally supposed that he was a good churchman. She had asked him what church he belonged to, and he had replied "The Episcopal." But as time went on she found that his association with it was vague.

Father's parents had been so fond of Mother and she had liked them so much, that it hadn't even occurred to her to cross-question them about Father's upbringing. His mother was a saint on earth, sweet and good; everyone loved her. His father was a newspaper publisher; philosophic and humorous. But it turned out that Grandpa's favorite authors were Voltaire and Shakespeare: he read almost nothing else, but his newspaper; and he had no use for religion. He had been brought up so strictly that he had got his fill of it, and had dismissed the whole subject.

Father had accordingly run about and done as he pleased. It was only through one of his schoolboy friends that he happened to go to a Sunday School. This school gave a party of some kind, at which they served cake; it was good cake, and whenever they had it Father went to that Sunday School.

When he grew older and decided that it was the proper thing to go to church sometimes, it seems that he had picked out an Episcopal church for this purpose. Not being a free-thinker, like my grandfather, he had approved of religion. But beyond this he hadn't looked into it. He had seen no necessity.

This rudimentary and semi-automatic approach to the church, as by a kind of molecular attraction, seemed pathetic to Mother. She was maternal, and she was compassionately eager to help Father in, and make him as good a churchman as anyone. But Father had felt he was already in, and to be confirmed was unnecessary. He didn't understand at all clearly what confirmation was anyhow. He declared it was only some folderol. He refused to be bothered with it. This was the root of all those conversations about whether he'd go to Heaven, when Mother said that to be on the safe side he ought to be confirmed first, and Father said that getting him into Heaven was her affair.

But this wasn't the worst. I don't know when Mother found out the whole truth about Father, but I don't think she knew it when she and I had those first talks. If not, it may have been my asking questions that led her to ask more herself, and thus to stumble on a strange and upsetting discovery.

Still, the discovery would have been almost sure to come some day. It was mere luck it hadn't come sooner. Nobody had purposely hidden Father's story from Mother—least of all poor

Father himself. He never kept anything from her. Not that he didn't try to; but he was far too unguarded to have any secrets.

I remember Father once had his pocket picked on the street-car, coming home. As an old New Yorker, born and bred, he was ashamed of this incident. He was also provoked; and when he unlocked the front door and came in, he was swearing to himself in loud whispers. Mother was upstairs in her room. She heard Father talking away to himself in the front hall, as he hung up his coat. "Damned rascals! if I ever catch them——." He flung his cane in the rack. "Not a word. I shan't say a word about it," he went on, to himself. He stamped up the stairs, muttering, "Yes, too much talk in this house." "Well, Vinnie," he said to Mother, and sat himself down by the fire, in what he evidently meant to be an impenetrable and innocent silence.

"Clare!" Mother said sharply.

"What is it?"

"Clare! What's the matter with you? What has happened?"

"Damnation!" Father said. "What's happened? How do you know that it's happened? There's entirely too much talk in this house. A man can't have any privacy in his own home, that's what it comes down to. I had my pocketbook stolen, that's what's happened. Are you satisfied now?"

"Your pocket-book? Oh! Why did you let them?"

"Let them!" said Father. "Good God! They picked my pocket on the street-car, I tell you. I had it when I left the club."

"Oh, Clare dear! How could you! You must be getting old. Did you have the cook's wages in it?"

Father sprang from his chair in a fury and left the room, saying: "I knew you'd ask that. Yes, damn it, I had the cook's wages. I want this prying to stop." And afterwards, when he came down to dinner, he was bursting to tell the whole story— just how a young whipper-snapper had jostled him, and what he had said to the fellow, while a confederate had stolen his money and jumped off the car. He added, with a baffled look at Mother, that he didn't know how she found out things.

"She finds out every damn thing I ever do," I heard him say

later, in his bathroom, in honest bewilderment. He usually chose the bathroom at night for his private communings, although an air-shaft connecting with the other bathrooms carried his words through the house.

A man who was so unselfconscious would have betrayed his religious shortcomings completely and promptly, if he himself had known the facts. Grandpa knew the facts, but they had seemed to him of no importance. So it wasn't until Mother chanced to ask him directly one day what church Father had been baptized at, that Grandpa said Father had never been baptized at all.

I doubt if I can even imagine what a shock this was to Mother. This was in the conventional eighteen-eighties, when women led sheltered lives, and when men in general conformed to religious requirements. Mother must have felt that she could hardly believe her own ears. She had taken it for granted that everyone in a civilized country was baptized as soon as he was born as a matter of course. She had never met or known about any man, woman or child, who had even dreamed of not being baptized. It was simply unheard of. Why, all the poor Indians in Mexico belonged to some church. Even in the wildest lands, anywhere, there were so many missionaries, that every half-naked savage—with any luck at all—seemed to get baptized. Yet here was her own husband—!

Grandpa explained to her that his idea had been to leave Father free: let the boy grow up and decide all such things for himself. As to Grandma, well, she always spoke of Grandpa as Mr. Day, and she was surprised to hear Mother take on so about this. She said to her gently and patiently, "But Vinnie, dear child, that was the way Mr. Day wished it; and he's generally right."

Mother didn't feel this way at all. She thought Grandpa was wrong about lots of things, and she always told him so to his face. Grandpa liked nothing better. She was young and impulsive and pretty, and very direct, and he used to egg her on by arguing with her in the most outrageous ways he could think of.

But this time there wasn't any argument, so far as I ever heard. Mother couldn't wait; she hurried home to Father with her terrible news, supposing that as soon as he heard it he would be baptized at once. There was some excuse for not being confirmed, since not everyone did it, but nobody would defy God to the extent of not at least being baptized. She had her second great shock when he flatly refused. He was dressing for dinner at the moment, and he said she must not interrupt him. Although he was surprised and displeased to hear he hadn't been christened, he at once declared that nothing could be done to correct matters now.

Mother cried when she talked with me about it, and couldn't give me his reasons. She didn't seem to think that he had any. He was just being obstinate. But I was sometimes allowed to be present when they debated the matter, and this gave me a picture—of some sort—of his state of mind.

"I simply can't understand why you won't be baptized," Mother said. "Clare dear, tell me, aren't you a Christian?"

"Why, confound it, of course I am a Christian," Father roundly declared. "A damned good Christian too. A lot better Christian than those psalm-singing donkeys at church."

"Oh hush, Clare!" Mother always was terrified when he bordered on blasphemy.

Now to say "hush" to Father was like pouring kerosene on a fire. I repeatedly saw Mother try to quench his flames in this way, and every such effort only made him blaze higher—far higher. Yet she tried it again the next time. Neither she nor Father seemed to study the other one's nature. They each insisted the other one's nature should work in some way it didn't. I never once saw either of them observe the other in a calm, detached spirit, to see how his or her ego operated, and how to press the right button. Instead they invariably charged at each other full tilt, and learned unwillingly and dimly—if at all—by collisions.

So Mother said "hush" to Father, and the conflagration was on. And Father, being maddened by the kerosene, swore more and more, and declared that there was no need whatever for him to go and get baptized, and that he was quite as good a Christian as Owen Lloyd Garden.

"But if you won't be baptized," Mother wailed, "you aren't a Christian at all."

Father said he would not be baptized, and he would be a Christian. He begged to inform Mother he would be a Christian in his own way.

In her desperation Mother went to Dr. Garden and pledged him to secrecy, and revealed to him the horrible fact that Father had never been baptized. Dr. Garden was greatly astonished, but said he would attend to it. He was still more astonished when he learned that he would not be allowed to.

Mother tried to explain Father's plan of being his own kind of Christian. Dr. Garden was agitated. He didn't seem to know what to make of this. He said it had never been heard of. Not even the Apostles had omitted being baptized, he explained. If Mr. Day was going to set himself above the Holy Apostles—

Mother felt more frightened than ever at this dreadful picture. That would be just like Father, she felt. That was exactly what he would do.

people it should come only when one was young. Since it hadn't
been attended to in his own case, why, let it go, damn it. It would
be ridiculous to baptize him now. It was far too late to do anything. He wasn't to blame. He would have been perfectly willing
to be baptized as a child, if they had done the thing soon enough.
Since they hadn't, it was no fault of his, and he didn't intend to
be bothered.

It was useless to try to make him see that being baptized was a
rite, and that it involved something holy and essential. He said
it was a mere technicality. As to obeying the Bible, there were
a lot of damn things in the Bible. A man would be in a pretty
fix if he gave all he had to the poor. No, a man had to use his
common-sense about obeying the Bible. And everything else. If
he had any.

He seemed to imagine that if he ever came to be tried, by his
God, he could easily establish the fact that his position was sound.
In any event, he wasn't going to be led around by the nose by
a parson. He didn't blame Mother for being upset; she was only
a woman; but even she would come to her senses eventually, and
see he was right.

At this point I went to Mother and asked her if she would let
me help out. It all seemed so simple and plain to me, that I was
sure I could make Father see it. I was in that stage between
infancy and adolescence when children will do strange things.
Besides, I wasn't neutral: it always upset me and shook me to
see Mother unhappy; and the strong emotional vortex before
me at last drew me in. Mother was pleased by my wanting to
help her, and said I might try. Perhaps she thought Father's
heart would be touched by the plea of his child. Needless to say,
he was not touched at all; he was merely disgusted.

I can see him now, ruddy and strong, and a little too stout, in
his evening clothes and bulging white shirt-front. He lit his
cigar after dinner, blew out a rich cloud of smoke, and took a sip
of his coffee. "God bless my soul," he said, heartily, and tasted
his cognac. "A—men!" He looked over at me. "It doesn't count
unless you say A—men," he said, with a wink.

I didn't smile back. I was worriedly waiting for an opening, and counting my weapons.

I had been reading a little devotional book. I don't recall ever willingly reading a book of that kind before; but this time it was almost a pleasure, because I wasn't reading it for my own improvement but Father's. The author was a person who wrote in a superior tone, and who seemed to feel bored and condescending when he explained things to groundlings. I immediately planned to use Father as my groundling, if possible, and to talk in such a calm, easy way to him, that he'd feel impressed. This author, for example, declared that baptism was "of course a matter of religious joy to any right-minded Christian." He also said that when we were baptized we were "buried with Christ." He went on to state that "remission of sins" was badly needed by everyone, and "it is absurd to suppose that we can be buried with Christ without receiving remission of sins." Things like that.

I tried, but without any success, to explain all this to Father. I also told him about a man called Nicodemus, who had argued against being baptized; and how he had been sternly refuted, and warned to behave himself.

But Father said he wasn't interested in Thing-a-ma-jig—Nicodemus. And I might have known, myself, that he took small stock in arguments. If he had ever debated things with me he might easily have won me over; but it didn't interest him, usually, to engage in discussion. He didn't care to marshal his reasons or describe the road he had taken. He preferred to begin by stating his conclusion, and by calling yours nonsense, and to end the debate then and there. There was nothing else to be said.

My picture of him, therefore, was that of a man blind and deaf to the anxious and intelligent warnings of Dr. Garden and me.

I was supposed to be a bright boy. I had a high rank at school. But I was so over-receptive and credulous that in effect I was stupid. I had none of a country boy's cautious approach to ideas. I could swallow ideas by the dozen, and did; good and bad. My mind hadn't any of the seasoning or the toughness of Father's. It was so logical that if it had accepted certain premises it would

have marched off a precipice. Or at least it would have marched
Father off one.

Father was looking quizzically at me. I went at him again.
My next weapon was one that I thought would strike fear to his
heart: a text that I had picked out as being especially strong and
conclusive. It had one weak point, it didn't specifically use the
word baptism, and I expected Father to pounce on this as an
objection; but when he did I planned to rebuke him for picking
at trifles, and for being concerned with its wording instead of its
spirit. But Father was not a man to niggle at small technicalities,
and he instinctively met this attack—like all others—head on.
The text was Christ's saying that unless people confessed Him
before men, neither would He confess them before His Father
in Heaven. When I read this to Father, to my astonishment he
was quite unconcerned. He felt that this was the mere empty
warning of a meddlesome middleman. Father was going to deal
direct with his Maker. Christ wasn't his Maker. Father felt he
had just as much right around Heaven as Christ.

In fact, now I think of it, Father was—if there is such a thing
—an Old Testament Christian. He permitted the existence of
Christ, but disapproved of all His ideas.

But I was in no mood to philosophise over this then. My emotions swept over me, and I became exalted and ardent. I told
Father that although we knew he had always been a good man,
still he hadn't taken this step that every Christian must take. If
he took it, he would go to Heaven and there be received by the
angels. If he didn't, I explained to him that he would be cast
into Hell. And I cried, and said there would be "weeping and
gnashing of teeth."

Instead of being moved to tears by this, and getting right down
on his knees, Father sat there, beside the dark book-case, fresh
and healthy and solid, breathing out a rich odor of Havana cigar
smoke and cognac. Every cell in his body seemed to be robustly
resisting destruction. I don't recall now what he said to me, but
he didn't say much. He reminded me that I was only a little boy.
This seemed to me quite irrelevant. What I wanted to know was,

how about those arguments; but he merely smiled at my earnest-
ness. A rather grave smile. Perhaps he was wondering how on
earth he had produced such a son. At any rate he showed great
forbearance, and sent me up to bed; while he got out the cards
from the game-box and played solitaire.

His situation looked pretty black to me, as I lay in bed. I pictured to myself how the rest of us would be standing around, up
in Heaven, and how very upset we'd all feel to see Father in Hell.

Yet somehow I felt more excitement than grief, at this scene.
I must have been deeply impressed by Father's intrepid firmness.
True, he was only too plainly shutting himself out of bliss; and
ordinarily I'd have felt a great horror at the thought of a loved
one in torment. But suppose Father positively refused to go to
Hell when they said to? He seemed so remarkably able to fend
for himself, that it would probably just be another of his fights.
He and Satan.

I began to cool off as a missionary, and go back to my toys. But
Mother of course kept right on. And suddenly it seemed for a
moment that she might prevail. She had a bad illness, which depressed and worried Father so much, that when she kept begging
and begging him to do this thing for her, and told him how
happy it would make her, he said that he would.

But when she was well again, and eager to take him around to
the font, he wouldn't go. His memory seemed to have got very
dim. Mother exclaimed that he had solemnly agreed to be baptized, but he said flatly he had no recollection of it.

I don't know what grounds he may have had for taking this
stand. He was never a man to justify, or explain, or excuse his
own conduct. He didn't refrain out of dignity; he merely didn't
examine it. He took himself, his thoughts and his actions, completely for granted, without introspection or analysis. Perhaps in
this instance, in her fever, Mother had misunderstood him. Or
perhaps his point of view was that he'd have done anything to
help her get well, but now that she had happily got well his end
was achieved, so how could she fairly expect him to proceed with

his sacrifice? All I know is he seemed entirely satisfied with his behavior.

Mother felt very badly, and told him he was breaking her heart. This did not upset him. He probably guessed that underneath her tears there was more exasperation than heart-break. She hated the feeling of impotence he gave her. There seemed to be no way to manage him. She kept telling him that she simply couldn't believe he would really go back on his Sacred Promise— as she now began calling it. She taunted him with it. She said she had always supposed he was a man of his word. Father was quite unperturbed. Downtown, his lightest word to anybody was binding, of course; but that was in the real world of business. Getting baptized was all poppycock.

But Mother began to feel surer now that she could make Father yield. At least she had got one Sacred Promise out of the obstinate man, and she wouldn't let him do any more forgetting if she could once get another. The more her self-confidence grew, the more her tactics improved. She was quite unconscious, probably, that she had handicapped herself, hitherto, by attacking Father only on religious grounds, where he had no soft spots to strike at. He became more vulnerable at once, when she begged him to do her a favor. They were in love with each other; and he would have done a good deal for Mother—"Anything in reason," he said.

He went into the whole matter as thoroughly as a railroad report. He asked just how wet would a man have to get to be baptized. Would he have to go to the River Jordan to please Mother, and do the thing properly? If not, then exactly what rigmarole would he have to go through. He said if it wasn't too complicated, perhaps he'd consider it.

Mother showed him the baptismal service in the prayer-book for those of riper years; but Father said that by persons of riper years it must mean those who knew better. It was nothing but a lot of prayers anyhow. That was the clergyman's part of it. What he wanted to know was how much trouble he himself would be put to. But when Mother impatiently answered his questions about this, he was startled. He said the thing was even more impracticable than he had supposed. It wasn't as though he could have an accommodating parson trot around to the house and baptize him quietly some morning, after his coffee and eggs; no, he learned that the performance would have to take place in a church; and, worse, there would have to be others present. A congregation, the book said. Father declared that that ended it. He said he certainly wasn't going around to the Peace Everlasting to be made a fool of in that way. He said, damn it, he'd be the laughing-stock of all his friends. Mother said, why, his friends would be proud of him for standing up for his Saviour; but Father said he'd never hear the last of it, around at the club.

MY FATHER ENTERS THE CHURCH

The way it ended was simple. Mother's family had lived at one time in a pretty little two-storied house, called "The Cottage," in East Twenty-ninth Street; it had casement windows, set with diamond-shaped panes of leaded glass, and a grass plot in front. On the other side of the street, at Fifth Avenue, stood the church that is now known as the Little Church Around the Corner. The first Dr. Houghton was the rector in those times, and Mother was fond of him. One day Mother heard that a young relative of his, the Reverend Mr. Morley, had taken a far-away parish near what was then Audubon Park, a mile or two north of where in later years they erected Grant's Tomb. This part of the city was so thinly settled that it was like a remote country suburb. There were dirt roads and lanes instead of streets; and thick, quiet old woods. Mother suddenly got the idea that perhaps this would suit Father, since he seemed bent on "confessing God before men" only where no one was looking. Besides, Mother knew young Mr. Morley, and she felt that here was someone she could go to with her curious problem. She asked him to come down and see her. He was sympathetic. He agreed to make everything as easy for Father as possible.

I don't know just why it was, but somehow that was all there was to it. Father still got in a very bad humor whenever the subject was mentioned; but at least Mother wasn't, any longer, asking the impossible of him. It was thoroughly distasteful and he hated it, but he supposed he could go through it sometime. Perhaps he even got to the point of wishing to get the thing over with.

So the day came on which Father had agreed he would enter the church. The only person who had to be reminded of it was

Father himself. I remember excitedly looking out of the window at breakfast, and seeing a hired brougham from Ryerson & Brown's in the street. The coachman had on a blue coat with a double row of bright buttons, and on his legs were faded green trousers from some other man's livery. He was looking up at our front door. His horse was as weather-beaten as the horse on the plains of Siberia, in the picture in my Geography; and he too seemed to be looking up at our house and wondering what would come out of it.

I stood out on our front stoop staring down at them, and listening to the sounds in our hallway. Father had come down to breakfast in a good temper that morning, and the bacon and eggs had suited him for once, and the coffee too had found favor. Mother gave a happy, tender look at this soul she was saving. The dining-room seemed full of sunshine, and the whole world light-hearted. But when Mother said it was nearly eight o'clock and the cab would soon be here, Father had demanded what cab. He listened to her answer in horror, and sprang up with a roar.

It was as though an elephant which had been tied up with infinite pains had trumpeted and burst every fetter, after the labor of months. It was all to do over again. Father not only had to be convinced that a day had been set, and that this was the day, but the whole question of baptism had to be reopened and proved. All the religious instruction that had been slowly inscribed on his mind had apparently utterly vanished—the slate was wiped clean. He was back at his original starting-point, that this thing was all folderol—it was nothing but a wild idea of Mother's with which he had no concern.

A woman of less determination would have given up, Father was so indignant. But Mother, though frightened and discouraged and tearful, was angry. She wasn't going to let Father off, after all she had done. At first I thought she surely had lost. He was completely intractable. She stood up to him, armed with God's word and the laws of the church, and also, as she despairingly reminded him, with his own "Sacred Promise," and again she learned that not a one of them was any good. But she had one other weapon: Ryerson & Brown's waiting cab.

There were some things that were unheard of in our family: they simply weren't done. One was wasting money on cabs. When we went to the length of ordering a cab, we did not keep it waiting. And the sight of this cab at the door seemed to hypnotize Father. It stood there like a link in some inevitable chain of events. At first he declared it could go to the devil, he didn't care if there were fifty cabs waiting. But he was by habit and instinct a methodical man. When he helped himself to a portion of anything at the table, for instance, he did his best to finish that portion, whether he liked it or not. He got all the more angry if it didn't taste right, but his code made him eat it. If he began a book he was bound to go on with it, no matter how much it bored him. He went through with any and every program to which he once felt committed. The fact that this cab had been ordered, and now stood at the door, prevailed in those depths of his spirit which God couldn't reach. Where I sat on the steps I could hear him upstairs in his room, banging doors and putting on his overcoat and cursing at fate.

Mother darted out and told the coachman where he was to take us; and then she got in, bonneted and cloaked, to wait for Father to come. The coachman looked puzzled when he found we were going to church. He could see we weren't dressed for a funeral, yet it was hardly a wedding. Perhaps he thought we were a very devout family, seeking for some extra worship.

Then Father came down the steps, blackly. He got in the cab. And the horse and the coachman both jumped as Father slammed the door shut.

The cab bumped along over the cobblestones, with its ironshod wheels. The steady-going rattle and jolting made me dreamy. It was soothing to see the landscape slide by, at five or six miles an hour. Milkmen, ladling milk out of tall cans. Chambermaids polishing door-bells. Ladies, with the tops of their sleeves built up high at each shoulder. Horses straining at street-cars. Flocks of sparrows hopping about, pecking at refuse and dung, and waiting until a horse almost stepped on them before flying off.

We drove up Madison Avenue to the Park, and out at West Seventy-second Street. Then under the Elevated, with its coaldust sifting down and stray cinders, blackening the pools in the street; and its little locomotives chuff-chuffing along overhead. At the Boulevard, as upper Broadway was then named, we turned northward. Over toward the river were rocky wastelands, old shanties and goats. The skyline along the Boulevard was one of telegraph poles, along bare blocks and rail fences. I liked the looks of this ungraded district; it was all up-and-down and had ponds in it. And it ought to have comforted Father. No members of the club or the stock exchange could be sighted for miles; they probably never set foot in such regions. What more could Father ask?

But Father was glaring about, looking like a caged lion. Apparently he had confidently believed up to this very moment that Heaven would intervene somehow, and spare him this dose. He had never done Heaven any harm; why should it be malignant? His disappointment was increasingly bitter as he saw he was trapped. Another sort of man would have opened the cab door and bolted. But Father was drinking his hemlock. He also was freely expressing his feelings about it. The hardships of marriage had never before impressed him so sharply. A woman's demands on her husband were simply beyond human reckoning. He felt, and he said plainly to Mother, as the cab rattled on, that if he did this thing for her, it must be understood that it was his supreme contribution. No diamond necklace. No other sacrifices of any kind. He must never be asked to do anything more all his life.

Mother tried to point out that he wasn't doing it for her but for God, but Father said: "Pshaw! I won't hear to it." He had never had any trouble with God till Mother appeared on the scene.

Mother quoted Dr. Garden again to him, but Father said "Pish!"

"Oh Clare, you mustn't," said Mother.

Next came a prayer in which Mr. Morley went back to the
ark, and spoke of how God saved Noah and his family from
perishing by water; and of how God also led the children of
Israel safely through the Red Sea; and of how Jesus was baptized in the Jordan. These three incidents were cited as proof
that God had sanctified "the element of Water to the mystical
washing away of sin."

"We beseech thee," Mr. Morley continued, "that thou wilt
mercifully look upon this thy Servant; wash him and sanctify him
with the Holy Ghost; that he, being delivered from thy wrath,
may be received into the ark of Christ's Church; and being steadfast in faith, joyful through hope, and rooted in charity, may
come to the land of everlasting life."

Father was getting restive by this time, but Mr. Morley kept
on. He read us a part of the Gospel of John, and a long exhorta-
tion and prayer; and after this he bravely turned and spoke as
follows to Father:

"Well-beloved, who are come hither desiring to receive holy
Baptism, you have heard how the congregation hath prayed that
our Lord Jesus Christ would release you of your sins, to give you
the kingdom of Heaven, and everlasting life. You have heard also
that our Lord hath promised to grant all those things that we
have prayed for. Wherefore you must also faithfully, in the presence of these your Witnesses and this whole congregation, promise and answer to the following questions:

"Dost thou renounce the devil and all his works, the vain pomp
and glory of the world, with all covetous desires of the same, and
the sinful desires of the flesh?"

The answer to this was rather long, and Father of course had
not learned it; but Mother whispered the words in his ear, and
he repeated some of them impatiently, in a harsh, stony voice.
He looked as though he might have been an annoyed Roman
general, participating much against his will in a low and barbaric
rite.

There were only three more questions, however, and the answers were short.

"O Merciful God," said Mr. Morley, when these were finished, "grant that the old Adam in this person may be so buried,
that the new man may be raised up in him. Amen." He had to
say this, because it was in the prayer-book; but Father's eyes were
on fire, and there was a great deal of the old Adam in him, and
it didn't look buried.

Four more little prayers followed, and then came the great
moment, when Mr. Morley tried to pour water on Father. Owing
to Father's being no longer an infant, the prayer-book didn't
require Mr. Morley to take him into his arms for this purpose,
and hold him over the font; but he did have to wet him a little.
I don't know how he managed it. I remember how Father stood,
grim and erect, in his tailed morning-coat; but when I saw Mr.
Morley make a pass at Father's forehead, I am sorry to say I
shut my eyes tightly at this frightful sacrilege, and whether he
actually landed or not I never knew. But he did go on to say, "I
baptize thee," and all the rest of it, to Father. "We receive this
person into the congregation of Christ's flock," he added; "and
do sign him with the sign of the Cross, in token that hereafter he
shall not be ashamed to confess the faith of Christ crucified, and
manfully to fight under his banner, against sin, the world, and
the devil; and to continue Christ's faithful soldier and servant
unto his life's end. Amen."

The baptism part was now over. Father started to leave, but
we managed somehow to detain him while we knelt and gave
thanks. And, to end with, Mr. Morley urged Father to "mortify
all his evil affections," and exhorted Mother and me to remember that it was our part and duty to put Father in mind what
a solemn vow he had now made, that so he might grow in grace
and the knowledge of Christ, "and live godly, righteously, and
soberly, in this present world."

We stood awkwardly still for a moment, but there was nothing
else. Mr. Morley started in being chatty, in a more everyday
voice. He stood next to me as he talked, and I remember how
absorbed I was, again, by his mellow aroma. The odor was so
grateful to my senses that it seemed almost nourishing. I sniffed

A HOLIDAY WITH FATHER

Once in a long while, as a great treat, Father took me down to his office. This could happen only on a Saturday morning, when there was no school. I felt very important and grown-up on the days I went to "The Office"—not after I got there, to be sure, but as I was leaving the house, with Mother and my three little brothers respectfully seeing me off.

If it was a rainy day, Father would prepare for rough weather by wearing a derby hat and a black rubber mackintosh over his usual tailed coat. (He seldom was informal enough to wear a sack suit in town except on warm days, or when he left New York to go to the country, in summer.) If the sun was out, he wore a silk hat and carried a cane, like his friends. When he and they passed each other on the street, they raised their canes and touched the brims of their hats with them, in formal salute.

I admired this rich and splendid gesture, and wished I could imitate it, but I was too young for a cane. I was soberly dressed in a pepper-and-salt sack suit with short pants and the usual broad flat white Eton collar that boys wore in the eighties—a collar that started out very stiff and immaculate every morning and was done for by dinner time. Black laced or buttoned shoes and black stockings. We only wore brown in the country in summer.

On one of these Saturdays, although it was sunny, Father put on his derby. I didn't know why until later. I hopped along by his side as he walked through the long rows of comfortable-looking brownstone houses from Madison Avenue over to Sixth, climbed the stairs of the Elevated, and stood on the platform, chatting with one of his friends, while we waited for the next train.

Soon a stubby little steam engine, with its open coal car piled

51

wells. It was fun to scamper around the streets carrying all the messages (which are telephoned nowadays), or to roll colored pencils down the clerks' slanting desks, or try to ring the bell on the typewriter. The latter was a new contraption which seldom was used except on important occasions, when the bookkeeper or one of the office boys had to stop work and pick at it.

All of a sudden it was noon. The customers left. The ticker came to a stop. At half past twelve Father called to me and we went out for lunch.

"Will you be back, Mr. Day?" the cashier asked respectfully, but eagerly too. On days when Father said yes, all the clerks looked disappointed. They bent over their desks, saying nothing, till Father went out of the door, but if I lingered behind for a moment I heard them slamming their ledgers about. Not only did they and the office boys all have to stay, but the rule was that they couldn't even smoke until Father had gone home for the day.

Today he said no, however. I saw them getting out their sulphur matches as he was crossing the threshold, and the instant he stepped into the hall they struck them on the seats of their pants.

I trotted along at Father's side down to Beaver Street, where there stood a mellow old building. It had the look of a friendly, hospitable country hotel. There were green blinds and little outside balconies on its upper floors, and windows with looped lacy curtains; and white pillars stood at the entrance, at the top of a low flight of steps.

This was Delmonico's, and the food was so good there that even I had heard it talked of, uptown. It was one of the places that just suited people like Father.

Delmonico's stood upon a triangular-shaped plot of ground, with the front doors at the apex, and when we arrived we met a bottle-necked jam at the entrance. Silk-hatted men, who had been lunching in a lingering way, had suddenly remembered apparently that they were due back in Wall Street, and they were shoving each other, politely but urgently, to force their way out. As Father and I went in the long crowded room, the head

waiter led us with a flourish to a table for two. The air was
fragrant with cigar smoke and the appetizing smell of rich, greasy
cooking. A stately-looking foreigner who was standing at the
side of the room caught Father's eye and bowed to him in a dignified way.

"Lorenzo," Father said to him, as he approached us, "this is
my son."

I bobbed my head at him, rather embarrassed, and Mr.
Lorenzo Crist Delmonico bowed and said he was happy to meet
me.

As he left us, old François, Father's regular waiter, hurried up
to our table, and he and Father had a talk, in French, about the
best dish to order. They spoke so rapidly that I couldn't understand a word of it, except that François kept assuring Father that
we could rely on the sauce. *"Parfaitement."* It seemed that the
last time that Father had relied on this sauce, an admittedly difficult kind, he had had a severe disappointment.

When anything of this sort occurred, I had noted, François
had a healing way of dealing with such a catastrophe. He seemed
even more shocked and perturbed at a failure than Father, and
he would snatch the offending dish away and come racing back
with a substitute. Usually he was accompanied at such moments
by one of the Delmonico family—Lorenzo or Charles—who bent
over the table to examine the new dish as it was placed before
Father, murmuring most sympathetically about the unhappy
misfortune.

Today the sauce and everything else was not only successful
but perfect, and Father and François smiled and nodded in a
congratulatory way to each other. I used to wonder why Father
never got into rages at Delmonico's as he did at home, but I see
now that he may have felt lonely at home, where there were no
brother experts.

Father was fond of French cooking and of being served by
French waiters. At home he had to put up with an Irish waitress
who was changed every few months, and with cooking which,
though excellent of its kind, after all wasn't French. He ate it

FATHER ON HORSEBACK

Father had been putting on weight and he didn't like it. He was a solidly-built man, but trim and erect, with a light easy step, and his extra pounds made him uncomfortable. He disapproved of them too. When the fat of fat men seemed to come natural to them, Father took it as a good joke; but he felt that it was slovenly to be careless about getting stout.

He talked about this at his club. What the saloon was to poor men and what coffee houses had once been to Londoners, his club was to Father. It was the font and center of his social life. He stopped there for half an hour or so on his way home from the office, or he walked down there at nine in the evening when Mother had gone up to bed. He played a game or two of billiards —not cards—or he had a whisky and soda with Commodore Brown, or he met and sized up distinguished foreigners, whom he usually didn't think much of. Or he sought for advice about fat.

Some members recommended long walks, but Father had always done a good deal of walking. The opinion of the club was that in that case he had better take up riding horseback.

The only proper way to ride horseback, Father felt, was to join one more club. He joined the Riding Club, in East Fifty-eighth Street, which provided stabling and other conveniences, and after practicing in there in the tanbark ring, he rode out in the Park.

The Park itself was only a ring on a larger scale, nothing wild or adventurous; but it suited Father. He disliked wildness—he preferred things like landscapes to be orderly, and suitably arranged for his use. From this time on, he was as critical of the Park as he was of his home. He felt personally affronted for instance when the bridle path wasn't raked properly, or when papers were left lying about.

His first horse was a powerful bay by the name of Rob Roy. This horse didn't like Father, and Father had still less affection for him. This was supposed to be of no importance—it was not even considered. Father bought him because he was spirited and sound, and able to stand work; handsome too. He paid three hundred dollars for him, and expected him to do what he was told.

Rob Roy never looked upon the transaction in this way, however. He had an independent and self-absorbed nature; he was always thinking of his own point of view. Even if he had been devoted to Father, which he never was, this would have made trouble.

One typical scene between them, I remember, occurred near the Park entrance. It was a warm autumn morning. Rob Roy and Father had trotted out of the club and into the Park, each thoroughly healthy and strong, and each intent on his thoughts. They made a fine sight as they went up the bridle path. All their plans coincided. But then a difference between them arose. Father wished to keep on. Rob Roy didn't. I don't know why Rob Roy wanted to stop; perhaps he didn't like the way Father rode him. Anyhow he came to a halt. Father gave him a cut with his whip. Rob Roy whirled around. Father reined him up sharply and struck him again. Rob Roy reared.

As they fought, Father in his anger kept hitting Rob Roy; and Rob Roy violently pawed the ground, and stamped on it, and tore it all up. They both perspired so freely that between them they must have lost gallons, and they both blindly stuck to their respective plans and would not give in.

But Rob Roy had the whole day before him, and Father did not—he had to get through his ride sometime and go to his office. He decided that Rob Roy was crazy, and they returned to the club. Rob Roy was led off to his stall and rubbed down by a groom, and Father went to the dressing-room for members and was rubbed dry by Jim, the attendant.

Jim was a friendly old soul. "Have a nice ride, Mr. Day?" he asked.

"Nice hell," Father shortly replied, and took his cane and went out.

These fierce morning combats gave our family a feeling of awe. We had never dreamed that anyone, man or beast, would resist Father's will. This rashness of Rob Roy's was like Satan's rebelling against God—it had a dark splendor about it, but it somehow filled me with horror.

In that fight between Satan and God, we had been told that God won. There were stray bits of evidence to the contrary lying around, but naturally we had accepted the official announcement. In the long war between Father and Rob Roy, we always assumed Father won, but there too I now see that Rob Roy may have looked at it differently. For the way that Father defeated Rob Roy was by deciding to sell him.

To us boys this seemed like a banishment. It made Rob Roy an outcast. Perhaps it only meant to him meeting a rider less uncongenial; but to us it seemed like obliterating him from the world, in the prime of his life. For years afterward he was spoken of as a strange being, a queer, insane creature, who had unaccountably and vainly attempted to disobey Father.

Rob Roy was a thorough-bred. His successor, a lanky brown horse named Brownie, was plain middle-class. Rob Roy was an adventurer. Brownie was a sad-eyed philosopher. Some philosophers are as great-hearted as adventurers, but they are mostly more docile. Brownie trotted wherever Father told him to, in any direction. He never once reared, never stamped on the ground, never snorted. There were sometimes little differences of opinion between him and Father, because Brownie got tired sooner than Father did, and wanted to rest. But he never made a direct issue of it, never fought for his rights; he tried to get them either by malingering or by passive resistance. For instance, Father would set out with the plan in his mind of having a glorious gallop, up hill and down dale. Well, Brownie, who had to do the galloping, would keep it up for a while—

would keep it up far longer at times than he had ever intended; for he found that a whip kept landing on his flank whenever he started to slacken. But, as he lost heart in the expedition, he also lost spring; and finally he would thump along so heavily that Father let up.

In general however the two got along very well. Father became enthusiastic about the pleasure of riding. Being a hearty, expansive man, he talked of this often, at home. He talked of it so much, in fact, that Mother began to feel he was selfish, in that he was keeping a pleasure for himself which should be shared with his family. If riding around the Park was so exhilarating, she said we all ought to do it.

Father said he wished that we could, but there was only one horse.

This silenced the family for a while; but soon Mother spoke up: she didn't see why the rest of us couldn't ride the horse when Father was through.

The unreasonableness and impracticability of this idea made Father hot. It showed how little Mother knew about anything, especially horses, he said. He explained that Brownie was already inclined to be sluggish, and that he wouldn't be fresh enough for a man to ride if he did extra work.

Mother said firmly, then Father should get some more horses.

This took him aback. He always meant to do the right thing by us; and he began to fear that his own goodness of heart might now get him in trouble. His feeling was that when he innocently had gone in for riding, himself, he had never contemplated having to spend enough to mount the whole family. He said that if he had foreseen that we all would be wanting to ride through the Park, just because he, a hard-working man, got a little relief in that way, he would have gone without the relief, damn it. He would now. He'd sell out.

Of course he had no intention of doing this. Instead he bought one more horse, a younger and happier one, and then gave us boys poor old Brownie.

FATHER IS FIRM WITH
HIS AILMENTS

Father got annoyed at us when we didn't stay well. He usually stayed well himself and he expected us to be like him, and not faint and slump on his hands and thus add to his burdens.

He was fearless about disease. He despised it. All this talk about germs, he said, was merely newfangled nonsense. He said that when he was a boy there had been no germs that he knew of. Perhaps invisible insects existed, but what of it? He was as healthy as they were. "If any damned germs want to have a try at me," he said, "bring 'em on."

From Father's point of view, Mother didn't know how to handle an ailment. He admired her most of the time and thought there was nobody like her; he often said to us boys, "Your mother is a wonderful woman"; but he always seemed to disapprove of her when she was ill.

Mother went to bed, for instance, at such times. Yet she didn't make noises. Father heard a little gasping moan sometimes, but she didn't want him to hear even that. Consequently he was sure she wasn't suffering. There was nothing to indicate it, he said.

The worse she felt, the less she ever said about it, and the harder it was for him to believe that there was anything really wrong with her. "He says he can't see why I stay in bed so long," she once wrote to me, when I was away, "but this colitis is a mean affair which keeps one perfectly flat. The doctor told him yesterday the meaning of colitis, but he said he 'had never heard of the damned thing, thank God.' He feels very abused that he should be 'so upset by people with queer things the matter with them and doctors all over the place.'" (Mother underlined the word "people.")

Even Mother's colds made him fretful. Whenever she had one, she kept going as long as she could, pottering about her room looking white and tired, with a shawl round her shoulders. But sometimes she had to give up and crawl into her bed.

Father pished and poohed to himself about this, and muttered that it was silly. He said Mother was perfectly healthy. When people thought they were ill, he declared, it didn't mean that there was anything the matter with them, it was merely a sign of weak character. He often told Mother how weak it was to give in to an ailment, but every time he tried to strengthen her character in this respect, he said she seemed to resent it. He never remembered to try except when she could hardly hold her head up. From his point of view, though, that was the very time that she needed his help.

He needed hers, too, or not exactly her help but her company, and he never hesitated to say so. When she was ill, he felt lost.

He usually came up from his office at about five or six. The first thing he did was to look around the house to find Mother. It made his home feel queer and empty to him when she wasn't there.

One night about six o'clock he opened the door of her bedroom. There was no light except for a struggling little fire which flickered and sank in the grate. A smell of witch-hazel was in the air, mixed with spirits of camphor. On the bed, huddled up under an afghan, Mother lay still, in the dark.

"Are you there, Vinnie?" Father said, in a voice even louder than usual because of his not being sure.

Mother moaned, "Go away."

"What?" he asked, in astonishment.

"Go away. Oh, go 'way."

"Damnation!" he said, marching out.

"Clare!"

"What is it?"

"Won't you *ple-e-ease* shut my door again!"

Father ground his teeth and shut it with such a bang that it made Mother jump.

He told himself she had nothing the matter with her. She'd be all right in the morning. He ate a good dinner. Being lonely, he added an extra glass of claret and some toasted crackers and cheese. He had such a long and dull evening that he smoked two extra cigars.

After breakfast the next morning, he went to her bedroom again. The fire was out. Two worn old slippers lay on a chair. The gray daylight was cheerless. Father stood at the foot of Mother's bed, looking disconsolately at her because she wasn't well yet. He had no one to laugh at or quarrel with; his features were lumpy with gloom.

"What is it?" Mother asked in a whisper, opening her weary eyes.

"Nothing," he said loudly. "Nothing."

"Well, for mercy's sake, don't come in here looking like that, Clare," Mother begged.

"What do you mean? Looking like what?"

"Oh, go away!" Mother shrieked. "When people are sick, they like to see a smile or something. I never will get well if you stand there and stare at me that way! And shut my door quietly this time. And let me alone."

Outside her door, when I asked him how Mother was, he said with a chuckle: "She's all right again. She isn't out of bed yet, but she sounds much better this morning."

Father's own experiences in a sick-room had been very few. When he was in his early thirties, he had an attack of gout which lasted three weeks. From that time until he was seventy-four and had pneumonia, he had no other serious illnesses. He said illnesses were mostly imaginary and he didn't believe in them.

He even declared that his pneumonia was imaginary. "It's only some idea of that doctor's," he said. "Nothing the matter with me but a cold." Our regular physician had died, and this new man and two trained nurses had all they could do, at first, to keep Father in bed.

The new doctor had pale-blue eyes, a slight build, and a way of inwardly smiling at the persons he talked to. He had a strong will in crises, and he was one of the ablest physicians in town. Mother had chosen him, however, chiefly because she liked one of his female cousins.

When Father got worse, the doctor kept warning him that it really *was* pneumonia, and that if he wouldn't be tractable, he might not get over it—especially at seventy-four.

Father lay in bed glowering at him and said: "I didn't send for you, sir. You needn't stand there and tell me what you want me to do. I know all about doctors. They think they know a damned lot. But they don't. Give your pills and things to Mrs. Day—she believes in them. That's all I have to say. There's no need to continue this discussion. There's the door, sir. Goodbye."

But somehow the discussion kept on, and much to his surprise Father at last became convinced he was ill. The doctor, leaving him alone in his bedroom to digest the bad news, came out in the hall, anxious and tired, to have a few words with Mother. As they stood outside Father's door whispering quietly, they heard his voice from within. Apparently, now that he knew he was in trouble, his thoughts had turned to his God. "Have mercy!" they heard him shouting indignantly. "I say have mercy, damn it!"

Any sufferings that Father ever had he attributed solely to God. Naturally, he never thought for a moment that God could mean him to suffer. He couldn't imagine God's wishing to punish him either, for his conscience was clear. His explanation seemed to be that God was clumsy, not to say muddle-headed.

However, in spite of God and the doctor, Father got over pneumonia, just as, some forty years before, he had got over his gout. Only, in conquering his gout, he had had the help of a cane and a masseur called Old Lowndes.

While the gout was besieging him, Father sat in a big chair by the fire with his bad foot on a stool, armed with a cane which he kept constantly ready. Not that he used the cane to walk with. When he walked, he hopped around on his other foot, uttering strong howls of fury. But he valued his cane highly, and needed it, too, as a war club. He threatened the whole family with it. When visitors entered the room he brandished it fiercely at them, to keep them away from his toe.

Old Lowndes was allowed to approach nearer than others, but he was warned that if he made any mistakes that cane would come down on his head. Father felt there was no knowing what harm Lowndes might have done if he hadn't shaken his cane at him and made him take care. As it was, owing largely to this useful stick, Father got well.

This experience convinced him that any disease could be conquered by firmness.

When he had a cold, his method of dealing with it was to try to clear it out by main force, either by violently blowing his nose or, still better, by sneezing. Mother didn't like him to sneeze, he did it with such a roar. She said she could feel it half across the room, and she was sure it was catching. Father said this was nonsense. He said his sneezes were healthy. And presently we'd hear a hearty, triumphant blast as he sneezed again.

Aside from colds, which he had very seldom, his only foes were sick headaches. He said headaches only came from eating, however. Hence a man who knew enough to stop eating could always get rid of one that way. It took time to starve it out thoroughly. It might take several hours. But as soon as it was gone, he could eat again and enjoy his cigar.

When one of these headaches started, Father lay down and shut his eyes tight and yelled. The severity of a headache could be judged by the volume of sound he put forth. His idea seemed to be to show the headache that he was just as strong as it was, and stronger. When a headache and he went to bed together, they were a noisy pair.

Father's code required him to be game, I suppose. He never spoke or thought of having a code; he wasn't that sort of person; but he denounced men whose standards were low, as to gameness or anything else. It didn't occur to him to conceal his sufferings, however: when he had any pains, he expressed them as fully as he knew how. His way of being brave was not to keep still but to keep on fighting the headache.

Mother used to beg him to be quiet at night, even if he did have a headache, and not wake up the whole house. He never paid the slightest attention to such a request. When she said, "Please don't groan so much, Clare," he'd look at her in disgust, as though he were a warrior being asked to stifle his battle-cries.

One evening he found Mother worrying because Aunt Emma was ill with some disease that was then epidemic.

"Oh, pooh!" Father said. "Nothing the matter with Emma. You can trust people to get any ailment whatever that's fashionable. They hear of a lot of other people having it, and the first thing you know they get scared and think they have it themselves. Then they go to bed, and send for the doctor. The doctor! All poppycock."

"Well, but Clare dear, if you were in charge of them, what would you do instead?"

"Cheer 'em up, that's the way to cure 'em."

"How would you cheer them up, darling?" Mother asked doubtfully.

"I? I'd tell 'em, *'Bah!'* "

FATHER WAKES UP THE VILLAGE

One of the most disgraceful features of life in the country, Father often declared, was the general inefficiency and slackness of small village tradesmen. He said he had originally supposed that such men were interested in business, and that that was why they had opened their shops and sunk capital in them, but no, they never used them for anything but gossip and sleep. They took no interest in civilized ways. Hadn't heard of them, probably. He said that of course if he were camping out on the veldt or the tundra, he would expect few conveniences in the neighborhood and would do his best to forego them, but why should he be confronted with the wilds twenty miles from New York?

Usually, when Father talked this way, he was thinking of ice. He strongly objected to spending even one day of his life without a glass of cold water beside his plate at every meal. There was never any difficulty about this in our home in the city. A great silver ice-water pitcher stood on the sideboard all day, and when Father was home its outer surface was frosted with cold. When he had gone to the office, the ice was allowed to melt sometimes, and the water got warmish, but never in the evening, or on Sundays, when Father might want some. He said he liked water, he told us it was one of Nature's best gifts, but he said that like all her gifts it was unfit for human consumption unless served in a suitable manner. And the only right way to serve water was icy cold.

It was still more important that each kind of wine should be served at whatever the right temperature was for it. And kept at it, too. No civilized man would take dinner without wine, Father said, and no man who knew the first thing about it would keep his wine in hot cellars. Mother thought this was a mere whim of

Father's. She said he was fussy. How about people who lived in apartments, she asked him, who didn't have cellars? Father replied that civilized persons didn't live in apartments.

One of the first summers that Father ever spent in the country, he rented a furnished house in Irvington on the Hudson, not far from New York. It had a garden, a stable, and one or two acres of woods, and Father arranged to camp out there with many misgivings. He took a train for New York every morning at eight-ten, after breakfast, and he got back between five and six, bringing anything special we might need along with him, such as a basket of peaches from the city, or a fresh package of his own private coffee.

Things went well until one day in August the ice-man didn't come. It was hot, he and his horses were tired, and he hated to come to us anyhow because the house we had rented was perched up on top of a hill. He said afterward that on this particular day he had not liked the idea of making his horses drag the big ice-wagon up that sharp and steep road to sell us fifty cents' worth of ice. Besides, all his ice was gone anyhow—the heat had melted it on him. He had four or five other good reasons. So he didn't come.

Father was in town. The rest of us waited in astonishment, wondering what could be the matter. We were so used to the regularity and punctilio of life in the city that it seemed unbelievable to us that the ice-man would fail to appear. We discussed it at lunch. Mother said that the minute he arrived she would have to give him a talking to. After lunch had been over an hour and he still hadn't come, she got so worried about what Father would say that she decided to send to the village.

There was no telephone, of course. There were no motors. She would have liked to spare the horse if she could, for he had been worked hard that week. But as this was a crisis, she sent for Morgan, the coachman, and told him to bring up the dog-cart.

The big English dog-cart arrived. Two of us boys and the coachman drove off. The sun beat down on our heads. Where the heavy harness was rubbing on Brownie's coat, he broke out into a thick, whitish lather. Morgan was sullen. When we boys were along he couldn't take off his stiff black high hat or unbutton his thick, padded coat. Worse still, from his point of view, he couldn't stop at a bar for a drink. That was why Mother had sent us along with him, of course, and he knew it.

We arrived at the little town after a while and I went into the Coal & Ice Office. A wiry-looking old clerk was dozing in a corner, his chair tilted back and his chin resting on his dingy shirt-front. I woke this clerk up. I told him about the crisis at our house.

He listened unwillingly, and when I had finished he said it was a very hot day.

I waited. He spat. He said he didn't see what he could do, because the ice-house was locked.

I explained earnestly that this was the Day family and that something must be done right away.

He hunted around his desk a few minutes, found his chewing tobacco, and said, "Well, sonny, I'll see what I can do about it."

I thanked him very much, as that seemed to me to settle the matter. I went back to the dog-cart. Brownie's check-rein had been unhooked, and he stood with his head hanging down. He looked sloppy. It wouldn't have been so bad with a buggy, but a slumpy horse in a dog-cart can look pretty awful. Also, Morgan was gone. He reappeared soon, coming out of a side door down the street, buttoning up his coat, but with his hat tilted back. He looked worse than the horse.

We checked up the weary animal's head again and drove slowly home. A hot little breeze in our rear moved our dust along with us. At the foot of the hill, we boys got out, to spare Brownie our extra weight. We unhooked his check-rein again. He dragged the heavy cart up.

Mother was sitting out on the piazza. I said the ice would come soon now. We waited.

It was a long afternoon.

At five o'clock, Brownie was hitched up again. The coachman and I drove back to the village. We had to meet Father's train.

We also had to break the bad news to him that he would have no ice-water for dinner, and that there didn't seem to be any way to chill his Rhine wine.

The village was as sleepy as ever, but when Father arrived and learned what the situation was, he said it would have to wake up. He told me that he had had a long, trying day at the office, the city was hotter than the Desert of Sahara, and he was completely worn out, but that if any ice-man imagined for a moment he could behave in that manner, he, Father, would take his damned head off. He strode into the Coal & Ice Office.

When he came out, he had the clerk with him, and the clerk had put on his hat and was vainly trying to calm Father down. He was promising that he himself would come with the ice-wagon if the driver had left, and deliver all the ice we could use, and he'd be there inside an hour.

Father said, "Inside of an hour be hanged, you'll have to come quicker than that."

The clerk got rebellious. He pointed out that he'd have to go to the stables and hitch up the horses himself, and then get someone to help him hoist a block of ice out of the ice-house. He said it was 'most time for his supper and he wasn't used to such work. He was only doing it as a favor to Father. He was just being neighborly.

Father said he'd have to be neighborly in a hurry, because he wouldn't stand it, and he didn't know what the devil the ice company meant by such actions.

The clerk said it wasn't his fault, was it? It was the driver's.

This was poor tactics, of course, because it wound Father up again. He wasn't interested in whose fault it was, he said. It was everybody's. What he wanted was ice and plenty of it, and he wanted it in time for his dinner. A small crowd which had collected by this time listened admiringly as Father shook his finger at the clerk and said he dined at six-thirty.

The clerk went loping off toward the stables to hitch up the big horses. Father waited till he'd turned the corner.

Followed by the crowd, Father marched to the butcher's.

After nearly a quarter of an hour, the butcher and his assistant came out, unwillingly carrying what seemed to be a coffin, wrapped in a black mackintosh. It was a huge cake of ice.

Father got in, in front, sat on the box seat beside me, and took up the reins. We drove off. The coachman was on the rear seat, sitting back-to-back to us, keeping the ice from sliding out with the calves of his legs. Father went a few doors up the street to a little house-furnishings shop and got out again.

I went in the shop with him this time. I didn't want to miss any further scenes of this performance. Father began proceedings by demanding to see all the man's ice-boxes. There were only a few. Father selected the largest he had. Then, when the sale seemed arranged, and when the proprietor was smiling broadly with pleasure at this sudden windfall, Father said he was buying that refrigerator only on two conditions.

The first was that it had to be delivered at his home before dinner. Yes, now. Right away. The shopkeeper explained over and over that this was impossible, but that he'd have it up the next morning, sure. Father said no, he didn't want it the next morning, he had to have it at once. He added that he dined at six-thirty, and that there was no time to waste.

The shopkeeper gave in.

The second condition, which was then put to him firmly, was staggering. Father announced that that ice-box must be delivered to him full of ice.

The man said he was not in the ice business.

Father said, "Very well then. I don't want it."

The man said obstinately that it was an excellent ice-box.

Father made a short speech. It was the one that we had heard so often at home about the slackness of village tradesmen, and he put such strong emotion and scorn in it that his voice rang through the shop. He closed it by saying, "An ice-box is of no use to a man without ice, and if you haven't the enterprise, the gumption, to sell your damned goods to a customer who wants them delivered in condition to use, you had better shut up your shop and be done with it. Not in the ice business, hey? You aren't in business at all!" He strode out.

The dealer came to the door just as Father was getting into the dog-cart, and called out anxiously, "All right, Mr. Day. I'll get that refrigerator filled for you and send it up right away."

Father drove quickly home. A thunderstorm seemed to be brewing and this had waked Brownie up, or else Father was putting some of his own supply of energy into him. The poor old boy probably needed it as again he climbed the steep hill. I got out at the foot, and as I walked along behind I saw that Morgan was looking kind of desperate, trying to sit in the correct position with his arms folded while he held in the ice with his legs. The big cake was continually slipping and sliding around under the seat and doing its best to plunge out. It had bumped against his calves all the way home. They must have got good and cold.

When the dog-cart drew up at our door, Father remained seated a moment while Morgan, the waitress, and I pulled and pushed at the ice. The mackintosh had come off it by this time. We dumped it out on the grass. A little later, after Morgan had unharnessed and hurriedly rubbed down the horse, he ran back to help us boys break the cake up, push the chunks around to the back door, and cram them into the ice-box while Father was dressing for dinner.

Mother had calmed down by this time. The Rhine wine was cooling. "Don't get it too cold," Father called.

Then the ice-man arrived.

The old clerk was with him, like a warden in charge of a prisoner. Mother stepped out to meet them, and at once gave the ice-man the scolding that had been waiting for him all day.

The clerk asked how much ice we wanted. Mother said we didn't want any now. Mr. Day had brought home some, and we had no room for more in the ice-box.

The ice-man looked at the clerk. The clerk tried to speak, but no words came.

Father put his head out of the window. "Take a hundred pounds, Vinnie," he said. "There's another box coming."

A hundred-pound block was brought into the house and heaved into the washtub. The waitress put the mackintosh over it. The ice-wagon left.

Just as we all sat down to dinner, the new ice-box arrived, full.

Mother was provoked. She said "Really, Clare!" crossly. "Now what am I to do with that piece that's waiting out in the wash-tub?"

Father chuckled.

She told him he didn't know the first thing about keeping house, and went out to the laundry with the waitress to tackle the problem. The thunderstorm broke and crashed. We boys ran around shutting the windows upstairs.

Father's soul was at peace. He dined well, and he had his coffee and cognac served to him on the piazza. The storm was over by then. Father snuffed a deep breath of the sweet-smelling air and smoked his evening cigar.

"Clarence," he said, "King Solomon had the right idea about these things. 'Whatsoever thy hand findeth to do,' Solomon said, 'do thy damnedest.' "

Mother called me inside. "Whose mackintosh is that?" she asked anxiously. "Katie's torn a hole in the back."

I heard Father saying contentedly on the piazza, "I like plenty of ice."

FATHER DECLINES TO BE KILLED

I don't know why Father and Mother chose Irvington to go to, that summer. There were lots of other places where we boys could have enjoyed ourselves better, but we weren't consulted of course, and we'd have been surprised if we had been. The family assumed that we could have a good time anywhere. We had supposed so ourselves. But everything was wrong about Irvington.

I used to sit up on our hill and stare down at the Hudson. It had a dirty yellow-brown color, it didn't make any noises, and I felt I never had seen such a tiresome river. Compared to the blue salt-water we were used to, it seemed too dull and lifeless to swim in. There was no bathing beach anyhow.

Down the road was the old Washington Irving house in Sleepy Hollow, which Mother insisted was lovely, but it was still as death, and two thin little old ladies who mustn't be disturbed sat and rocked on the porch.

About an hour's walk in the other direction there was a fat boy who had rabbits, but we didn't think much of either those rabbits or the fellow who owned them.

On our hill we were surrounded by great, silent, park-like estates, belonging to great, silent, rich men who didn't want boys around. We occasionally explored these parks uninvited, but they weren't any good. And the hill that we lived on was as limited a hill as we'd ever seen.

Our garden seemed to be owned by the gardener. He wouldn't let us go in it. He doled out flowers from it to Mother and he scowled when he brought in the vegetables. When Mother asked him when he'd have more tomatoes or peas, he used to think deeply and say, "She be up in two day." He complained of the

Sunday mornings, she arrived at the church door shaken loose on top and bunched up below. And the combination of rain and a dog-cart didn't suit her at all.

The very first drive that we took in it, there was a shower. The dog-cart was stopped. Father and Mother and I and Morgan, the coachman, stood up and put on our rubber coats, and Morgan got out the large rubber apron. Mother then raised her umbrella to protect her big ribbony hat.

Father, sitting on the box seat beside her, stared at this in horror. "You can't put up that thing," he said.

"I can so," Mother answered indignantly.

"I can't drive if you do," Father said. "How the devil can a man see to drive with you bobbing that big thing in front of us?"

"I'm *not* bobbing it," Mother cried. "It's the wind. Do please hurry, Clare. This is awful!"

"Awful?" said Father, trying to hold his whip crosswise, with the umbrella jerking and beating against it. "It's damnable."

"Well then, why didn't you get a buggy, as I told you?" said Mother.

"Will you kindly hold that thing out of my way?" Father shouted. "Upon my soul, this is positively disgraceful. Stop, Vinnie! Stop! You're poking it right in my eye! You can't carry an umbrella in a dog-cart."

When we arrived at the house, half an hour later, with the rain pouring down, they were still hotly debating this question. I don't remember that it ever was settled, though it was debated for years.

One windy night, a week later, there was another and heavier storm, which began just as Father and Cousin Julie were going out to a dinner party. Neither of them wanted to go, and Julie hadn't even been invited, but Mother declared that they had to. She had written and accepted the invitation for Father and herself ten days ago, she explained, and it was only because she really felt too ill to stir that she was sending Julie instead. Father said he felt sick himself, a lot sicker than Mother, but Mother said he couldn't back out at the last moment and there was no

time to send word. So she hurried them off in their evening finery
in that cold wind and rain, up high in the air on that shelterless
dog-cart, along the unlighted roads.

In general, the roads around Irvington were dusty but good.
The great trouble was they were hilly. So far as we boys were
concerned, we liked them, but Brownie did not. Brownie was not
made for hills, and neither, of course, was the dog-cart. Father
said it would have been better to have had a short, stocky cob
for such work. Brownie was of an opposite type, he was lanky and
limp—so limp that Mother said he was becoming unnaturally
elongated, pulling that cart up those hills.

On the other hand, it was because of those hills that our horseback rides were such fun. Father rode every morning before he
took the train to the city, and we boys took turns going with him.
Little by little we explored every inch of that beautiful country-
side.

I was riding with Father one day in September when he found
a new road. I galloped ahead, up a hill. Just over the crest of it,
hidden from sight till it was too late to stop, was a wash-out—a
deep, ditchlike chasm across the road—which my horse luckily
jumped, almost before I had seen it. A little farther on I reined
him in and looked back, to see if Father had cleared it.

Father was lying face downward in the road. His horse, which
had fallen beside him, was thrashing around with its feet. It
scrambled up just as I turned, and I saw it step over Father.

I galloped back, dismounted, and managed to roll and push
Father over. He was senseless. I sat down in the road with his
head on my lap and wiped the blood off his face. I had never seen
him helpless before. It gave me a strange feeling.

I had slung the reins of the two horses over my arm. They kept
pulling and tugging to get at the grass on the bank.

As Father didn't come to, or stir, I began shouting for help.
It was a still Sunday morning. The road ran through cornfields
and pastures, and there were no passers-by.

Presently, as I sat there, making all the noise I could, I saw
Father frown. His eyes were shut; gravel and mud were ground

into his face and he looked done for; but I now felt more hope. I threw back my head, and yelled louder than ever. "Hi! Hi! Hi there, help!"

'Way off in a hollow was a yellow farmhouse. At last I saw a man coming out of it. He shut the door and walked down a grassy path and up the hill toward us.

He got Father to his feet, after a while. We went slowly along to the house with Father stumbling between us. We put him in a chair, on the grass, and washed his face. He held his head up better after this, but he didn't seem to understand questions.

The farmer and I anxiously discussed different plans. We decided I'd better unsaddle my horse and hitch him up to the farmer's buggy, put Father in, and drive him home just as quick as I could.

Father paid no attention to what we were doing. When the buggy was ready, however, and we tried to pick him up and dump him in, he objected. He was so groggy and his muscles were so slumpy he could hardly sit up, but he clung to the idea that he was out for a nice morning ride. He absolutely refused to have anything to do with a buggy. "Take that damn thing away," he said, and added that he wanted his horse.

The farmer and I were taken aback by this. We had naturally supposed that we were in charge of things, and that Father's ideas didn't count. I still thought so. I told the farmer that all Father needed was a little persuasion. We tried a great deal of it. We got nowhere at all. Shaken up though he was, Father's firm belief in his impregnability remained unimpaired, and he was still somehow the master of the whole situation.

He kept on demanding his horse so imperiously that I gave in. I unharnessed my own horse and resaddled him, put the buggy back in the barn, and with the greatest misgivings the farmer and I hoisted Father up on his mount. He looked as though he'd fall off every minute, but to our amazement he didn't. I said goodbye to the farmer, and Father and I rode up the hill.

It was a long, silent ride. Father came out of his stupor at moments better than I had hoped. At other times he sank back and wobbled about in the saddle. But his knees held on, even when he shut his eyes and seemed not to know what was happening.

We got back to the main road at last. Farther on we came to Dr. Coudert's place. I got off and rang the front doorbell.

Dr. Coudert was upstairs, dressing for church. He looked out of his bedroom window.

"Why, good morning, Day," he called down to Father. "What's the matter?"

"Marrer is," Father said thickly, "some accident. Want you come my house. Fix it."

He turned and trotted away, lurching in the saddle. I hurried off after him.

At our doorway, when he saw Mother come running out, exclaiming at our being late, he tried to dismount by himself. "Vinnie, dear Vinnie," he muttered, and toppled into our arms.

We got him to bed. Dr. Coudert found a great, dull, dark-red place at the nape of his neck, and said that it was pretty serious, but that there was nothing to do but apply icebags and wait.

Mother immediately telegraphed to Uncle Hal. He was Father's elder brother; he had retired from business and he was taking his ease at some summer resort, which he did not wish to leave, but he took a train and got up to Irvington that same afternoon. Mother explained to him that Father had to have somebody run the office for him, and that Uncle Hal was the only one whom he would trust. Uncle Hal knew Father too well to take this as a compliment. Father trusted him more than others, yes; but, as Uncle Hal knew from long experience, Father didn't like to trust anyone.

However, Uncle Hal began spending his days down in Wall Street, and faithfully coming up to Irvington to make his reports. He was a large, stout, phlegmatic man, with a face that seemed to be carved from old wood, he could make it so completely expressionless. In behind this, if you watched his eye closely, you could sometimes see a twinkle.

One afternoon when I was in Father's room, changing his icebags, Uncle Hal tiptoed heavily in, and sat down at the side of the bed. He told Father about a few routine matters, in his deliberate way, and then put his fingers together and waited to be cross-examined.

Father feverishly began firing questions at him. "What did you do about those Rome Watertown bonds?" he demanded. "Did you straighten out those legal matters with Choate & Larocque?" The answers to these and other questions were only half-satisfactory. Uncle Hal was a thoroughly sound, careful man; he had made no mistakes, and there was nothing that Father could reasonably object to, exactly, but it exasperated him to discover that his office was not being conducted in quite his own regular manner. "I won't have my office run that way!" he finally roared.

Uncle Hal looked at him stolidly.

Mother rushed in. "Oh, Hal, what *are* you doing!" she shrieked. "I begged you not to excite him!"

Uncle Hal turned his large frame half around in his chair and regarded Mother stolidly too.

"Never knew such a damned way of doing things in my life," Father groaned.

"Come, Hal!" Mother cried. "Come out here in the hall with me, and let me explain *again* to you! Don't sit there, Hal, making things worse like this."

They went out together.

Later on, looking out of the window, I saw Uncle Hal slowly heave himself up into the dog-cart, which always shook him up like a jelly, and which he hated like poison. The coachman drove him off, jiggetty-jig, jiggetty-jog, to the station.

It was weeks before Father got up again. I suppose he had had a concussion of the brain, but we boys weren't told any details. All we knew was that Father had to stay in bed and that he was strangely quiet at first, although later he became his old self again and made a great deal of noise about it. Meanwhile I had a fine time riding his horse, which had more spirit than ours.

After Father got well, he seemed to want to forget the whole incident. He never went back to see that farmer who had tried to lend him his buggy. He didn't seem appreciative of what Mother had done either, she felt, until one day, as a surprise, he gratefully bought her a beautiful ring with three rubies. When Dr. Coudert heard about this, he strongly approved. He told Father that he owed his life to Mother, she had been such a good nurse; and when Mother heard him say it, she nodded her head violently and said that was true.

FATHER HIRES A COOK

One late afternoon when Father came up from downtown, he found his home much upset. Our cook had walked out and left us. I was a child of four, George was two, and there was a new baby besides. Mother was ill. She hadn't been able to leave us to go to an agency. And as she was no hand at cooking herself, the outlook for dinner was poor.

This state of affairs was unprecedented in all Father's experience. In his father's home, they never changed their servants suddenly; they seldom changed them at all; and as his mother was a past mistress of cooking, he had always been doubly protected. Since his marriage, he had had to live a much bumpier life. But this was the worst yet.

He asked Mother, who was lying in bed, what she was going to do about it. There were no telephones then, and she couldn't do anything at all, at the moment; but she said she would try to go to an agency in the morning and see what she could find. "In the morning? Good God!" Father said. "Where is the place, anyhow?" And he clapped on his hat and strode out again, over toward Sixth Avenue.

As I heard the story years afterward, it was late when he got there, and he bounded up the front stoop two or three steps at a time, and went quickly into the little office, where the gaslights were burning. He had never been in such a place before, and to his surprise it was empty, except for a severe-looking woman who sat at a desk at one side. "Where do you keep 'em?" he urgently demanded, his mind on the question of dinner.

She looked at him, got out her pen, and opened a large book deliberately. "I will take your name and address," she informed

him, "and then, if you please, you may give me the details as to
what kind of person you require and when you would wish her
to call."

But Father had no time, he told her, for any damned fol-de-rol.
"Where do you keep 'em?" he said again. She was standing in the
way of his dinner. I can imagine how his face must have reddened
and how his eyes must have blazed at her. "I am asking you
where you keep them!" he roared.

"Why, the girls are in there," the lady explained, to calm him,
"but clients are not allowed in that room. If you will tell me the
kind of position you wish me to fill for you, I will have one come
out."

Before she'd half finished, Father had thrown open the door
and gone in. There sat a crowd of the girls, young and old, sickly
and brawny, of all shapes and sizes; some ugly, some pretty and
trim and stylish, some awkward; nurses, ladies' maids, waitresses,
washerwomen, and cooks.

The manager was by now at Father's elbow, trying to make
him get out, and insisting that he tell her the position he wished
her to fill. But Father was swiftly glancing around at the crowd,
and he paid no attention. He noticed a little woman in the
corner, with honest gray eyes, who sat there, shrewd-looking and
quiet. He pointed his cane over at her and said, "I'll take that
one."

The manager was flustered, but still she kept trying to enforce
her authority. She protested she didn't yet know the position. . . .

"Cook," Father said, "cook."

"But Margaret doesn't wish to be a cook, she wants—"

"You can cook, can't you?" Father demanded.

Margaret's plain little face was still pink with excitement and
pleasure at being chosen above all that roomful by such a mas-
terful gentleman. Father had probably smiled at her, too, for they
liked each other at once. Well, she said, she had cooked for one
family.

"Of course she can cook," Father said.

He said afterward, when describing the incident, "I knew at once she could cook."

The manager didn't like this at all. The discipline of the office was spoiled. "If you are going to take her anyhow," she said acidly, "what day would you wish her to come, and will you please give me your name?"

"Yes, yes," Father said, without giving it. "Come on, Margaret." And he planked down the fee and walked out.

Margaret followed him through the door and trotted over to our home at his heels. He sent her down to the kitchen immediately, while he went upstairs to dress.

"I don't know why you make such a fuss about engaging new servants. It's simple enough," he said comfortably to Mother that evening, after Margaret's first dinner.

It was the first of a long series, for she stayed with us twenty-six years.

FATHER FEELS STARVED

In the summers, when we went to the country, our usual plan was to hire a temporary cook to go with us, so that Margaret could stay in town. We hated to leave her, but the idea was that somebody must stay to take care of the house. There were no electric burglar alarms in those days, and few special watchmen. Little Margaret made a pretty small watchman, for she was no size at all, but she had an indomitable spirit. So we'd leave her on guard while we went up to our summer home in Harrison with a substitute cook.

But this didn't work well. No matter how few the substitute's faults were, Father had no patience with them. One summer, I remember, there was a nice woman, Delia, who got on well with Mother because she was so obliging and pleasant, but who didn't suit Father at all. "I don't give a damn how obliging she is," he kept saying. "If she won't oblige me by cooking something fit to eat, she can go."

This didn't sound unreasonable, but Delia cooked well enough for the rest of us, and Mother hated to risk getting someone else who'd be temperamental. Our dining-room consequently became a battleground morning and night. At breakfast, Father would put down his coffee cup in disgust and roar: "Slops! Damn it, slops! Does she call this confounded mess coffee? Isn't there a damned soul in Westchester County who knows how to make coffee but me? I swear to God I can't even imagine how she concocts such atrocities. I come down to this room hungry every morning, and she tries to fill me with slops! Take it away, I tell you!" he would bellow to the waitress. "Take this accursed mess away!" And while she and Delia were frantically hurrying to

87

make a fresh pot, he would savagely devour his omelet and bacon, and declare that his breakfast was ruined.

The longer Delia stayed with us, the more alarmed Father became. He ate heartily, as Mother kept pointing out to him, but he said he didn't feel nourished. He said it was no use to argue about it; he felt all gone inside. One night after he had had a four-course dinner, he fretfully got up from the table, went into the library with his cigar, and moaned that he was starved. His moans were, as always, full-throated, and they came from the heart. Every now and then, when his miserable condition seemed to strike him afresh, he laid down his book and shouted "Starved! Starved!" in a grief-stricken roar.

When Mother went in the library to quiet him, he told her he'd be damned if he'd stand it. "I refuse to be sent to my grave, do you hear me, by that infernal bog-trotting imbecile you keep in my kitchen."

"Now Clare, a Japanese is coming tomorrow, I told you. This is Delia's last night. I do hope you'll like Tobo. He won't know our ways right at the start, of course, but he is a very good cook."

Father was appeased for the moment by the dismissal of Delia. But the next night, when he found that the first dish was too Oriental, he said in an annoyed tone to Mother, "Will you kindly explain to your man Tobo that I am not a coolie?" And after eating the rest of his dinner, he pushed his plate away and went up to his bedroom, declaring vehemently that he was poisoned. He undressed, lay down on his sofa, and filled the air with deep groans.

From time to time he stopped and dozed a little, or listened to what he could hear of our talk. His feeling was that we shouldn't be talking at all. We ought to be sitting with bowed heads in silence until he recovered. "Poisoned!" he suddenly boomed, to remind us. "Oh, God! I am poisoned!"

At this point, Mother, who was down in the library, laughed. Father heard her. He jumped up from his sofa and marched from his bedroom indignantly into the hall. "I'm a sick man!" he thundered robustly. "And nobody in this house gives a damn!"

Mother hurried upstairs to see what he wanted. He insisted on her rubbing his back. Sick or well, that always soothed him, and he would have liked her to do it for hours. He loved to close his eyes, with someone's hand moving quietly on him, while a feeling of comfort flowed into his thoughts and his nerves.

Mother didn't think much of rubbing, however. She didn't like it herself. When anyone rubbed her, she stiffened and resisted at once. Consequently she had no idea of the right way to do it. When she had to rub Father, she always got tired of it in a very few minutes.

She gave him some hasty little rubs and digs as well as she could, but just as he was beginning to relax, she said, "There now, Clare, that's enough." Father was so disappointed by this that it reminded him that he was poisoned, and the only cure he could think of was the dismissal of Tobo.

The next day old Margaret was sent for to come at once to the country, and the house in town was locked up and left to take care of itself.

She came in a hack from the Harrison station. She was an odd sight. Her face looked familiar in her little black bonnet, tied under her chin, but she seemed strangely swollen and bulky; she stuck out in queer places; and as she crowded through the back door, she bruised me with her hard, bony hip. Only it wasn't her hip, it turned out; it was her favorite saucepan, which was tied to her waist under her skirt. Several large spoons, a dipper, a skillet, and two pair of shoes were made fast under it elsewhere. In her arms she had some bundles wrapped in newspapers, which Mother thought at first held her clothes, but when Margaret opened them we found they contained cheeses, melons, fresh coffee, a leg of lamb, some sweet potatoes, and other provisions. Margaret had no faith at all in being able to buy any supplies in the country. She had brought as complete a larder to Harrison as though we were at the North Pole.

"But didn't you bring any clothes with you, Margaret? Not even an apron?" asked Mother.

Little Margaret pursed her lips closely together and didn't

answer at first. Then, as Mother stood waiting, she said unwillingly, "I have me other clothes on me."

She had wanted to have her hands free, it seemed, to bring us something good to eat. So under her street dress she was wearing two other dresses on that hot summer day, a collection of stiffly starched petticoats, three aprons, two night-gowns, and pretty much all the rest of her wardrobe.

As she was climbing upstairs to unpeel and unpack herself, Father saw her. "Is that you, Margaret?" he called, suddenly feeling much better. "Thank God!"

FATHER THUMPS ON THE FLOOR

Old Margaret was just the kind of cook that we wanted. Lots of cooks can do rich dishes well. Margaret couldn't. But she cooked simple, everyday dishes in a way that made our mouths water. Her apple pies were the most satisfying pies I've ever tasted. Her warmed-up potatoes were so delicious I could have made my whole dinner of them.

Yet even Margaret sometimes miscalculated. A large, royal-looking steak would be set before Father, which, upon being cut into, would turn out to be too underdone. Father's face would darken with disappointment. If the earth had begun to wobble and reel in its orbit he could scarcely have been more disapproving. He would raise his foot, under the table, and stamp slowly and heavily three times on the rug. Thud; thud; thud.

At this solemn signal, we would hear Margaret leave the kitchen below us and come clumping step by step up the stairs to the dining-room door.

"Margaret, look at that steak."

Margaret would step nearer and peer with a shocked look at the platter. "The Lord bless us and save us," she would say to herself in a low voice. She would then seize the platter and make off with it, to better it the best way she could, and Father would gloomily wait and eat a few vegetables and pour out a fresh glass of claret.

Father and Margaret were united by the intense interest they both took in cooking. Each understood the other instinctively. They had a complete fellow-feeling. Mother's great interest was in babies—she had never been taught how to cook. All she wanted was to keep Father pleased somehow; and if it was too difficult she didn't always care about even that.

At table it was Father who carved the fowl, or sliced the roast lamb or beef. I liked to watch him whet the knife and go at it. He had such a fine, easy hand. To a hungry boy, he seemed over-deliberate and exact in his strokes, yet in a moment or two he had done. And usually the cooking had been as superb as the carving. Sometimes it was so perfect that Father's face would crinkle with pleasure, and with a wink at us he'd summon Margaret with his usual three measured thumps. She would appear, clutching her skirts with both hands, and looking worried. "What's wanting?" she'd ask.

"Margaret," Father would tell her affectionately, "that fricas-seed chicken is *good*."

Margaret would turn her wrinkled face aside, and look down, and push the flat of her hand out toward Father. It was the same gesture she used when she said "Get along with you" to flatterers. She couldn't say that to Father, but she would beam at him, and turn and go out, and stump back down the dark little stairs with-out ever a word.

Every once in a while, when the household bills were getting too high, a platter with three tiny French chops on it would be placed before Father, and a larger dish full of cold corned beef or Irish stew before Mother. At this sight we boys would stop talking and become round-eyed and still.

Father would look over at Mother's dish to see if it seemed appetizing, for he often said there was nothing better than one of Margaret's stews. The stew usually seemed possible enough to him, yet not quite what he wanted. He would then ask Mother if she'd have a chop.

Mother always said, "No."

"They look nice and juicy," Father would urge her, but she would say again she didn't want any, and turn her eyes away from the platter.

Father would then look around at the rest of us, doubtfully. He had four sons, all with appetites. He would clear his throat as though getting ready to offer a chop to each boy in turn; but he usually compromised by saying, "Will anyone else have a chop?"

"No, Clare," Mother would quickly and impatiently reply, "they're for you. The rest of us are going to have stew tonight." And she'd smile brightly but a little watchfully around at us boys, to be sure that we were making no fuss about it, while she hurried to get the thing settled.

We boys would then earnestly watch Father while he ate the three chops.

Not that we didn't like Margaret's stew, which was the best in the world, but we regarded dinner as a special occasion, and we often had stew for lunch.

If some of us had taken up Father's offer, and left him with only one chop or none, I suppose that he would have asked Mother, "Where are the rest of the chops?" and been very cross about it when she told him there weren't any more. But his offer of them to us was sincere, though it cost him a struggle. He wanted plenty of food bought for everyone. His instincts were generous. Only, it made him cross if he suffered for those generous instincts.

Long after Margaret died, Father was speaking one night of how good her things always had tasted.

"I wish she could hear you," said Mother. She smiled tenderly at the thought of that gallant and dear little figure. "If anybody ever was sure of going to Heaven," she added, "I know it was Margaret."

This struck Father as a recommendation of the place. He took a sip of cognac and said casually, "I'll look her up when I get there. I'll have her take care of me."

Mother started to say something but checked herself.

"What's the matter?" he asked.

"Well, Clare dear," said Mother, "Margaret must be in some special part of Heaven, she was so good. You'd be very fortunate, Clare, to get to the same part as Margaret."

"Hah!" Father said, suddenly scowling. "I'll make a devil of a row if I don't."

THE GIFT OF SONG

One day when I was about ten years old, and George eight, Father suddenly remembered an intention of his to have us taught music. There were numerous other things that he felt every boy ought to learn, such as swimming, blacking his own shoes, and bookkeeping; to say nothing of school work, in which he expected a boy to excel. He now recalled that music, too, should be included in our education. He held that all children should be taught to play on something, and sing.

He was right, perhaps. At any rate, there is a great deal to be said for his program. On the other hand, there are children and children. I had no ear for music.

Father was the last man to take this into consideration, however: he looked upon children as raw material that a father should mold. When I said I couldn't sing, he said nonsense. He went to the piano. He played a scale, cleared his throat, and sang *Do, re, mi,* and the rest. He did this with relish. He sang it again, high and low. He then turned to me and told me to sing it, too, while he accompanied me.

I was bashful. I again told him earnestly that I couldn't sing. He laughed. "What do *you* know about what you can or can't do?" And he added in a firm, kindly voice, "Do whatever I tell you." He was always so sure of himself that I couldn't help having faith in him. For all I knew, he could detect the existence of organs in a boy of which that boy had no evidence. It was astonishing, certainly, but if he said I could sing, I could sing.

I planted myself respectfully before him. He played the first note. He never wasted time in explanations; that was not his way; and I had only the dimmest understanding of what he wished me

94

to do. But I struck out, haphazard, and chanted the extraordinary syllables loudly.

"No, no, no!" said Father, disgustedly.

We tried it again.

"No, no, no!" He struck the notes louder.

We tried it repeatedly. . . .

I gradually saw that I was supposed to match the piano, in some way, with my voice. But how such a thing could be done I had no notion whatever. The kind of sound a piano made was different from the sound of a voice. And the various notes—I could hear that each one had its own sound, but that didn't help me out any: they were all total strangers. One end of the piano made deep noises, the other end shrill; I could make my voice deep, shrill, or medium; but that was the best I could do.

At the end of what seemed to me an hour, I still stood at attention, while Father still tried energetically to force me to sing. It was an absolute deadlock. He wouldn't give in, and I couldn't. Two or three times I had felt for a moment I was getting the hang of it, but my voice wouldn't do what I wanted; I don't think it could. Anyhow, my momentary grasp of the problem soon faded. It felt so queer to be trying to do anything exact with my voice. And Father was so urgent about it, and the words so outlandish. *Do, re, mi, fa, sol, la, si, do!* What a nightmare! though by this time he had abandoned his insistence on my learning the scale; he had reduced his demands to my singing one single note: *Do.* I continually opened my mouth wide, as he had instructed me, and shouted the word *Do* at random, hoping it might be the pitch. He snorted, and again struck the piano. I again shouted *Do.*

George sat on the sofa by the parlor door, watching me with great sympathy. He always had the easy end of it. George was a good brother; he looked up to me, loved me, and I couldn't help loving him; but I used to get tired of being his path-breaker in encounters with Father. All Father's experience as a parent was obtained at my hands. He was a man who had many impossible hopes for his children, and it was only as he tried these on me that he slowly became disillusioned. He clung to each hope tenaciously; he surrendered none without a long struggle; after which he felt baffled and indignant, and I felt done up, too. At such times if only he had repeated the attack on my brothers, it might have been hard on them but at least it would have given me a slight rest. But no, when he had had a disappointment, he turned to new projects. And as I was the eldest, the new were always tried out on me. George and the others trailed along happily, in comparative peace, while I perpetually confronted Father in a wrestling match upon some new ground. . . .

Mother came into the room in her long swishing skirts. Father was obstinately striking the piano for the nine thousandth time, and I was steadily though hopelessly calling out *Do*.

"Why Clare! What *are* you doing?" Mother cried.

Father jumped up. I suppose that at heart he was relieved at her interruption—it allowed him to stop without facing the fact of defeat. But he strongly wished to execute any such maneuver without loss of dignity, and Mother never showed enough regard for this, from his point of view. Besides, he was full of a natural irritation at the way things resisted him. He had visited only a part of this on me. The rest he now hurled at her. He said would she kindly go away and leave him alone with his sons. He declared he would not be interfered with. He banged the piano lid shut. He said he was "sick and tired of being systematically thwarted and hindered," and he swore he would be damned if he'd stand it. Off he went to his room.

"You'll only have to come right back down again," Mother called after him. "The soup's being put on the table."

"I don't want any dinner."

"Oh Clare! Please! it's oyster soup!"

"Don't want any." He slammed his room door.

We sat down, frightened, at table. I was exhausted. But the soup was a life-saver. It was more like a stew, really. Rich milk, oyster juice, and big oysters. I put lots of small hard crackers in mine, and one slice of French toast. That hot toast soaked in soup was delicious, only there wasn't much of it, and as Father par-

ticularly liked it, we had to leave it for him. But there was plenty
of soup: a great tureen full. Each boy had two helpings.

Father came down in the middle of it, still offended, but he
ate his full share. I guess he was somewhat in need of a life-
saver himself. The chops and peas and potatoes came on. He
gradually forgot how we'd wronged him.

There were too many things always happening at our family
dinners, too many new vexations, or funny things, for him to
dwell on the past.

But though he was willing enough, usually, to drop small re-
sentments, nevertheless there were certain recollections that
remained in his mind—such as the feeling that Mother sometimes
failed to understand his plans for our welfare, and made his
duty needlessly hard for him by her interference; and the impression that I was an awkward little boy, and great trouble to
train.

Not that these thoughts disturbed him, or lessened at all his
self-confidence. He lit his cigar after dinner and leaned back
philosophically, taking deep vigorous puffs with enjoyment, and
drinking black coffee. When I said, "Good night, Father," he
smiled at me like a humorous potter, pausing to consider—for
the moment—an odd bit of clay. Then he patted me affectionately on the shoulder and I went up to bed.

THE NOBLEST INSTRUMENT

Father had been away, reorganizing some old upstate railroad. He returned in an executive mood and proceeded to shake up our home. In spite of my failure as a singer, he was still bound to have us taught music. We boys were summoned before him and informed that we must at once learn to play on something. We might not appreciate it now, he said, but we should later on. "You, Clarence, will learn the violin. George, you the piano. Julian—well, Julian is too young yet. But you older boys must have lessons."

I was appalled at this order. At the age of ten it seemed a disaster to lose any more of my freedom. The days were already too short for our games after school; and now here was a chunk to come out of playtime three days every week. A chunk every day, we found afterward, because we had to practice.

George sat at the piano in the parlor, and faithfully learned to pound out his exercises. He had all the luck. He was not an inspired player, but at least he had some ear for music. He also had the advantage of playing on a good robust instrument, which he didn't have to be careful not to drop, and was in no danger of breaking. Furthermore, he did not have to tune it. A piano had some good points.

But I had to go through a blacker and more gruesome experience. It was bad enough to have to come in from the street and the sunlight and go down into our dark little basement where I took my lessons. But that was only the opening chill of the struggle that followed.

The whole thing was uncanny. The violin itself was a queer, fragile, cigar-boxy thing, that had to be handled most gingerly. Nothing sturdy about it. Why, a fellow was liable to crack it putting it into its case. And then my teacher, he was queer too. He had a queer pickled smell.

I dare say he wasn't queer at all really, but he seemed so to me, because he was different from the people I generally met. He was probably worth a dozen of some of them, but I didn't know it. He was one of the violins in the Philharmonic, and an excellent player; a grave, middle-aged little man—who was obliged to give lessons.

He wore a black, wrinkled frock coat, and a discolored gold watch-chain. He had small, black-rimmed glasses; not tortoise-shell, but thin rims of metal. His violin was dark, rich, and polished, and would do anything for him.

Mine was balky and awkward, brand new, and of a light, common color.

The violin is intended for persons with a passion for music. I wasn't that kind of person. I liked to hear a band play a tune that we could march up and down to, but try as I would, I could seldom whistle such a tune afterward. My teacher didn't know this. He greeted me as a possible genius.

He taught me how to hold the contraption, tucked under my chin. I learned how to move my fingers here and there on its handle or stem. I learned how to draw the bow across the strings, and thus produce sounds. . . .

Does a mother recall the first cry of her baby, I wonder? I still remember the strange cry at birth of that new violin.

My teacher, Herr M., looked as though he had suddenly taken a large glass of vinegar. He sucked in his breath. His lips were drawn back from his teeth, and his eyes tightly shut. Of course, he hadn't expected my notes to be sweet at the start; but still, there was something unearthly about that first cry. He snatched the violin from me, examined it, readjusted its pegs, and comforted it gently, by drawing his own bow across it. It was only a new and not especially fine violin, but the sounds it made for him were more natural—they were classifiable sounds. They were not richly musical, but at least they had been heard before on this earth.

He handed the instrument back to me with careful directions. I tucked it up under my chin again and grasped the end tight. I held my bow exactly as ordered. I looked up at him, waiting.

"Now," he said, nervously.

I slowly raised the bow, drew it downward. . . .

This time there were *two* dreadful cries in our little front basement. One came from my new violin and one from the heart of Herr M.

Herr M. presently came to, and smiled bravely at me, and said if I wanted to rest a moment he would permit it. He seemed to think I might wish to lie down awhile and recover. I didn't feel any need of lying down. All I wanted was to get through the lesson. But Herr M. was shaken. He was by no means ready to let me proceed. He looked around desperately, saw the music book, and said he would now show me that. We sat down side by side on the window-seat, with the book in his lap, while he pointed out the notes to me with his finger, and told me their names.

After a bit, when he felt better, he took up his own violin, and instructed me to watch him and note how he handled the strings. And then at last, he nerved himself to let me take my violin up again. "Softly, my child, softly," he begged me, and stood facing the wall. . . .

We got through the afternoon somehow, but it was a ghastly experience. Part of the time he was maddened by the mistakes I kept making, and part of the time he was plain wretched. He covered his eyes. He seemed ill. He looked often at his watch, even shook it as though it had stopped; but he stayed the full hour.

That was Wednesday. What struggles he had with himself before Friday, when my second lesson was due, I can only dimly imagine, and of course I never even gave them a thought at the time. He came back to recommence teaching me, but he had changed—he had hardened. Instead of being cross, he was stern; and instead of sad, bitter. He wasn't unkind to me, but we were no longer companions. He talked to himself, under his breath;

and sometimes he took bits of paper, and did little sums on them, gloomily, and then tore them up.

During my third lesson I saw the tears come to his eyes. He went up to Father and said he was sorry but he honestly felt sure I'd never be able to play.

Father didn't like this at all. He said he felt sure I would. He dismissed Herr M. briefly—the poor man came stumbling back down in two minutes. In that short space of time he had gallantly gone upstairs in a glow, resolved upon sacrificing his earnings for the sake of telling the truth. He returned with his earnings still running, but with the look of a lost soul about him, as though he felt that his nerves and his sanity were doomed to destruction. He was low in his mind, and he talked to himself more than ever. Sometimes he spoke harshly of America, sometimes of fate.

But he no longer struggled. He accepted this thing as his destiny. He regarded me as an unfortunate something, outside the human species, whom he must simply try to labor with as well as he could. It was a grotesque, indeed a hellish experience, but he felt he must bear it.

He wasn't the only one—he was at least not alone in his sufferings. Mother, though expecting the worst, had tried to be hopeful about it, but at the end of a week or two I heard her and Margaret talking it over. I was slaughtering a scale in the front basement, when Mother came down and stood outside the door in the kitchen hall and whispered, "Oh, Margaret!"

I watched them. Margaret was baking a cake. She screwed up her face, raised her arms, and brought them down with hands clenched.

"I don't know what we shall do, Margaret."

"The poor little feller," Margaret whispered. "He can't make the thing go."

This made me indignant. They were making me look like a lubber. I wished to feel always that I could make anything go. . . .

I now began to feel a determination to master this thing. History shows us many examples of the misplaced determinations of men—they are one of the darkest aspects of human life, they spread so much needless pain: but I knew little history. And I viewed what little I did know romantically—I should have seen in such episodes their heroism, not their futility. Any role that seemed heroic attracted me, no matter how senseless.

Not that I saw any chance for heroism in our front basement, of course. You had to have a battlefield or something. I saw only that I was appearing ridiculous. But that stung my pride. I hadn't wanted to learn anything whatever about fiddles or music, but since I was in for it, I'd do it, and show them I could. A boy will often put in enormous amounts of his time trying to prove he isn't as ridiculous as he thinks people think him.

Meanwhile Herr M. and I had discovered that I was nearsighted. On account of the violin's being an instrument that sticks out in front of one, I couldn't stand close enough to the music book to see the notes clearly. He didn't at first realize that I often made mistakes from that cause. When he and I finally comprehended that I had this defect, he had a sudden new hope that this might have been the whole trouble, and that when it was corrected I might play like a human being at last.

Neither of us ventured to take up this matter with Father. We knew that it would have been hard to convince him that my eyes were not perfect, I being a son of his and presumably made in his image; and we knew that he immediately would have felt we were trying to make trouble for him, and would have shown an amount of resentment which it was best to avoid. So Herr M. instead lent me his glasses. These did fairly well. They turned the dim grayness of the notes into a queer bright distortion, but the main thing was they did make them brighter, so that I now saw more of them. How well I remember those little glasses. Poor, dingy old things. Herr M. was nervous about lending them to me; he feared that I'd drop them. It would have been safer if they had been spectacles: but no, they were pince-nez; and I had to learn to balance them across my nose as well as I could. I couldn't wear them up near my eyes because my nose was too thin there; I had to put them about half-way down where there was enough flesh to hold them. I also had to tilt my head back, for the music-stand was a little too tall for me. Herr M. sometimes mounted me on a stool, warning me not to step off. Then when I was all set, and when he without his glasses was blind, I would smash my way into the scales again.

All during the long winter months I worked away at this job. I gave no thought, of course, to the family. But they did to me. Our house was heated by a furnace, which had big warm air pipes; these ran up through the walls with wide outlets into each room, and sound traveled easily and ringingly through their roomy, tin passages. My violin could be heard in every part of the house. No one could settle down to anything while I was practicing. If visitors came they soon left. Mother couldn't even sing to the baby. She would wait, watching the clock, until my long hour of scalework was over, and then come downstairs and shriek at me that my time was up. She would find me sawing away with my forehead wet, and my hair wet and stringy, and even my clothes slowly getting damp from my exertions. She would feel my collar, which was done for, and say I must change it. "Oh, Mother! Please!"—for I was in a hurry now to run out and play. But she wasn't being fussy about my collar, I can see, looking back; she was using it merely as a barometer or gauge of my pores. She thought I had better dry myself before going out in the snow.

It was a hard winter for Mother. I believe she also had fears for the baby. She sometimes pleaded with Father; but no one could ever tell Father anything. He continued to stand like a rock against stopping my lessons.

Schopenhauer, in his rules for debating, shows how to win a weak case by insidiously transferring an argument from its right field, and discussing it instead from some irrelevant but impregnable angle. Father knew nothing of Schopenhauer, and was never insidious, but, nevertheless, he had certain natural gifts for debate. In the first place his voice was powerful and stormy, and he let it out at full strength, and kept on letting it out with a vigor that stunned his opponents. As a second gift, he was convinced at all times that his opponents were wrong. Hence, even if they did win a point or two, it did them no good, for he dragged the issue to some other ground then, where he and Truth could prevail. When Mother said it surely was plain enough that I had no ear, what was his reply? Why, he said that the violin was the noblest instrument invented by man. Having silenced her with this solid premise he declared that it followed that any boy was lucky to be given the privilege of learning to play it. No boy should expect to learn it immediately. It required persistence. Everything, he had found, required persistence. The motto was, Never give up.

All his life, he declared, he had persevered in spite of discouragement, and he meant to keep on persevering, and he meant me to, too. He said that none of us realized what he had had to go through. If he had been the kind that gave up at the very first obstacle, where would he have been now—where would any of the family have been? The answer was, apparently, that we'd either have been in a very bad way, poking round for crusts in the gutter, or else nonexistent. We might have never even been born if Father had not persevered.

Placed beside this record of Father's vast trials overcome, the little difficulty of my learning to play the violin seemed a trifle. I faithfully spurred myself on again, to work at the puzzle. Even my teacher seemed impressed with these views on persistence. Though older than Father, he had certainly not made as much money, and he bowed to the experience of a practical man who was a success. If he, Herr M., had been a success he would not have had to teach boys; and sitting in this black pit in which his need of money had placed him, he saw more than ever that he must learn the ways of this world. He listened with all his heart, as to a god, when Father shook his forefinger, and told him how to climb to the heights where financial rewards were achieved. The idea he got was that perseverance was sure to lead to great wealth.

Consequently our front basement continued to be the home of lost causes.

Of course, I kept begging Herr M. to let me learn just one tune. Even though I seldom could whistle them, still I liked tunes; and I knew that, in my hours of practicing, a tune would be a comfort. That is, for myself. Here again I never gave a thought to the effect upon others.

Herr M., after many misgivings, to which I respectfully listened —though they were not spoken to me, they were muttered to himself, pessimistically—hunted through a worn old book of selections, and after much doubtful fumbling chose as simple a thing as he could find for me—for me and the neighbors.

It was spring now, and windows were open. That tune became famous.

What would the musician who had tenderly composed this air, years before, have felt if he had foreseen what an end it would have, on Madison Avenue; and how, before death, it would be execrated by that once peaceful neighborhood. I engraved it on their hearts; not in its true form but in my own eerie versions. It was the only tune I knew. Consequently I played and re-played it.

Even horrors when repeated grow old and lose part of their sting. But those I produced were, unluckily, never the same. To be sure, this tune kept its general structure the same, even in my sweating hands. There was always the place where I climbed unsteadily up to its peak, and that difficult spot where it wavered, or staggered, and stuck; and then a sudden jerk of resumption— I came out strong on that. Every afternoon when I got to that difficult spot, the neighbors dropped whatever they were doing to wait for that jerk, shrinking from the moment, and yet fever-ishly impatient for it to come.

But what made the tune and their anguish so different each day? I'll explain. The strings of a violin are wound at the end around pegs, and each peg must be screwed in and tightened till the string sounds just right. Herr M. left my violin properly tuned when he went. But suppose a string broke, or that some-how I jarred a peg loose. Its string then became slack and soundless. I had to re-tighten it. Not having an ear, I was highly uncertain about this.

Our neighbors never knew at what degree of tautness I'd put such a string. I didn't myself. I just screwed her up tight enough to make a strong reliable sound. Neither they nor I could tell which string would thus appear in a new role each day, nor foresee the profound transformations this would produce in that tune.

All that spring this unhappy and ill-destined melody floated out through my window, and writhed in the air for one hour daily, in sunshine or storm. All that spring our neighbors and I daily toiled to its peak, and staggered over its hump, so to speak, and fell wailing through space.

Things now began to be said to Mother which drove her to act. She explained to Father that the end had come at last. Absolutely. "This awful nightmare cannot go on," she said.

Father pooh-poohed her.

She cried. She told him what it was doing to her. He said that she was excited, and that her descriptions of the sounds I made were exaggerated and hysterical—must be. She was always too vehement, he shouted. She must learn to be calm.

"But you're downtown, *you* don't have to hear it!"

Father remained wholly skeptical.

She endeavored to shame him. She told him what awful things the neighbors were saying about him, because of the noise I was making, for which he was responsible.

He couldn't be made to look at it that way. If there really were any unpleasantness then I was responsible. He had provided me with a good teacher and a good violin—so he reasoned. In short, he had done his best, and no father could have done more. If I made hideous sounds after all that, the fault must be mine. He said that Mother should be stricter with me, if necessary, and make me try harder.

This was the last straw. I couldn't try harder. When Mother told me his verdict I said nothing, but my body rebelled. Self-discipline had its limits—and I wanted to be out: it was spring.

I skimped my hours of practice when I heard the fellows playing outside. I came home late for lessons—even forgot them. Little by little they stopped.

Father was outraged. His final argument, I remember, was that my violin had cost twenty-five dollars; if I didn't learn it the money would be wasted, and he couldn't afford it. But it was put to him that my younger brother, Julian, could learn it instead, later on. Then summer came, anyhow, and we went for three months to the seashore; and in the confusion of this Father was defeated and I was set free.

In the autumn little Julian was led away one afternoon, and imprisoned in the front basement in my place. I don't remember how long they kept him down there, but it was several years. He had an ear, however, and I believe he learned to play fairly well. This would have made a happy ending for Herr M. after all; but it was some other teacher, a younger man, who was engaged to teach Julian. Father said Herr M. was a failure.

FATHER TRIES TO MAKE MOTHER LIKE FIGURES

Father was always trying to make Mother keep track of the household expenses. He was systematic by nature and he had had a sound business training. He had a full set of account books at home in addition to those in his office—a personal cashbook, journal, and ledger—in which he carefully made double entries. His home ledger showed at a glance exactly how much a month or a year his clothes or his clubs or his cigar bills amounted to. Every item was listed. He knew just how every one of his expenses compared with those of former years, and when he allowed the figures to mount up in one place, he could bring them down in another.

Before he got married, these books had apparently given him great satisfaction, but he said they were never the same after that. They had suddenly stopped telling him anything. He still knew what his personal expenses were, but they were microscopic compared to his household expenses, and of those he knew nothing, no details, only the horrible total. His money was flowing away in all directions and he had no record of it.

Every once in so often he tried to explain his system to Mother. But his stout, leather-bound ledgers, and his methodical ruling of lines in red ink, and the whole business of putting down every little expense every day, were too much for her. She didn't feel that women should have anything to do with accounts, any more than men should have to see that the parlor was dusted. She had been only a débutante when she married, not long out of school, and though she had been head of her class, and wrote well and spelled well, and spoke beautiful French, she had never laid eyes on a ledger. Every time Father showed her his, she was unsympathetic.

Figures were so absorbing to Father that for a long time he couldn't believe Mother really disliked them. He hoped for years that her lack of interest was due only to her youth and that she would outgrow it. He said confidently that she would soon learn to keep books. It was simple. Meanwhile, if she would just make a memorandum for him of whatever she spent, he would enter it himself in the accounts until he could trust her to do it.

That day never arrived.

Father knew where some of the money went, for part of the expenses were charged. But this was a poor consolation. Although the household bills gave him plenty of data which he could sit and stare at, in horror, he said that many of the details were not clear to him, and most of the rest were incredible.

He tried to go over the bills regularly with Mother, as well as he could, demanding information about items which he did not understand. But every now and then there were items which she didn't understand, either. She said she wasn't sure they were mistakes, but she couldn't remember about them. Her mind was a blank. She behaved as though the bill were a total stranger to her.

This was one of the features that annoyed Father most.

Mother didn't like these sessions a bit. She told us she hated bills, anyhow. When they were larger than she expected, she felt guilty and hardly dared to let Father see them. When some of them seemed small to her, she felt happy, but not for long, because they never seemed small to Father. And when she spotted an error—when she found, for instance, that Tyson, the butcher, had charged too much for a broiler—she had to fly around to the shop to have it corrected, and argue it out, and go through a disagreeable experience, and then when she told Father how hard she had worked he took it as a matter of course, and she indignantly found that she never got any credit for it.

Sometimes I had to do this kind of thing, too. There was a man named Flannagan over on Sixth Avenue who supplied us with newspapers, and I used to be sent to rebuke him when he overcharged. Father said Flannagan had no head for figures.

After checking up the addition and recomputing the individual items, he would generally discover that the bill was anywhere from three to fourteen cents out. He then sent for me, handed me the correct amount of change and the bill, and told me to go over to see Flannagan the next day, after school, and warn him that we wouldn't stand it.

I got used to this after a while, but the first time I went I was frightened. Flannagan was a large man who looked like a barkeeper and whose face was tough and belligerent. When I marched into his dark little shop and shakily attempted to warn him that we wouldn't stand it, he leaned over the counter, stared down at me, and said loudly, "Har?"

"Excuse me, Mr. Flannagan," I repeated, "here is your bill but it's wrong."

"*Har?*"

"It seems to be just a little wrong, sir. Eight cents too much for the *Sun.*"

Flannagan snatched the bill from me and the money, and went to his desk. After working over it with a thick pencil, and smudging the bill all up, front and back, he snarled to himself, and receipted it the way Father wished. Then he chucked it disdainfully on the counter. I picked it up and got out.

"Confound it all," Father said when he got it, "don't muss my bills up so."

"It was Mr. Flannagan, Father."

"Well, tell him he must learn to be tidy."

"Yes, sir," I said, hopelessly.

I liked figures myself, just as Father did, and I thought it was queer Mother didn't. She was as quick at them as anybody, yet she didn't get any fun out of writing them down and adding them up. I liked the problems in my school arithmetic, and I deeply admired Father's account books. I didn't dare tell him this, somehow. He never offered to let me examine those big, handsome books. He kept them locked up in a desk he had, down in the front basement.

If I showed Father one of my arithmetic lessons, he was inter-

ested—he got up from his chair and put down his newspaper
and sat at the dining-room table with a pencil and paper, to see
how well I had done. But Mother didn't want to go into such
matters.

Every month when the bills came in, there was trouble. Mother
seemed to have no great extravagances. But she loved pretty
things. She had a passion for china, for instance. She saw hundreds of beautiful cups and saucers that it was hard to walk away
from and leave. She knew she couldn't buy them, and mustn't,
but every so often she did. No one purchase seemed large by
itself, but they kept mounting up, and Father declared that she
bought more china than the Windsor Hotel.

Father couldn't see why charge accounts should be a temptation to Mother. They were no temptation to him. He knew that
the bill would arrive on the first of the month and that in a few
days he would pay it. He said he had supposed that Mother
would have the same feelings that he had about this.

But Mother was one of those persons for whom charge accounts were invented. When she bought something and charged
it, the first of the next month seemed far away, and she hoped
that perhaps Father wouldn't mind—he might be nice about it
for once. Her desire for the thing was strong at that moment, the
penalty was remote, and she fell.

She was a different woman entirely when she had to pay cash.
It was hard to get cash out of Father, she never got much at
one time, and as she looked in her pocketbook she could see her
precious little hoard dwindling. She fingered a purchase and
thought twice about it before she could bear to part with the
money. But shopping on a charge account was fun. She tried not
to let herself be tempted, but of course she was, all the time, and
after she had conscientiously resisted nine lovely temptations, it
didn't seem really wicked to yield to the tenth.

Father did his level best to take all the fun out of it for her.
Once every month regularly he held court and sat as a judge,
and required her to explain her crimes and misdemeanors. When
she cried, or showed that she was hurt, it appeared that Father,

FATHER AND HIS HARD-
ROCKING SHIP

Father said that one great mystery about the monthly household expenses was what made them jump up and down so. "Anyone would suppose that there would be some regularity after a while which would let a man try to make plans, but I never know from one month to another what to expect."

Mother said she didn't, either. Things just seemed to go that way.

"But they have no business to go that way, Vinnie," Father declared. "And what's more I won't allow it."

Mother said she didn't see what she could do about it. All she knew was that when the bills mounted up, it didn't mean that she had been extravagant.

"Well, it certainly means that you've spent a devil of a lot of money," said Father.

Mother looked at him obstinately. She couldn't exactly deny this, but she said that it wasn't fair.

Appearances were often hopelessly against Mother but that never daunted her. She wasn't afraid of Father or anybody. She was a woman of great spirit who would have flown at and pecked any tyrant. It was only when she had a bad conscience that she had no heart to fight. Father had the best of her there because he never had a bad conscience. And he didn't know that he was a tyrant. He regarded himself as a long-suffering man who asked little of anybody, and who showed only the greatest moderation in his encounters with unreasonable beings like Mother. Mother's one advantage over him was that she was quicker. She was particularly elusive when Father was trying to hammer her into shape.

When the household expenses shot up very high, Father got frightened. He would then, as Mother put it, yell his head off. He always did some yelling anyhow, merely on general principles, but when his alarm was genuine he roared in real anguish.

Usually this brought the total down again, at least for a while. But there were times when no amount of noise seemed to do any good, and when every month for one reason or another the total went on up and up. And then, just as Father had almost resigned himself to this awful outgo, and just as he had eased up on his yelling and had begun to feel grim, the expenses, to his utter amazement, would take a sharp drop.

Mother didn't keep track of these totals, she was too busy watching small details, and Father never knew whether to tell her the good news or not. He always did tell her, because he couldn't keep things to himself. But he always had cause to regret it.

When he told her, he did it in as disciplinary a manner as possible. He didn't congratulate her on the expenses having come down. He appeared at her door, waving the bills at her with a threatening scowl, and said, "I've told you again and again that you could keep the expenses down if you tried, and this shows I was right."

Mother was always startled at such attacks, but she didn't lose her presence of mind. She asked how much less the amount was and said it was all due to her good management, of course, and Father ought to give her the difference.

At this point Father suddenly found himself on the defensive and the entire moral lecture that he had intended to deliver was wrecked. The more they talked, the clearer it seemed to Mother that he owed her that money. Only when he was lucky could he get out of her room without paying it.

He said that this was one of the things about her that was enough to drive a man mad.

The other thing was her lack of system, which was always cropping up in new ways. He sometimes looked at Mother as though he had never seen her before. "Upon my soul," he said,

"I almost believe you don't know what system is. You don't even want to know, either."

He had at last invented what seemed a perfect method of recording expenses. Whenever he gave any money to Mother, he asked her what it was for and made a note of it in his pocket notebook. His idea was that these items, added to those in the itemized bills, would show him exactly where every dollar had gone.

But they didn't.

He consulted his notebook. "I gave you six dollars in cash on the twenty-fifth of last month," he said, "to buy a new coffee-pot."

"Yes," Mother said, "because you broke your old one. You threw it right on the floor."

Father frowned. "I'm not talking about that," he answered. "I am simply endeavoring to find out from you, if I can—"

"But it's so silly to break a nice coffeepot, Clare, and that was the last of those French ones, and there was nothing the matter with the coffee that morning; it was made just the same as it always is."

"It wasn't," said Father. "It was made in a damned barbaric manner."

"And I couldn't get another French one," Mother continued, "because that little shop the Auffmordts told us about has stopped selling them. They said the tariff wouldn't let them any more, and I told Monsieur Duval he ought to be ashamed of himself to stand there and say so. I said that if I had a shop, I'd like to see the tariff keep me from selling things."

"But I gave you six dollars to buy a new pot," Father firmly repeated, "and now I find that you apparently got one at Lewis & Conger's and charged it. Here's their bill: 'one brown earthenware drip coffeepot, five dollars.' "

"So I saved you a dollar," Mother triumphantly said, "and you can hand it right over to me."

"Bah! What nonsense you talk!" Father cried. "Is there no

way to get this thing straightened out? What did you do with the six dollars?"

"Why, Clare! I can't tell you now, dear. Why didn't you ask at the time?"

"Oh, my God!" Father groaned.

"Wait a moment," said Mother. "I spent four dollars and a half for that new umbrella I told you I wanted, and you said I didn't need a new one, but I did, very much."

Father got out his pencil and wrote "New Umbrella for V." in his notebook.

"And that must have been the week," Mother went on, "that I paid Mrs. Tobin for two extra days' washing, so that was two dollars more out of it, which makes it six-fifty. There's another fifty cents that you owe me."

"I don't owe you anything," Father said. "You have managed to turn a coffeepot for me into a new umbrella for you. No matter what I give you money for, you buy something else with it, and if this is to keep on, I might as well not keep account books at all."

"I'd like to see you run this house without having any money on hand for things," Mother said.

"I am not made of money," Father replied. "You seem to think I only have to put my hand in my pocket to get some."

Mother not only thought this, she knew it. His wallet always was full. That was the provoking part of it—she knew he had the money right there, but he tried to keep from giving it to her. She had to argue it out of him.

"Well, you can put your hand in your pocket and give me that dollar-fifty this minute," she said. "You owe me that, anyhow."

Father said he didn't have a dollar-fifty to spare and tried to get back to his desk, but Mother wouldn't let him go till he paid her. She said she wouldn't put up with injustice.

Mother said it hampered her dreadfully never to have any cash. She was always having to pay out small amounts for demands that she had forgot to provide for, and in such emergencies the only way to do was to juggle things around. One result, however, of all these more or less innocent shifts was that in this way she usually took care of all her follies herself. All the small ones, at any rate. They never got entered on Father's books, except when they were monstrous.

She came home one late afternoon in a terrible state. "Has it come yet?" she asked the waitress.

The waitress said nothing had come that she knew of.

Mother ran upstairs with a hunted expression and flung herself down on her bed. When we looked in, she was sobbing.

It turned out that she had gone to an auction, and she had become so excited that she had bought but not paid for a grandfather's clock.

Mother knew in her heart that she had no business going to auctions. She was too suggestible, and if an hypnotic auctioneer once got her eye, she was lost. Besides, an auction aroused all her worst instincts—her combativeness, her recklessness, and her avaricious love of a bargain. And the worst of it was that this time it wasn't a bargain at all. At least she didn't think it was now. The awful old thing was about eight feet tall, and it wasn't the one she had wanted. It wasn't half as nice as the clock that old Miss Van Derwent had bought. And inside the hood over the dial, she said, there was a little ship which at first she hadn't noticed, a horrid ship that rocked up and down every time the clock ticked. It made her ill just to look at it. And she didn't have the money, and the man said he'd have to send it this evening, and what would Father say?

She came down to dinner, and left half-way through. Couldn't stand it. But an hour or two later, when the doorbell rang, she bravely went to tell Father.

She could hardly believe it, but she found that luck was with her, for once. If the clock had come earlier, there might have been a major catastrophe, but Father was in a good mood and he had had a good dinner. And though he never admitted it or spoke of it, he had a weakness for clocks. There were clocks all over the house, which he would allow no one to wind but himself. Every Sunday between breakfast and church he made the rounds, setting them at the right time by his infallible watch, regulating their speed, and telling us about every clock's little idiosyncrasies. When he happened to be coming downstairs on the hour, he cocked his ear, watch in hand, to listen to as many of them as he could, in the hope that they would all strike at once. He would reprove the impulsive pink clock in the spare room for striking too soon, and the big solemn clock in the dining-room for being a minute too late.

So when Mother led him out in the hall to confess to him and show him what she had bought, and he saw it was a clock, he fell in love with it, and made almost no fuss at all.

The let-down was too much for Mother. She tottered off to her room without another word and went straight to bed, leaving Father and the auctioneer's man setting up the new clock along-side the hatrack. Father was especially fascinated by the hard-rocking ship.

FATHER HAS TROUBLE
WITH THE LAND OF EGYPT

One winter when most of us boys were away, Mother was invited
to go to Egypt with Mrs. Tytus and two or three others. Mrs.
Tytus's son, Bob, was in charge of the party. They were going
to sail up the Nile in a houseboat, they would see Luxor and
Memphis, and altogether it seemed to be an ideal opportunity.
Mother loved travel. She was eager to see any place that was
new to her, even a place that was comparatively near-by like the
Whitneys' camp up in Maine, and as Egypt was ten times as far
away it seemed ten times as attractive.

She explained to Father what a wonderful chance it was. He
was not impressed. He said she wanted to go anywhere, always,
and he had never seen such a woman. Most women were glad
to have a home, he said, and knew enough to appreciate it, but
the only thing Mother seemed to want was to be on the go.

He went on to say that he himself had some sense, however,
and that he would no more think of going to Egypt than to the
North Pole. In a year or two, if he could get away from business,
they might go to London and Paris once more, but not one of
the Day family had ever even set foot in Egypt, and nobody else
he knew had, either, except Charlie Bond, who was one of those
restless fellows anyhow and was always doing queer things. He
said it was a wild and entirely unsuitable country, and that never
in any circumstances whatever would he take Mother to Egypt.

"But that's just why I want to go, Clare, dear. You don't
understand."

Father stared at her, and said, "What! What's why you want
to go? Of course I don't understand."

"Why, because you don't like it. I thought it would please you."

The veins in Father's forehead began to swell. "You thought it would *please* me?"

"Oh Clare, dear, don't be stupid. I knew you wouldn't want to take me over to Egypt yourself, but don't you see, if Mrs. Tytus takes me, you won't have to."

This theory that Mother was only trying to save him trouble by getting on a ship and going to Egypt completely dumfounded Father. But Mother clung firmly to it. She said of course she hated to have him miss seeing the Pyramids, but still she wouldn't enjoy dragging him off there if he was so unwilling, so he could just stay home and be comfortable in his own way while she went quietly over with Mrs. Tytus and hurried straight back.

To help clinch the matter, she brought Mrs. Tytus to see him. She brought young Bob Tytus, too. She told Father how much her letter of credit should be, and when he protested, she said she was saving him money, because it would be nearly twice as much if he took her himself.

When Father said violently that he wished her to remain at his side, she said everybody had to go away sometimes, and Dr. Markoe had warned her she must.

Dr. Markoe was a man Father liked. Mrs. Tytus was tactful and beautiful. Mother was pertinacious. Between them all, they actually bore Father down, and on the appointed day Mother got aboard the ship, letter of credit and all, with Father swearing that now he would have to worry about her all winter, and he wouldn't be happy for a minute until she got back.

"Goodbye, darling," she said. "Do be quiet and nice while I'm gone."

"I won't!" he shouted, kissing her, and he marched stiffly off, saying, "I hope you are satisfied," and then turned back at the foot of the gangplank, calling loudly, "Dear Vinnie!" Mother waved her hand, the whistles blew hoarsely, and the crowds swirled and jostled, hiding these two from each other as the ship slid away.

Father began looking for letters the very next morning, and when none came he cursed the pilot and the postman, and said that he had a bad headache. But a letter did arrive in a few days, when the pilot had had time to mail it, and after the first three or four weeks we heard from Mother often.

Some of the letters told us how she was constantly meeting people she knew, not only on the ship but at every port where Mrs. Tytus and she went ashore. "Your mother has the damnedest number of friends I ever heard of," said Father. "She's everlastingly meeting some old friend or other wherever she goes. I never see people I know when I'm traveling. But there isn't a city in Europe where your mother wouldn't spot a friend in five minutes." And when a letter came saying she had just climbed Mt. Vesuvius and had found old Mr. and Mrs. Quintard of Rye at the top, peering down into the crater, Father said that upon his soul he never knew anyone like her.

Other letters were full of household advice and instructions about menus, or warnings to Father to keep an eye on the rubber tree and to speak about washing the curtains. Others abused the bad habits of foreigners and the inconveniences and troubles she met. "Well, why doesn't she stay home, then?" Father demanded triumphantly. Though he swore at every foreigner who dared to inconvenience her, he relished the complaints in these letters.

But when Mother left civilization behind her, even a far outpost like Cairo, and went off up the Nile in a thing called a dahabeah, manned by native boatmen, and when letters came from queer-sounding ancient cities in the interior, Father got nervous. He said it was a wild, harum-scarum thing to do. Moreover, it was entirely needless. He said he could see all of Egypt he wanted to without leaving New York—there were enough musty old mummies in the Museum to satisfy anybody. "But your mother wouldn't look at them; no, they weren't dead enough for her; she had to go traipsing off to see a mummy on its native heath. Why, somebody even brought an obelisk over here at great expense," he went on, "and left it to crumble away in the Park, where people can see it for nothing, but for some reason or other it isn't crumbly enough for your mother."

There were letters about the strange range of hills back of

Thebes, and the great colonnades at Karnak, and the statues and tombs, which Father pished at impatiently; and there were letters about fleas, and moonlight and Nubian songs, and finally letters with snapshots. Father said he hated these photographs. He spent a great deal of time staring at them in deep disapproval. There was one in particular of Mother looking very roguish and chic in her voluminous dress, sitting way up on top of a tall and insolent camel, with two big black men in white turbans standing off at one side. No other member of the party around. Not a soul in sight but the black men and Mother. Father looked at that photograph often and groaned about it at night, and kept shouting things to himself about "the ends of the earth."

Soon after that, Mother turned around and headed for home. Father grew more and more eager to have her back, every day. Up to this time he had been comparatively quiet, for him, but the nearer the day of her return came the more noisy and impatient he got. Even at the pier, he made indignant remarks about how slow the ship was, getting in.

He forgot this mood, however, the minute he hugged her, and he instantly took charge of her things—all except her black bag, which she would never let anyone touch—and he ordered all the customs inspectors around and got Mother through in a jiffy, and he found a man to shoulder her trunk and he picked out the best hackman, and as the carriage rattled off over the cobblestones, Mother said she was glad to be back.

Father had taken particular pains to have everything in the house in its place, so that when Mother came in the door, she would say that home was just the way she had left it. Instead, what she actually said was "Oh, this poor room! Why, I never!" and she put down the black bag and began setting the chairs at different angles and moving her favorite ornaments affectionately as she straightened them out. "Poor things," she said, as she patted them, "didn't anybody know enough to turn you around the way you belong?" Father followed her, looking puzzled at these minute changes, and calling her attention to the rubber tree, which had grown half a foot. "Well," Mother said, "of all the forlorn objects, with those dead leaves left hanging there!" But when Father's face fell and she saw how disappointed he looked, she smiled at him to console him and said, "You did the best you could, darling." And she climbed upstairs to unpack.

The letter of credit had been very much on Father's mind. He had never before given Mother the management of any such sum. He was so happy to have her back that he said nothing about this at first. He was waiting for Mother to speak of it. But she said nothing either.

He had two expectations about it, and he didn't know which to trust. One was hopeful but slightly unreal. The other, based on long experience, was pessimistic.

It had been a large letter of credit, not as much as Mrs. Tytus had recommended but still, he felt, generous. He felt he had a right to expect that Mother hadn't spent all of it, but had left a substantial balance undrawn which he could now restore to his bank account. His other and realer expectation was that she had spent every cent and had possibly even had to borrow from Mrs. Tytus besides. The fact that she was avoiding the subject pointed to this latter outcome.

One night, after she had gone up to bed, she came back down for a moment to hand him some papers. "You might be going over these, Clare," she said. "I couldn't keep track of everything for you; I tried my best but I couldn't. But I saved all the bills." And she went off to bed again.

Father checked them over, one by one, carefully. They were full of strange-looking details:

CAIRO, FEB. 24, 1900.

MRS. DAY,
  Room 195,
    Shepheard's Hotel.

To 1 Passage to Second Cataract	£ 23. 0.0.
To 60 days on Dahabeah Tih	85.16.0.
	£108.16.0.

"Second Cataract!" Father muttered to himself vehemently. What would such a woman do next?

These bills supplied Father with more details than he had hoped to keep track of, and there was none of them that he felt much inclined to dispute. But as there were still several hundred dollars unaccounted for, he waited for Mother to confess what she had done with the balance.

Day after day went by without her saying one word. He began to fear that things must be serious. He became so alarmed that it would have been a relief to him to know the worst and be done with it. But do what he could—without direct questioning—he could get nothing out of her.

Mother had noticed his fumbling hints of course, and she did have a confession to make. But first she went and had a long talk with a young girl she was fond of—a girl whose name was Wilhelmine Johnson, whom George afterward married. Mother confided to Wilhelmine in secret that the situation was this: she hadn't spent all her letter of credit but she hated to give up the balance. It was wicked of her to feel that way, she supposed, but she meant to keep it herself.

Wilhelmine instantly took a strong stand about this. She said that on no account should Mother hand over that money to Father. Mother had always wanted to have some money of her own, Wilhelmine reminded her, and now here was her chance.

As Mother listened to this advice she felt happy, but she also felt frightened. It seemed to her far more daring to hang onto that money than it had been to ride on a camel. But while she was away all those months she had had a taste of what independence was like, and she was reluctant to drop back into her Victorian role.

When at last she nerved herself to tell Father, he felt better at once, but he smilingly reproved her for not having come to him sooner; and as to her keeping the money he said that that was all nonsense. He said that she was home now, thank God, and as he always paid all her bills at home she had no use for this money.

"Yes I have too," Mother said.

"Well, what will you use it for, then?" Father asked.

Mother didn't wish to explain. As a matter of fact she had no very definite ideas as to what she wanted some cash of her own for—she only knew that she wanted it. She said: "Oh, there are lots of little things I could use it for, Clare. Things I'd like to get when I need them, without so much talk."

This seemed unconvincing to Father. He demanded the balance. He felt that he was the natural custodian of any such fund and the only safe place for it was in his bank account, as Mother, of course, didn't have one. But Mother insisted on hiding it away in her own bureau drawer. Father pointed out how reckless this was, but he could do nothing with her. That voyage to Egypt had changed her; she was always much harder to manage after that sail up the Nile.

As a gracious concession, however, she presented Father with a large pale blue scarab, mounted to use as a scarfpin, which she said she hadn't really meant to let him have until Christmas. Father looked at this object without enthusiasm and asked what it was. When he was told that it was the image of a sacred beetle, he immediately pushed it away. He didn't want any dead beetles in his scarf, he declared. He told Mother she could send it right back to the tomb it had come from. He said that he begged to inform her that he was not a mummy.

FATHER TEACHES ME TO
BE PROMPT

Father made a great point of our getting down to breakfast on time. I meant to be prompt, but it never occurred to me that I had better try to be early. My idea was to slide into the room at the last moment. Consequently, I often was late.

My brothers were often late, too, with the exception of George. He was the only thoroughly reliable son Father had. George got down so early, Father pointed out to me, that he even had time to practice a few minutes on the piano.

The reason George was so prompt was that he was in a hurry to see the sporting page before Father got hold of the newspaper, and the reason he then played the piano was to signal to the rest of us, as we dressed, which team had won yesterday's ball game. He had made up a code for this purpose, and we leaned over the banisters, pulling on our stockings and shoes, to hear him announce the results. I don't remember now what the titles were of the airs he selected, but the general idea was that if he played a gay, lively air it meant that the Giants had won, and when the strains of a dirge or lament floated up to us, it meant that Pop Anson had beaten them.

As Father didn't approve of professional baseball, we said nothing to him about this arrangement. He led his life and we led ours, under his nose. He took the newspaper away from George the moment he entered the room, and George said good morning to him and stepped innocently into the parlor. Then, while Father watched him through the broad doorway and looked over the political headlines, George banged out the baseball news for us on the piano. Father used to admonish him with a chuckle not to thump it so hard, but George felt that he had to.

We were at the top of the house, and he wanted to be sure that we'd hear him even if we were brushing our teeth. George always was thorough about things. He not only thumped the piano as hard as he could but he hammered out the tune over and over besides, while Father impatiently muttered to himself, *"Trop de zèle."*

Upstairs, there was usually some discussion as to what kind of news George was sending. He had not been allowed to learn popular tunes, which it would have been easy for us to recognize, and the few classic selections which were available in his little music book sounded pretty much alike at a distance. George rendered these with plenty of good will and muscle but not a great deal of sympathy. He regarded some of the rules of piano-playing as needlessly complicated.

The fact remained that he was the one boy who was always on time, and Father was so pleased by this that he bought a watch for him with "George Parmly Day, Always on Time" engraved on the back. He told me that as I was the eldest he had meant to give me a watch first, and he showed me the one he had bought for me. It was just like George's except that nothing had been engraved on it yet. Father explained that to his regret he would have to put it away for a while, until I had earned it by getting down early to breakfast.

Time went on, without much improvement on my part. Dawdling had got to be a habit with me. Sometimes my lateness was serious. One morning, when breakfast was half over and I had nothing on but a pair of long woolen drawers, Father called up from the front hall, napkin in hand, that he wouldn't stand it and that I was to come down that instant. When I shouted indignantly that I wasn't dressed yet, he said he didn't care. "Come down just as you are, confound it!" he roared. I was tempted to take him at his word, but thought there might be some catch in it and wouldn't, though I hurried, of course, all I could. Father ate his usual hearty breakfast in a stormy mood, and I ate my usual hearty breakfast in a guilty and nervous one. Come what might, we always ate heartily. I sometimes wished afterward that I hadn't, but it never seemed to hurt Father.

Mother told Father that if he would give me the watch, she was sure I'd do better. He said that he didn't believe it, and that that was a poor way to bring a boy up. To prove to him that he was wrong, Mother at last unlocked her jewel box and gave me a watch which had belonged to one of her elderly cousins. It was really too valuable a watch for a boy to wear, she said, and I must be very careful of it. I promised I would.

This watch, however, turned out to be painfully delicate. It was old, I was young. We were not exactly made for each other. It had a back and front of thin gold, and as Mother had had the former owner's monogram shaved off the front cover, that cover used to sink in the middle when pressed. Also, the lid fitted so closely that there was barely room for the glass crystal over the face. Such a very thin crystal had to be used that any pressure on the lid broke it.

I didn't press on the lid, naturally, after the first time this happened. I was careful, and everything would have gone well enough if other boys had been careful, too. It was not practicable, however, for me to make them be careful enough. When I had a fight, friendly or otherwise, I used to ask my opponent if he would be so kind as not to punch me on the left side of my stomach. He might or might not listen. If he and I were too excited and kept on long enough, the watch crystal broke anyway. There was never time to take off my watch first, and anyhow there was no place to put it. A watch that goes around the streets in a boy's pocket has to take life as it comes. This watch had never been designed for any such fate.

The first two crystals I broke Mother paid for, as Father disapproved of the whole business and would have nothing to do with it. Mother was always short of small change, however, and I hated to trouble her—and she hated to be troubled, too. "Oh, Clarence, dear! You haven't broken your watch again?" she cried when I opened the cover the second time, to show her the shattered fragments. She was so upset that I felt too guilty to tell her the next time it happened, and from then on I was reduced to the necessity of paying for the damage myself.

My pocket money never exceeded a dollar a month. Every new crystal cost twenty-five cents. It was a serious drain.

Wrestling and rolling around on the floor with Sam Willets, my watch quite forgotten, I would suddenly hear a faint tinkle and know that I was once more insolvent. I would pick out the broken glass and leave the watch with no crystal till I had twenty-five cents on hand, but these delays made me nervous. I knew that Mother wanted to feel sure I was taking good care of the watch, and that she might look at it any evening. As soon as I had the money, I hurried over to Sixth Avenue, where two old Germans kept a tiny watch shop, and left it there to be fixed. One of my most dismal memories is of that stuffy little shop's smell of sauerkraut, and how tall the glass counter then seemed, and the slowness of those two old Germans. When I got there late and they made me leave the watch overnight, I didn't have one easy moment until I got it back the next day. Again and again I argued with them that twenty-five cents was too much, especially for a regular customer, but they said it didn't pay them to do the work even for that, because those thin old-fashioned crystals were hard to get.

I gave up at last. I told Mother I didn't want to wear the watch any more.

Then I found, to my amazement, that this way out of my troubles was barred. The watch was an heirloom. And an heirloom was a thing that its recipient must value and cherish. No good Chinese, I read later on in life, fails to honor his ancestors; and no good boy, I was told in my youth, fails to appreciate heirlooms.

I left Mother's room in low spirits. That night, as I wound up my watch with its slender key, I envied George. Father had selected the right kind for George; he knew what a boy needed. It had a thick nickel case, it had an almost unbreakable crystal, and it endured daily life imperturbably, even when dropped in the bathtub.

It seemed to me that I was facing a pretty dark future. The curse of great possessions became a living thought to me, instead of a mere phrase. The demands that such possessions made on their owners for upkeep were merciless. For months I had had no money for marbles. I couldn't even afford a new top. In some way that I didn't fully understand I was yoked to a watch I now hated—a delicate thing that would always make trouble unless I learned to live gingerly.

Then I saw a way out. All this time I had kept on being late for breakfast at least once a week, out of habit, but it now occurred to me that if I could reform, perhaps Father might relent and give me that reliable nickel watch he had bought. I reformed. I occasionally weakened in my new resolution at first, but every time that crystal got broken I was spurred on to fresh efforts. When I had at length established a record for promptness that satisfied Father, he had my name engraved on the watch he had bought, and presented it to me. He was a little surprised at the intense pleasure I showed on this occasion, and as he watched me hopping around the room in delight he said "There, there" several times. "Don't be so excited, confound it," he added. "You'll knock over that vase."

Mother said she couldn't see why Father should give me a nickel watch when I had a gold one already, but he laughed and told her that "that old thing" was no kind of a watch for a boy. She reluctantly laid it away again to rest in her jewel box.

Her parting shot at Father was that anyhow she had been right; she had said all along that a watch was what I needed to teach me how to be prompt.

FATHER INTERFERES
WITH THE TWENTY-THIRD PSALM

When we boys were little, we used to go to Mother's room Sunday evenings, on our way upstairs to bed, and sit in a circle around her, while she told us a story from the Bible or talked to us about how good we ought to be and how much we ought to love God. She loved God herself as much as she dared to, and she deeply loved us, and she was especially tender and dear on those Sunday evenings. One of my brothers told me years afterward how much they had meant to him in those days, and how he had cherished the memory of them all his life.

I was a little older than my brothers, though, and my feelings were mixed. I loved Mother and hated to disappoint her, but I couldn't respond as easily as the other boys to her gentle appeals. I never seemed to have the emotions that she waited for me to show. I wish now that I could have listened uncritically and have thought only of the look in her eyes. What difference need it have made to me whether we had the same ideas about God, or whether the stories Mother thought lovely seemed less so to me? But there I sat, staring uncomfortably at the carpet and trying to avoid answering questions.

One night she repeated the Twenty-third Psalm to us and asked us to learn it by heart. "The Lord is my shepherd," she whispered, softly. "He maketh me to lie down in green pastures: he leadeth me beside the still waters." She raised her eyes and went on bravely, although with a quiver of fear: "Thy rod and thy staff they comfort me." She had often felt the Lord's rod.

I heard Father going by in the hall. He looked in at the doorway and smiled affectionately at us and at Mother. Then he went off, and I heard his firm step as he walked on toward his room.

He hadn't meant to interfere with Mother's teachings. He hadn't spoken one word. But I found myself speculating, all of a sudden, on what his opinion would be of the Twenty-third Psalm.

I couldn't imagine Father being comforted by the Lord's rod and staff, or allowing anybody whatever to lead him to a pasture and get him to lie down somewhere in it. I could see him in my mind's eye, in his tailed coat and top hat, refusing point-blank even to enter a pasture. He would as soon have thought of wearing overalls. In spite of my admiring him for this attitude, it seemed wicked of him. I felt resentful about it. It would have been so much easier for me to be properly reverent if he had not been around. My idea was that if Mother was too religious, Father wasn't religious enough.

"Good night, Clarence," I heard Mother saying. "You won't forget, darling?"

I kissed her and went out, wondering what I was not to forget. Oh, yes—she had asked us to learn that psalm by heart.

Up in my bedroom, I got out my Bible. It was full of paper bookmarks, to help me find texts that I'd had to memorize, and these bookmarks in turn were full of pictures I had drawn of Biblical scenes. A picture of Adam looking doubtfully at the Tree of Knowledge in Eden, with a complete set of school books dangling heavily down from its boughs. A picture of Sarah "dealing hardly with Hagar," driving her out with a broomstick. A picture of the sun, moon, and stars bowing politely to Joseph.

I sat down and added to the collection a picture of Job in pajamas, weeping copiously as he endeavored, on top of all his other trials, to learn the Twenty-third Psalm. I also drew his three unsatisfactory friends, sitting in a row staring at Job. Each friend wore a sardonic expression and had a large mustache and imperial like Napoleon the Third.

I got out another Bible that Mother had lent me. This one was in French, and it sometimes shocked me deeply to read it. As my belief was that when God had created the world He had said, "Let there be light," it seemed to me highly irreverent to put

French words in His mouth and have Him exclaim, *"Que la lumière soit!"* Imagine the Lord talking French! Aside from a few odd words in Hebrew, I took it completely for granted that God had never spoken anything but the most dignified English.

The French were notoriously godless, however. It made me laugh, though it frightened me, too, to see what liberties they had taken. In my English Bible, David was a fine Anglo-Saxon type, "a youth, ruddy and of a fair countenance." In the French, he was a revolting little snip from the boulevards, *"un enfant, blond, et d'une belle figure."* Where my Bible spoke of "leviathan," the French said *"le crocodile,"* which ruined the grandeur and mystery of that famous beast. And where mine said, "Behold now behemoth," they said, *"Voici l'hippopotame!"*

Instead of the children of Israel fearing lest the Lord should be wroth, the French said *"les enfants d'Israel"* were afraid lest *"le Seigneur"* should be *"irrité."* This word *"irrité"* appeared everywhere in the French version. It wasn't only the Lord. Cain was *"très irrité."* Moïse (which seemed to me a very jaunty way of referring to Moses) was *"irrité"* again and again. Everybody was *"irrité."* When my regular Bible, the real one, impressively described men as "wroth," their anger seemed to have something stately and solemn about it. If they were full of mere irritation all the time, they were more like the Day family.

I turned at last to the Twenty-third Psalm. They had spoiled that, too. They had twisted it around until it read as though the scene were in Paris. "Green pastures" were changed into *"parcs herbeux,"* and "thy rod and thy staff" had become *"ton bâton,"* as though the Lord were leading David up and down the Bois de Boulogne like a drum major.

I decided to go to bed and let that psalm wait for a day or two. But before putting the books back on my shelf, I hunted up the one place in the French Bible that I really liked. "Blessed are the meek," my English Bible said, "for they shall inherit the earth." I had always hated that verse. It made all religion so difficult. Uriah Heep typified the meek, to my mind. The meek were a snivelling, despicable, and uncomfortable lot. But in poring over the French Bible one evening, I had found to my delight that some daring Frenchman had altered this passage, and had changed the Sermon on the Mount into something that a fellow could stand. *"Heureux les débonnaires,"* he had represented Jesus as saying, *"car ils hériteront de la terre."*

The debonair! That was more like it! I cheerfully jumped into bed.

MOTHER AND THE ARMENIAN

Mother used to take us boys to a summer resort in our vacations. In all such places there was usually an Armenian, prowling around the hotel piazza. Blue-black hair, dark skin, gleaming eyes, a hooked nose, perfect teeth. Mother said that there wasn't a lady on the piazza who didn't envy those teeth. The Armenian was always trying to catch the eye of one of them to see if he couldn't persuade her to look at his rugs or his silks. "Not buy, Madam! Just look!" She would say no; but he would tell her they were "Oh, so beautiful," and offer to give her some perfume, till perhaps if it were a dull afternoon she would roll up her knitting, and saunter down to the end of the hall where his dark little room was.

Since Mother had both a kind heart and a weakness for rugs, she was occasionally snared in this fashion and shown some bargain, some rug that was intrinsically priceless and could never be duplicated, but which could be had for a few hundred dollars, as it happened, that morning. The crisis that made such a price possible would tomorrow be gone, but today it was here, and a wise and clever woman would seize it. Whoever did would be helping a most grateful young man get through college. He was no dealer; he was just a poor student with a few priceless rugs, and if the lady would only make him an offer she could buy at her own figure. She could make him an offer, surely, *some* offer; let it be what it might.

It began to seem unreasonable to Mother not to make him some offer, especially as he was trying to get through college, and it might be a bargain. So she silently tried to figure how much she'd have had to pay at places like Sloane's; and then she took a lot off; and then she felt a little ashamed at taking so much off—she didn't wish to cheat the young man. He seemed to mean well, poor creature. So she worked her price up a little, in her mind, and then got a bit frightened because, after all, it was a good deal of money—though it did seem perfectly safe to pay that much, since Lord & Taylor's or Arnold Constable's would have charged more. Still, you never could tell about a rug, because it might not be genuine, and she wished the young man had let her alone and could get through college without her, though he didn't much look as though he would manage it; he could hardly speak English—and how could the poor thing talk to the professors, or the professors to him, when even on the subject of rugs he had to use a sort of sign language which consisted of hunching his shoulders till she feared he would dislocate them, and picking out sums on his fingers in the most confusing manner. However, she had better make him an offer, she felt, and then perhaps he'd stop smiling, which no doubt he intended as pleasant, but his breath was so bad.

So she finally said, fingering the rug in a dissatisfied way, that she supposed she could give him a hundred for it. The Armenian's smile instantly disappeared. He walked off in gloom. Then he rushed back, excited and jerky, and began a long, rapid expostulation that threatened to deafen us. Mother reluctantly raised her bid to a hundred and twenty to stop him, whereupon it suddenly appeared that he had misunderstood her first offer. He had supposed it to be two hundred, not one. She meant *two* hundred and twenty? Mother said, No, one hundred and twenty was all she had offered. The Armenian then tottered around, sank into a chair, and sort of hissed through his teeth, with such a ghastly look that it made Mother fear he might be having a fit. It began to seem advisable to her to do anything she could to get out of it, and then never buy anything again for the rest of her life. So she miserably and angrily said she would make it one-fifty. She had to say it several times, however, before he seemed to hear her, and even then he received it only with low shrieks and groans in Armenian. He said that now he would have to give up college, because he could not bear such losses. All he had ever hoped of

FATHER OPENS MY MAIL

There was a time in my boyhood when I felt that Father had handicapped me severely in life by naming me after him, "Clarence." All literature, so far as I could see, was thronged with objectionable persons named Clarence. Percy was bad enough, but there had been some good fighters named Percy. The only Clarence in history was a duke who did something dirty at Tewkesbury, and who died a ridiculous death afterwards in a barrel of malmsey.

As for the Clarences in the fiction I read, they were horrible. In one story, for instance, there were two brothers, Clarence and Frank. Clarence was a "vain, disagreeable little fellow," who was proud of his curly hair and fine clothes, while Frank was a "rollicking boy who was ready to play games with anybody." Clarence didn't like to play games, of course. He just minced around looking on.

One day when the mother of these boys had gone out, this story went on, Clarence "tempted" Frank to disobey her and fly their kite on the roof. Frank didn't want to, but Clarence kept taunting him and daring him until Frank was stung into doing it. After the two boys went up to the roof, Frank got good and dirty, running up and down and stumbling over scuttles, while Clarence sat there, giving him orders, and kept his natty clothes tidy. To my horror, he even spread out his handkerchief on the trapdoor to sit on. And to crown all, this sneak told on Frank as soon as their mother came in.

This wasn't an exceptionally mean Clarence, either. He was just run-of-the-mill. Some were worse.

So far as I could ever learn, however, Father had never heard of these stories, and had never dreamed of there being any-

thing objectionable in his name. Quite the contrary. And yet as
a boy he had lived a good rough-and-tumble boy's life. He had
played and fought on the city streets, and kept a dog in Grandpa's
stable, and stolen rides to Greenpoint Ferry on the high, lurching
bus. In the summer he had gone to West Springfield and had
run down Shad Lane through the trees to the house where
Grandpa was born, and had gone barefoot and driven the cows
home just as though he had been named Tom or Bill.

He had the same character as a boy, I suppose, that he had
as a man, and he was too independent to care if people thought
his name fancy. He paid no attention to the prejudices of others,
except to disapprove of them. He had plenty of prejudices himself, of course, but they were his own. He was humorous and
confident and level-headed, and I imagine that if any boy had
tried to make fun of him for being named Clarence, Father
would simply have laughed and told him he didn't know what
he was talking about.

I asked Mother how this name had ever happened to spring
up in our family. She explained that my great-great-grandfather
was Benjamin Day, and my great-grandfather was Henry, and
consequently my grandfather had been named Benjamin Henry.
He in turn had named his eldest son Henry and his second son
Benjamin. The result was that when Father was born there was
no family name left. The privilege of choosing a name for Father
had thereupon been given to Grandma, and unluckily for the
Day family she had been reading a novel, the hero of which was
named Clarence.

I knew that Grandma, though very like Grandpa in some respects, had a dreamy side which he hadn't, a side that she usually
kept to herself, in her serene, quiet way. Her romantic choice of
this name probably made Grandpa smile, but he was a detached
sort of man who didn't take small matters seriously, and who
drew a good deal of private amusement from the happenings of
everyday life. Besides, he was partly to blame in this case, because
that novel was one he had published himself in his magazine.

from some person I never heard of. I can't see what it's about."
By the time it had occurred to him that possibly the letter might
be for me, I was red and embarrassed and even angrier at the
girl than at Father. And on days when he had read some of the
phrases aloud to the family, it nearly killed me to claim it.

Lots of fellows whom I knew had been named after their
fathers without having such troubles. But although Father
couldn't have been kinder-hearted or had any better intentions,
when he saw his name on a package or envelope it never dawned
on him that it might not be for him. He was too active in his
habits to wait until I had a chance to get at it. And as he was
also single-minded and prompt to attend to unfinished business,
he opened everything automatically and then did his best to dis-
pose of it.

This went on even after I grew up, until I had a home of my
own. Father was always perfectly decent about it, but he never
changed. When he saw I felt sulky, he was genuinely sorry and
said so, but he couldn't see why all this should annoy me, and
he was surprised and amused that it did. I used to get angry once
in a while when something came for me which I particularly
hadn't wished him to see and which I would find lying, opened,
on the hall table marked "For Jr.?" when I came in; but nobody
could stay angry with Father—he was too utterly guiltless of
having meant to offend.

He often got angry himself, but it was mostly at things, not at
persons, and he didn't mind a bit (as a rule) when persons got
angry at him. He even declared, when I got back from college,
feeling dignified, and told him that I wished he'd be more careful,
that he suffered from these mistakes more than I did. It wasn't
his fault, he pointed out, if my stupid correspondents couldn't
remember my name, and it wasn't any pleasure to him to be
upset at his breakfast by finding that a damned lunatic company
in Battle Creek had sent him a box of dry bread crumbs, with
a letter asserting that this rubbish would be good for his stomach.
"I admit I threw it into the fireplace, Clarence, but what else
could I do? If you valued this preposterous concoction, my dear

boy, I'm sorry. I'll buy another box for you today, if you'll tell me where I can get it. Don't feel badly! I'll buy you a barrel. Only I hope you won't eat it."

In the days when Mrs. Pankhurst and her friends were chaining themselves to lamp-posts in London, in their campaign for the vote, a letter came from Frances Hand trustfully asking "Dear Clarence" to do something to help Woman Suffrage—speak at a meeting, I think. Father got red in the face. "Speak at one of their meetings!" he roared at Mother. "I'd like nothing better! You can tell Mrs. Hand that it would give me great pleasure to inform all those crackpots in petticoats exactly what I think of their antics."

"Now, Clare," Mother said, "you mustn't talk that way. I like that nice Mrs. Hand, and anyhow this letter must be for Clarence."

One time I asked Father for his opinion of a low-priced stock I'd been watching. His opinion was that it was not worth a damn. I thought this over, but I still wished to buy it, so I placed a scale order with another firm instead of with Father's office, and said nothing about it. At the end of the month this other firm sent me a statement, setting forth each of my little transactions in full, and of course they forgot to put the "Jr." at the end of my name. When Father opened the envelope, he thought at first in his excitement that this firm had actually opened an account for him without being asked. I found him telling Mother that he'd like to wring their damned necks.

"That must be for me, Father," I said, when I took in what had happened.

We looked at each other.

"You bought this stuff?" he said incredulously. "After all I said about it?"

"Yes, Father."

He handed over the statement and walked out of the room.

Both he and I felt offended and angry. We stayed so for several days, too, but we then made it up.

Once in a while when I got a letter that I had no time to an-

swer I used to address an envelope to the sender and then put
anything in it that happened to be lying around on my desk—
a circular about books, a piece of newspaper, an old laundry bill
—anything at all, just to be amiable, and yet at the same time to
save myself the trouble of writing. I happened to tell several
people about this private habit of mine at a dinner one night—
a dinner at which Alice Duer Miller and one or two other writers
were present. A little later she wrote me a criticism of Henry
James and ended by saying that I needn't send her any of my
old laundry bills because she wouldn't stand it. And she forgot
to put on the "Jr."

"In the name of God," Father said bleakly, "this is the worst
yet. Here's a woman who says I'd better not read *The Golden
Bowl,* which I have no intention whatever of doing, and she
also warns me for some unknown reason not to send her my
laundry bills."

The good part of all these experiences, as I realize now, was
that in the end they drew Father and me closer together. My
brothers had only chance battles with him. I had a war. Neither
he nor I relished its clashes, but they made us surprisingly intimate.

FATHER SENDS ME TO THE WORLD'S FAIR

Father and Mother and my brothers went out to the World's Fair in Chicago in 1893. I was finishing my freshman year at Yale, and by the time I got home they had gone. Father had written me that I had better follow on and join them, but I couldn't. I had spent all my allowance. There would be no more money coming to me until college opened again in September. In the meantime I didn't even have carfare or money enough for tobacco. It wasn't this that bothered me, however, or not going out to Chicago. It was the fact that for the first time in my life I had got deep in debt.

I owed Warner Hall forty-two dollars for seven weeks' board, I owed Dole for a heavy turtleneck sweater, and De Bussy, Manwaring & Co. for ascot ties and shirts and a pair of pointed-toed shoes. I owed Heublein's for the rounds of drinks I had signed for, on what had once seemed jolly nights. I was in debt to Stoddard the tobacconist for sixty or seventy dollars for all sorts of fancy pipes—one of them was a meerschaum head of a bull with large amber horns. The total due to these and other tradesmen was nearly three hundred dollars, and I didn't see how I could have been so reckless, or when I could ever pay up. Worst of all, my creditors too had become pessimistic.

I borrowed a nickel for carfare from old Margaret, after she had cooked me my breakfast, put a sandwich and a banana in my pocket, and went downtown at once to Father's office to ask for a job. They didn't have any work for me down there and didn't want me around, but it was lucky I went, because while I was eating my sandwich one of my creditors entered. He had come down to New York with a bundle of overdue bills to see whether he could collect any of them by calling upon his customers' parents.

I was appalled. It had never occurred to me that anyone would come to Father's office like this. It seemed to me most underhanded. If Father had been there and I hadn't, I'd have been in serious trouble, for Father had warned me repeatedly to keep out of debt. I was thoroughly frightened, and I attempted to frighten that creditor. I said in a loud, shaky voice that if he was going to behave in this manner, I would never buy anything more from him as long as I lived.

He said he was sorry to hear it. But he didn't sound very sorry. Times were bad, he explained, and he had to have money. I didn't believe him. Looking back, I realize that the long depression of the nineties had started and banks were beginning to close, but I knew nothing about this at that time. I was preoccupied with my own troubles. These looked blacker than ever to me when my creditor said, as he left, that since my father was out, he would have to call on him again the next time he came to New York.

I didn't know what to do. But one thing was clear. I saw I must stick around Father's office for the rest of that summer. So as soon as he got back from the Fair, I begged him to give me a job. I didn't need any vacation, I told him, and I would be getting a lot of valuable experience if he would let me go to work.

After thinking it over, he said that perhaps I could make myself useful as an office boy while his clerks were taking turns going on their vacations. I started the very next day at four dollars a week.

I might have got slightly better wages elsewhere, but I couldn't have made enough anyway to pay much on my bills, and the most important thing was not to make a few dollars extra but to stand on guard at the door of Father's office to keep my creditors out. When I was sent out on an errand, I ran all the way there and back. When I was in the office, turning the big iron wheel on the letter press, I always kept one eye on the grated window where the cashier sat at his counter, to make sure that no old buzzards from New Haven were coming in to see Father.

But late in the summer I got into trouble. The cashier told Father that I had taken hold better than he had expected, and that although I was not very accurate I was punctual and quick and seemed to be especially interested in getting down early. Father was so pleased that he sent for me to come into his inner office and told me that he had decided I had earned a vacation.

I said that honestly and truly a vacation was the last thing I wanted.

He smiled at the immense pleasure I seemed to be taking in sealing envelopes and filling inkwells, but he explained that he wanted me to have some rest and recreation before college opened, and he added that he would advise me to go to Chicago and see the World's Fair.

I said I didn't care about seeing the Fair.

Father didn't quite like this. "I have just told you, Clarence," he said, "that I would advise you to go." I saw that he would regard it as disrespectful of me if I refused.

I uncomfortably made a partial confession. I said I couldn't afford to go to Chicago. I didn't have any money.

Father was surprised. "What about your allowance?" he asked.

"I'm sorry to say I've spent it all, Father."

"That was very imprudent of you," he observed.

I said in a low voice that I knew it.

Father said that he hoped this would be a lesson to me to be more careful in future. By failing to exercise even the most ordinary prudence, he explained in his firm, friendly way, I had deprived myself of seeing a sight that might never come again in my lifetime. He said he felt badly about it.

I didn't, however. I went back to working the letter press. I liked to turn the big, painted iron wheel and tighten the plates. We didn't use carbons. Instead, after writing letters by hand in copying ink or else on the typewriter, we pressed them down hard on damp tissue paper to make copies to file. It took a good deal of practice to do this correctly. If the tissue was too dry, the copy was so faint it could hardly be read, and if I got it too wet, it made the ink run and smudged the whole letter.

The next day, Father interrupted me at this interesting occupation again. He had had a long talk with Mother, it seemed, and, as all the rest of the family had seen the Fair, they wanted me to go, too. He said that he would therefore help me out this once and give me some money, and he asked how much I had saved from my wages.

I had saved nearly all of them, as a matter of fact. I had spent less than a dollar a week. Margaret had wrapped up little lunches for me, and my only other needs had been a haircut and carfares and a new pair of cuffs. But as I had been using all I saved to pay small installments to those men in New Haven, I had only forty-eight cents on hand.

"Well, the devil!" Father laughed disappointedly. "You have attended to your duties here faithfully enough, I suppose, but I see you have a damn lot to learn."

I thought to myself that he little knew how much I was learning.

He lit a cigar and looked at me reflectively. "Clarence," he said, "I think I should reproach myself afterward if I allowed you to miss seeing this Fair. It is a great educational opportunity that may never recur. So I will make you a present of one hundred dollars to enable you to go to Chicago."

"Thank you very much, Father," I said, as he shook hands with me, "but if you wouldn't mind, I'd rather have the money, sir."

Father frowned.

I stood beside his desk, waiting. A hundred dollars would be a magnificent windfall for me and my creditors.

His reply killed my hopes. "I see no point in giving you a hundred dollars to fritter away as you have done with your other funds," he said. "If you don't choose to avail yourself of this educational—"

"Oh, I do, sir," I said. If the only way to get that hundred dollars was to go to Chicago and back, I saw that of course I'd better go. I felt sure I could save at least some of it to use in paying my bills.

I went to the cashier and begged him to keep an eye out for my creditors and not let any of them in, in my absence. He said he would do all he could, but he wouldn't like to be caught surreptitiously keeping out callers. I argued that these people would annoy Father if they saw him, and that they ought to be treated like book-agents; but he said Father might regard their disclosures as important, however unwelcome, and that he couldn't keep anyone out who came on legitimate business.

I almost gave up going, at this. But Father and Mother were so eager to give me a treat that I couldn't. I had to pretend to be eager myself, with my heart in my boots.

I wrote to my creditors that I would begin paying my bills very soon and that I hoped they would wait.

Father asked me what road I was getting a ticket on. He said the Lake Shore was the best. I made some vague answer to that. I didn't like to tell him, after he had been so generous to me, that I had bought a cut-rate ticket to Chicago and back, for eleven dollars, on an Erie Special Excursion. The Erie was so awful in those days that it was a joke. It didn't go nearly as far as Chicago, of course, but it had arranged for trackage rights over a number of other one-horse railroads for its Special Excursions.

It took that train three days and two nights, if I remember correctly, to get to Chicago. We stopped at every small station. We waited for hours on sidings. Most of the time I had very little idea where we were. The Excursion wandered around here and there, in various parts of this country and Canada, trying to pick up extra passengers. Of course, the train had no sleeping cars or diner—only day coaches. There was quite a crowd of us in them —men, women, and children. In the seat back of mine was a woman with two babies. I had my seat pretty much to myself, however, because the old man who sat with me spent most of his time in the smoker. I didn't go to the smoker myself. I had nothing to smoke.

All the windows were open, it was so hot. We were coated with coal dust. The washroom got out of order and had to be locked. The little drinking tank was soon emptied. Most of us had nothing to eat, and we slept sitting up. But it was fun. Nearly everybody but the overworked trainmen was good-natured and friendly. At every stop we'd all pile out of the cars and bolt for the washroom in the station, or try to buy pie and sandwiches and stand in line at the water-cooler, and those of us who went dry at one stop would try again at the next. At one little place where the station was locked and there was no other building in sight, we had the best luck of all, because there was a pond near the tracks, rather yellow, but with plenty of water for everybody. I was rinsing my undershirt in it when the whistle blew, and I only just managed to scramble aboard the train as it started. The day before that, at a little place where the eating was good, several passengers who didn't run fast enough had been left behind.

At Chicago, I hunted up a boarding house. As those near the Fair Grounds were expensive, I went to the outskirts, where I found an old boarding house near the railroad which was clean and decent. I sent off a postcard to Mother saying that the Fair was simply fine, and got a good bath and sleep.

I went to the Fair the next day. My boarding house was so far out that I had to go by train, but the fare was low and the station was handy. And when I walked into the Fair Grounds, I was deeply impressed. They were a wonderful sight. The vast buildings weren't solid stone, of course, and they wouldn't be there a hundred years hence, but in the meanwhile they provided a vision of grandeur, at least for innocent eyes. The eyes, for example, of persons who had come on the Erie.

I sat in the Court of Honor, I walked admiringly around the artificial lagoon, I sauntered through one or two of the exhibition halls, and went back to my boarding house.

On my next visit, I explored the grounds more thoroughly and I was upset to find that all the places which I wanted to see most cost money. This was particularly true of the Midway Plaisance, a broad promenade lined with sideshows. There were Bedouins, a Ferris Wheel, a fearsome (canvas) Hawaiian volcano, a won-

derful captive balloon, and a "Congress of Beauty." And there
was also a real Dahomey village of genuine savages. I could reach
out and touch them as they stalked about, scowling; and whenever I did I could hear them muttering things to themselves. They
occasionally danced in a threatening manner uttering genuine
war-cries; and the guide-book said, "They also sell products of
their mechanical skill." And, what had excited the most talk of
all in the newspapers, there were dancing girls with bare stom-
achs, who wriggled in what clergymen said was a most abandoned way, right before everybody.

I had heard so much about these girls that I forgot all my vows
to economize and went into their tent. They didn't come up to
my hopes. I had already noticed in New Haven that such things
never did.

That night in my boarding house, I counted my money, and
I saw that if I had good times on the Midway, I'd have a bad
time with creditors. My creditors won and I didn't go to the
Midway again.

There was a great deal else to see, however, and I saw nearly
all of it, because it was free. But as Father had said, it was educational. I spent hours and hours roaming through the principal
exhibits which were supposed to be good for the mind. They
were interesting but monotonous. It was like visiting a hundred
museums at once. A few of these palaces fascinated me when I
came to them fresh; the Krupp guns were better than anything
on the Midway. But the showmanship wasn't. Herr Krupp had
announced, by the way, that he was presenting the biggest gun
of all to America, "for the defense of the great port of Chicago."

These free exhibits increased my expenses, some days; they
made me so hungry. I had a hard time trying to be economical
at the White Horse Inn, I remember. This was a reproduction
of an old English inn, swollen to an extraordinary size, and the
big chops at the next table looked juicy and the steaks smelled
delicious. And every time I went to the Transportation Building
and got in a coma, I had to revive myself on beer and cheese
afterward in a place called Old Vienna.

Father had especially enjoined upon me the duty of studying the Transportation Exhibits, because he was an officer or director of several small railroads, and he hoped that by and by I might be too. It was quite an assignment. That building had eighteen acres of floor-space. It was built in the form of several large train sheds. The guide-book explained that "in style it is somewhat Romanesque," and it added that "the ornamental color designs, in thirty different shades, of its exterior, produce an effect almost as fine as embroidery."

On rainy days I didn't go to the Fair Grounds. I sat in my boarding house and saved money. But this was dull and I felt lonely, so I bought a chameleon for company. He wasn't much company. On the other hand, as the end of his tail had been broken off, he only cost twenty cents. He wore a chain with a little brass collar at one end and a pin at the other, and I stuck the pin in the window curtain to tether him, and fed him live flies.

I wanted to go home after a week of this, but I figured that I'd better not. Father might think I had been too lavish with his money if it only lasted a week. So I stayed on for over a fortnight to inspire him with confidence in me, and make him see that I wasn't always a spendthrift in spite of my bad freshman record.

When I wasn't at the Fair, I wandered around Chicago. There was something about Chicago I liked. It seemed bigger and busier to me than New York, and much fatter, much more spread-out and roomy.

At last, when I thought Father must surely be feeling that I had used up that hundred dollars, I packed my suitcase, pinned the chameleon to the lapel of my coat, and embarked again on the Erie. The chameleon had a miserable time on the train and the rest of his tail got joggled off, but even so he was luckier than he knew, for we made much better time going east than we had made going west.

I had gone away worried and alarmed, but I came home in triumph. No creditors had gone to the office, I learned, and I had saved fifty-two dollars to send to New Haven. I hadn't brought home any presents for the family, but I presented the chameleon to Mother.

Father and I had a little talk about what I had liked. "Did you see the Midway?" he asked.

"I saw a little of it," I said cautiously. "Did you see it, Father?"

"Yes," he said, "I was interested in those filthy Hottentots. How people can live in that disgusting manner I don't understand. I didn't know it was allowed."

He was pleased when he found I had gone only once to the Midway and had apparently spent all the rest of my time in the right places.

"Well," he finally said in approval, "I gather, then, that you found it was an educational experience for you."

"Yes, Father," I told him, "I did."

FATHER'S OLD TROUSERS

Father didn't care much for jewelry. He disliked the heavy watch-chains which were worn by the men of his time, chains with charms dangling down from the middle. His had none of these things on it; it was strong and handsome but simple. His studs and cuff-links were on the same order, not ornate like those then in fashion. His ring was a solid plain band of gold, set with a rectangular sapphire. All these objects we regarded with a reverence which we felt was their due. There was a special sort of rightness about Father's things, in our eyes, and we had a special respect for them because they were Father's.

Father had had a lighter ring once, with a smaller sapphire, which he had worn as a young man. He had discarded it as less suitable for him, however, as he got on in life, and it had been put away long ago in the safe in our pantry.

Mother didn't like to have it lying idle there, year after year. After I left college, she decided that I had better wear it, so that the family would get some good out of it once more. One afternoon she and I went into the crowded pantry, with its smell of damp washcloths, and she took it out of the safe.

I did not want a ring, but Mother presented this one to me with such affection that I saw no way to get out of accepting it. She put it on my finger and kissed me. I looked at the thing. The sapphire was a beautiful little stone. I thought that after a while I might learn to like it, perhaps. At any rate, there was nothing to get out of order or break.

I soon discovered, however, that this ring was a nuisance—it was such hard work not to lose it. If I had bought and paid for it myself, I suppose I'd have cherished it, but as it had been wished on me, it was only a responsibility. It preyed on my mind. After a little while, I stopped wearing it and put it away.

When Mother noticed that it wasn't on my finger, she spoke out at once. She said there wasn't much point in my having a ring if I merely kept it in my bureau drawer. She reminded me that it was a very handsome ring and I ought to be proud to wear it.

I explained that I couldn't get used to remembering that I was wearing a ring, and had several times left it on public washstands and got it back only by sheer luck. Mother was frightened. She instantly agreed that it would be a terrible thing to lose Father's ring. It went back into the safe in the pantry.

Several years later, it was taken out again, and after another little ceremony it was entrusted to George. He had even more trouble with it than I'd had. He, too, decided that he didn't wish to wear it himself, so, as he had married, he gave it to his wife, who adored it. Everyone was happy for a while until Mother happened to see Father's ring nestling on Wilhelmine's finger. Mother was very fond of Wilhelmine, but this strange sight disturbed her. She felt that the only right and appropriate use for that ring was for it to be worn by one of Father's sons. She asked George to take it away from Wilhelmine and return it. He silently did so, and back it went again to the pantry.

It was a curious fact that everything that Father had ever owned seemed to be permanently a part of him. No matter what happened to it, it remained impressed with his personality. This isn't unusual in the case of a ring, I suppose, but the same thing was true even of Father's old neckties, especially from his point of view. I don't think he cared what became of that ring, the way Mother did, but when he gave me an old necktie or a discarded pair of trousers, they still seemed to him to be his. Not only did he feel that way about it but he made me feel that way, too. He explained to me that he gave things which he didn't care about to the coachman or the Salvation Army, but that when he had a particularly handsome tie which had plenty of wear in it yet, or a pair of trousers which he had been fond of, he saved anything of that sort for me.

A pair of striped trousers which he had worn to church on
Sundays for years went up to New Haven with me one Christmas,
when I was a junior, and as I was short of clothes at the time,
they came in very handy. I had to be careful not to take off my
coat while I was wearing them, though. They looked oddly baggy
in the seat when exposed to full view—on nights when I was
playing billiards in a poolroom, for instance. They also made it
harder for me to climb Osborn Hall's iron gate. This gate was
ten feet high, with a row of long, sharp spikes at the top, and
to get quickly over it in Father's trousers was quite a feat.

There was no point in getting over it quickly. In fact, there
was no point in getting over it at all. Osborn Hall was used solely
for lectures, and we saw quite enough of it in the daytime without trying to get in there at night. Besides, we couldn't get in
anyhow, even after climbing the gate, because the big inside doors
were locked fast. After standing in the vestibule a minute, between
the doors and the gate, there was nothing to do but climb back
again and go home to bed. This seemed like a useful or stimu-
lating performance, though, when we had been drinking.

On nights like these, as I was undressing in my bedroom, I
sometimes had moral qualms over the way that I was making
Father's trousers lead this new kind of life. Once in a while such
misgivings would even come over me elsewhere. They were not
clear-cut or acute, but they floated around in the back of my
mind. Usually I paid little attention to what clothes I had on,
but when I did happen to notice that I was wearing those trousers
into places which were not respectable, I didn't feel right about it.

Then one week I lent them to a classmate of mine, Jerry Ives,
to wear in his role of a fat man in some Psi U play. Father wasn't
fat, but he was much more full-bodied than Jerry, and there was
plenty of room in his trousers for a pillow and Jerry besides. I
thought no more of the matter until the night of the play, but when
the curtain went up and I saw Father's Sunday trousers running
across the stage pursued by a comic bartender who was yelling
"Stop thief!" I felt distinctly uncomfortable.

After that, nothing seemed to go right with them. The fact was, they simply didn't fit into undergraduate life. The night that I most fully realized this, I remember, was when a girl whom Father would have by no means approved of sat on what was my lap but his trousers. Father was a good eighty miles away and safely in bed, but I became so preoccupied and ill at ease that I got up and left.

FATHER LETS IN THE TELEPHONE

Up to the late eighteen-nineties, when Father walked in the front door of his home and closed it behind him, he shut out the world. Telephones had been invented but, like most people, he hadn't installed one. There was no way for anybody to get at us except by climbing up the front stoop and ringing the bell; and if the bell rang late at night, Father looked out of the window to see who it was. He thought nothing of this—homes had always been shut off since men began building them, and it seemed only natural.

Once in a long while a messenger boy would bring him or Mother a telegram—maybe two or three times a year. As this generally meant bad news, we were nervous about getting telegrams.

No telegraph poles were allowed on Fifth Avenue, but they stood in long rows on other thoroughfares. Old Margaret was mystified by all those wires, up in the air. We had wires in our house, to be sure; they had been strung inside the walls to ring bells with; but they were good, honest, old-fashioned wires and to make them work we had to pull them. There was none of this dangerous stuff called electricity in them. Electricity was much too risky a thing to put in a home, and neither we boys nor Margaret could make out what it was. All we knew about it was that there were electric batteries in the Eden Musée which could and did give anyone who paid twenty-five cents a shock. You were supposed to give yourself as big a shock as you could stand. We had been cautious in trying them, except George, who had had a startling experience. He had taken hold of one end of the thing in his right hand and moved it way up, till the indicator pointed to far more "current" than the rest of us had been able to stand, and yet he stood there at ease for a while as though

he were completely immune. Then the lady in charge noticed that
George hadn't taken the other end in his left hand at all. He
hadn't understood that he ought to. When she told him that the
way to feel the current was to hold one end in each hand, he
immediately seized the left hand one without lowering the right
from its height. It was grandly exciting to the rest of us to see
how violently this shook him up, and how the lady screamed until
attendants rushed over and managed to shut off the current.

After a while the telegraph company persuaded Father to let
them install a brand new invention, just inside of one of our back
bedroom windows, where it couldn't do any harm. This was a
small metal box with a handle. A wire led from it which was
connected with a telegraph pole, but although there was some
electricity in it there was only a little, and the company guaranteed it was safe. The handle was made to look just like those on
the pull-bells which we were used to. When we pulled it, the box
began to buzz, and somehow that sent a signal to the nearest
telegraph office, where a row of little messenger boys was supposed to be waiting. The office then sent a boy to our house ready
to run any errand.

This "buzzer," as we called it, seemed almost as remarkable
to us as that lamp of Aladdin's. By giving some extra pulls on it
and making it buzz enough times, the directions said, a policeman
could be summoned, or even a fire engine.

How long it would have taken for a policeman to come we
never had occasion to learn. It took a messenger boy from twenty
to forty-five minutes—that is, if we were lucky. The branch office
was nearly a mile away and it had only one little benchful of boys.
If the boys were all out when we buzzed for one, the manager
had no way to tell us. We might be impatient. He wasn't. He
peacefully waited till some boy got through other errands.

On stormy days sometimes, when a friend wished to send us a
message or break an engagement, a messenger would surprise us
by coming without being buzzed for. He stood outside the front
door, with a black rubber hood dripping with rain hanging down
from his cap, blowing on his cold fingers and stamping, and ringing away at the bell. And when one of us opened the door, the

boy would thrust in a wet letter and hoarsely ask us to sign the name and the hour on a small, smudgy slip.

All these delays were more or less put up with, however. There was no other service to turn to. And anyway people seldom used messengers—they were not only slow but expensive. We ran our own errands.

When the telephone was invented and was ready to use, hardly anybody cared to install one. We all stuck to our buzzers. Messenger boys were quite enough of a nuisance, suddenly appearing at the door with a letter and expecting an answer. But they came only a few times a year, and a telephone might ring every week. People admitted that telephones were ingenious contraptions and wondered just how they worked, but they no more thought of getting one than of buying a balloon or a diving suit.

As a matter of fact, for a long time they were of little use in a home. Since almost nobody had them but brokers, there was no one to talk to. The telephone company sent us circulars in which they made large claims: they said that an important department store now had a telephone, and three banks had ordered one apiece, and some enterprising doctors were getting them. But though people saw vaguely that a telephone might be a convenience if every household installed one, they decided to wait in a body until everyone did.

Father had to have one downtown, but he wouldn't use it himself; he had it put in the back office, where the bookkeeper dealt with it, bringing Father the message if necessary. The typewriter and a gelatine hektograph were in the back office, too. But the idea of putting these business conveniences in a home seemed absurd.

Mother agreed with Father—she didn't like telephones either. She distrusted machines of all kinds; they weren't human, they popped or exploded and made her nervous. She never knew what they might do to her. And the telephone seemed to her, and many other people, especially dangerous. They were afraid that if they stood near one in a thunderstorm they might get hit by lightning. Even if there wasn't any storm, the electric wiring might give them a shock. When they saw a telephone in some hotel or office, they stood away from it or picked it up gingerly. It was a freak way to use electricity, and Mother wouldn't even touch the queer toy. Besides, she said, she had to see the face of any person she talked to. She didn't want to be answered by a voice coming out of a box on the wall.

Little by little, however, and year by year, telephones came into use. Some of the large markets and groceries installed them. The livery stable. Some druggists. And once in a while, when Father had a bad cold and couldn't go to the office, he saw it would be a business convenience to have one at home.

After ten or fifteen years, in spite of his still having misgivings, he got one. It was put on a wall on the second floor, where everybody could hear its loud bell. We didn't give it much of a welcome. It seemed to us rude and intrusive, and from the first it made trouble. It rang seldom but it always chose a bad moment, when there was nobody on that floor to answer. Mother would pick up her skirts and run upstairs, calling to it loudly "I'm coming! I'm coming!" but the fretful thing kept right on ringing. Father couldn't regard it as inanimate either. He refused to be hurried like Mother, but he scolded and cursed it.

The outer world now began intruding upon us at will. This was hard to get used to. Even Mother felt there was too much of it. As for Father, he met these invasions with ferocious resentment. When somebody telephoned him and he couldn't make out at once who it was, and when there was nothing he could shake his fist at but a little black receiver which was squeaking at him, he said it was horrible. "Speak up, speak up, damn it!" he would shout at the telephone, getting red in the face. "What is it, who are you? I can't hear a word you are saying. I can't hear a damned word, I tell you."

"Clare, give me that telephone!" Mother would cry, rushing in.

"I will not give you this telephone!" Father would roar in reply, without taking his lips from the transmitter. "Will you let me alone? I am trying to find out who the devil this person is. Halloa! I say halloa there, do you hear me? Who are you? Halloa! . . . What's that? . . . Oh, it's you, Mrs. Nichols." Here his voice would grow a little less forbidding, and sometimes even friendly. "Yes, Mrs. Day's here. How are you? . . . Oh, do you wish to speak to Mrs. Day? . . . Eh? . . . Very well then. Wait a moment." And he would at last allow Mother to get at the box on the wall.

When Father called a number himself, he usually got angry at "Central." He said she was deaf, she was stupid, he told her she wasn't attending to her duties in a suitable manner. If she said a number was busy, he'd protest: "I can't sit here waiting all day. Busy? Busy be damned!"

He always assumed when the bell rang that it was a message for him. The idea that it might be a call for Mother or one of the rest of us seemed wholly improbable. If he let anyone but himself answer, he would keep calling out and asking who it was and what it was all about anyhow, while we tried, in the midst of his shouts, to hear some of the message. When we said it was something that didn't concern him, he was incredulous, and had to have it explained to make sure.

One day a new friend of mine, a girl who had moved down to live in a settlement house in the slums, telephoned to invite me to lunch with some visiting Russians. Father answered the telephone. "Yes, this is Mr. Day. Speak up, hang it! Don't mumble at me. Who are you? . . . *What?* Come to lunch? I've had lunch. . . . Next Friday? Why, I don't want to lunch with you next Friday. . . . No. . . . Where? Where do you say? . . . In Rivington Street? The devil! . . . Yes, my name is Clarence Day and I told you that before. Don't repeat. . . . Lunch with you in Rivington Street? Good God! I never heard of such a thing in my life! . . . Russians? I don't know any Russians. . . . No, I don't want to, either. . . . No, I haven't changed. I never change. . . . What? . . . Goodbye, Madam. Damn!"

"I think that was a friend of mine, Father," I said.

"A friend of yours!" he exclaimed. "Why, it sounded to me like some impudent peddler's wife this time, arguing with me about lunching with her somewhere down in the slums. I can't stand it, that's all I have to say. I'll have the confounded thing taken out."

FATHER ISN'T MUCH HELP

In Father's childhood it was unusual for boys to take music lessons, and his father hadn't had him taught music. Men didn't play the piano. Young ladies learned to play pretty things on it as an accomplishment, but few of them went further, and any desire to play classical music was rare.

After Father grew up, however, and began to do well in his business, he decided that music was one of the good things of life. He bought himself a piano and paid a musician to teach him. He took no interest in the languishing love songs which were popular then, he didn't admire patriotic things such as "Marching Through Georgia," and he had a hearty distaste for songs of pathos—he always swore if he heard them. He enjoyed music as he did a fine wine or a good ride on horseback.

The people he associated with didn't care much for this kind of thing, and Father didn't wish to associate with the longhaired musicians who did. He got no encouragement from anyone and his progress was lonely. But Father was not the kind of man who depends on encouragement. He had long muscular fingers, he practiced faithfully, and he learned to the best of his ability to play Beethoven and Bach.

His feeling for music was limited but it was deeply rooted, and he cared enough for it to keep on practicing even after he married and in the busy years when he was providing for a house full of boys. He didn't go to symphonic concerts and he never liked Wagner, but he'd hum something of Brahms while posting his ledger, or play Mozart or Chopin after dinner. It gave him a sense of well-being.

Mother liked music too. We often heard her sweet voice gently singing old songs of an evening. If she forgot parts here or there, she swiftly improvised something that would let the air flow along without breaking the spell.

Father didn't play that way. He was erecting much statelier structures, and when he got a chord wrong, he stopped. He took that chord apart and went over the notes one by one, and he kept on going over them methodically. This sometimes drove Mother mad. She would desperately cry "Oh-oh-oh!" and run out of the room.

Her whole attitude toward music was different. She didn't get a solid and purely personal enjoyment from it like Father. It was more of a social function to her. It went with dancing and singing. She played and sang for fun, or to keep from being sad, or to give others pleasure.

On Thursday afternoons in the winter, Mother was always "at home." She served tea and cakes, and quite a few people dropped in to see her. She liked entertaining. And whenever she saw a way to make her Thursdays more attractive, she tried it.

About this time, Mother's favorite niece, Cousin Julie, was duly "finished" at boarding school and came to live with us, bringing her trunks and hatboxes and a great gilded harp. Mother at once made room for this beautiful object in our crowded parlor, and the first thing Julie knew she had to play it for the Thursday-afternoon visitors. Julie loved her harp dearly but she didn't like performing at all—performances frightened her, and if she fumbled a bit, she felt badly. But Mother said she must get over all that. She tried to give Julie self-confidence. She talked to her like a determined though kind impresario.

These afternoon sessions were pleasant, but they made Mother want to do more. While she was thinking one evening about what a lot of social debts she must pay, she suddenly said to Father, who was reading Gibbon, half-asleep by the fire, "Why not give a musicale, Clare, instead of a series of dinners?"

When Father was able to understand what she was talking about, he said he was glad if she had come to her senses sufficiently to give up any wild idea of having a series of dinners, and that she had better by all means give up musicales, too. He informed her he was not made of money, and all good string quartets were expensive; and when Mother interrupted him, he raised his voice and said, to close the discussion: "I will not have my peaceful home turned into a Roman arena, with a lot of hairy fiddlers prancing about and disturbing my comfort."

"You needn't get so excited, Clare," Mother said. "I didn't say a word about hairy fiddlers. I don't know where you get such ideas. But I do know a lovely young girl whom Mrs. Spiller has had, and she'll come for very little, I'm sure."

"What instrument does this inexpensive paragon play?" Father inquired sardonically.

"She doesn't play, Clare. She whistles."

"Whistles!" said Father. "Good God!"

"Very well, then," Mother said after an argument. "I'll have to have Julie instead, and Miss Kregman can help her, and I'll try to get Sally Brown or somebody to play the piano."

"Miss Kregman!" Father snorted. "I wash my hands of the whole business."

Mother asked nothing better. She could have made a grander affair of it if he had provided the money, but even with only a little to spend, getting up a party was fun. Before her marriage, she had loved her brother Alden's musicales. She would model hers upon those. Hers would be different in one way, for Uncle Alden had had famous artists, and at hers the famous artists would be impersonated by Cousin Julie. But the question as to how expert the music would be didn't bother her, and she didn't think it would bother the guests whom she planned to invite. The flowers would be pretty; she knew just what she would put in each vase (the parlor was full of large vases); she had a special kind of little cakes in mind, and everybody would enjoy it all thoroughly.

But no matter what kind of artists she has, a hostess is bound to have trouble managing them, and Mother knew that even her homemade material would need a firm hand. Julie was devoted to her, and so was the other victim, Sally Brown, Julie's schoolmate. But devoted or not, they were uneasy about this experiment. Sally would rather have done almost anything than perform at a musicale, and the idea of playing in public sent cold chills down Julie's back.

The only one Mother worried about, however, was Julie's teacher, Miss Kregman. She could bring a harp of her own, so she would be quite an addition, but Mother didn't feel she was decorative. She was an angular, plain-looking woman, and she certainly was a very unromantic sight at a harp.

Father didn't feel she was decorative either, and said, "I'll be hanged if I come." He said musicales were all poppycock anyway. "Nothing but tinkle and twitter."

"Nobody's invited you, Clare," Mother said defiantly. As a matter of fact, she felt relieved by his announcement. This wasn't like a dinner, where she wanted Father and where he would be of some use. She didn't want him at all at her musicale.

"All I ask is," she went on, "that you will please dine out for once. It won't be over until six at the earliest, and it would make things much easier for me if you would dine at the club."

Father said that was ridiculous. "I never dine at the club. I won't do it. Any time I can't have my dinner in my own home, this house is for sale. I disapprove entirely of these parties and uproar!" he shouted. "I'm ready to sell the place this very minute if I can't live here in peace, and we can all go and sit under a palm tree and live on breadfruit and pickles!"

On the day of the musicale, it began to snow while we were at breakfast. Father had forgotten what day it was, of course, and he didn't care anyhow—his mind was on a waistcoat which he wished Mother to take to his tailor's. To his astonishment, he found her standing on a stepladder, arranging some ivy, and when he said "Here's my waistcoat," she gave a loud wail of self-pity at this new infliction. Father said in a bothered way: "What is the matter with you, Vinnie? What are you doing up on that ladder? Here's my waistcoat, I tell you, and it's got to go to the tailor at once." He insisted on handing it up to her, and he banged the front door going out.

Early in the afternoon, the snow changed to rain. The streets were deep in slush. We boys gave up sliding downhill on the railroad bridge in East Forty-eighth Street and came tramping in with our sleds. Before going up to the playroom, we looked in the parlor. It was full of small folding chairs. The big teakwood armchairs with their embroidered backs were crowded off into corners, and the blue velvety ottoman with its flowered top could hardly be seen. The rubber tree had been moved from the window and strategically placed by Miss Kregman's harp, in such a way that the harp would be in full view but Miss Kregman would not.

Going upstairs, we met Julie coming down. Her lips were blue. She was pale. She passed us with fixed, unseeing eyes, and when I touched her hand it felt cold.

Looking over the banisters, we saw Miss Kregman arrive in her galoshes. Sally Brown, who was usually gay, entered silently later. Miss Kregman clambered in behind the rubber tree and tuned the majestic gold harps. Mother was arranging trayfuls of little cakes and sandwiches, and giving a last touch to the flowers. Her excited voice floated up to us. There was not a sound from the others.

At the hour appointed for this human sacrifice, ladies began arriving in long, swishy dresses which swept bits of mud over the carpet. Soon the parlor was packed. I thought of Sally, so anxious and numb she could hardly feel the piano keys, and of Julie's icy fingers plucking valiantly away at the strings. Then Mother clapped her hands as a signal for the chatter to halt, the first hesitating strains of music began, and someone slid the doors shut.

When we boys went down to dinner that evening, we heard the news, good and bad. In a way it had been a success. Julie and Sally had played beautifully the whole afternoon, and the ladies had admired the harps, and applauded, and eaten up all the cakes. But there had been two catastrophes. One was that although Miss Kregman herself had been invisible, everybody had kept looking fascinatedly at her feet, which had stuck out from the rubber tree, working away by themselves, as it were, at the pedals, and the awful part was she had forgotten to take off her galoshes. The other was that Father had come home during a sweet little lullaby and the ladies had distinctly heard him say "Damn" as he went up to his room.

FATHER SEWS ON A BUTTON

It must have been hard work to keep up with the mending in our house. Four boys had to be kept in repair besides Father, and there was no special person to do it. The baby's nurse did some sewing, and Cousin Julie turned to and did a lot when she was around, but the rest of it kept Mother busy and her work basket was always piled high.

Looking back, I wonder now how she managed it. I remember her regularly going off to her room and sewing on something, right after dinner or at other idle moments, when she might have sat around with the rest of us. My impression as a boy was that this was like going off to do puzzles—it was a form of amusement, or a woman's way of passing the time.

There was more talk about Father's socks and shirts than anything else. Most of this talk was by Father, who didn't like things to disappear for long periods, and who wanted them brought promptly back and put in his bureau drawer where they belonged. This was particularly true of his favorite socks. Not the plain white ones which he wore in the evening, because they were all alike, but the colored socks that were supplied to him by an English haberdasher in Paris.

These colored socks were the one outlet of something in Father which ran contrary to that religion of propriety to which he adhered. In that day of somber hues for men's suits and quiet tones for men's neckties, most socks were as dark and severe as the rest of one's garments; but Father's, hidden from the public eye by his trousers and his high buttoned shoes, had a really astonishing range both of color and fancy. They were mostly in excellent taste, but in a distinctly French way, and Wilhelmine used to tease him about them. She called them his "secret joys."

Father got holes in his socks even oftener than we boys did
in our stockings. He had long athletic toes, and when he lay
stretched out on his sofa reading and smoking, or absorbed in
talking to anyone, these toes would begin stretching and wiggling
in a curious way by themselves, as though they were seizing on
this chance to live a life of their own. I often stared in fascination
at their leisurely twistings and turnings, when I should have been
listening to Father's instructions about far different matters. Soon
one and then the other slipper would fall off, always to Father's
surprise, but without interrupting his talk, and a little later his
busy great toe would peer out at me through a new hole in his
sock.

Mother felt that it was a woman's duty to mend things and
sew, but she hated it. She rather liked to embroider silk lambre-
quins, as a feat of womanly prowess, but her darning of Father's
socks was an impatient and not-too-skillful performance. She
said there were so many of them that they made the back of her
neck ache.

Father's heavily starched shirts, too, were a problem. When
he put one on, he pulled it down over his head, and thrust his
arms blindly out right and left in a hunt for the sleeves. A new
shirt was strong enough to survive these strains without splitting,
but life with Father rapidly weakened it, and the first thing he
knew he would hear it beginning to tear. That disgusted him.
He hated any evidence of weakness, either in people or things.
In his wrath he would strike out harder than ever as he felt
around for the sleeve. Then would come a sharp crackling noise
as the shirt ripped open, and a loud wail from Mother.

Buttons were Father's worst trial, however, from his point of
view. Ripped shirts and socks with holes in them could still be
worn, but drawers with their buttons off couldn't. The speed
with which he dressed seemed to discourage his buttons and make
them desert Father's service. Furthermore, they always gave out
suddenly and at the wrong moment.

He wanted help and he wanted it promptly at such times,
of course. He would appear at Mother's door with a waistcoat

in one hand and a disloyal button in the other, demanding that it be sewn on at once. If she said she couldn't just then, Father would get as indignant as though he had been drowning and a life-guard had informed him he would save him tomorrow.

When his indignation mounted high enough to sweep aside his good judgment, he would say in a stern voice, "Very well, I'll sew it on myself," and demand a needle and thread. This announcement always caused consternation. Mother knew only too well what it meant. She would beg him to leave his waistcoat in her work basket and let her do it next day. Father was inflexible. Moreover, his decision would be strengthened if he happened to glance at her basket and see how many of his socks were dismally waiting there in that crowded exile.

"I've been looking for those blue polka-dotted socks for a month," he said angrily one night before dinner. "Not a thing is done for a man in this house. I even have to sew on my own buttons. Where is your needle and thread?"

Mother reluctantly gave these implements to him. He marched off, sat on the edge of his sofa in the middle of his bedroom, and got ready to work. The gaslight was better by his bureau, but he couldn't sit on a chair when he sewed. It had no extra room on it. He laid his scissors, the spool of thread, and his waistcoat down on the sofa beside him, wet his fingers, held the needle high up and well out in front, and began poking the thread at the eye.

Like every commander, Father expected instant obedience, and he wished to deal with trained troops. The contrariness of the needle and the limp obstinacy of the thread made him swear. He stuck the needle in the sofa while he wet his fingers and stiffened the thread again. When he came to take up his needle, it had disappeared. He felt around everywhere for it. He got up, holding fast to his thread, and turned around, facing the sofa to see where it was hiding. This jerked the spool off onto the floor, where it rolled away and unwound.

The husbands of two of Mother's friends had had fits of apoplexy and died. It frightened her horribly when this seemed about to happen to Father. At the sound of his roars, she rushed in. There he was on the floor, as she had feared. He was trying to get his head under the sofa and he was yelling at something, and his face was such a dark red and his eyes so bloodshot that Mother was terrified. Pleading with him to stop only made him more apoplectic. He said he'd be damned if he'd stop. He stood up presently, tousled but triumphant, the spool in his hand. Mother ran to get a new needle. She threaded it for him and he at last started sewing.

Father sewed on the button in a violent manner, with vicious haulings and jabs. Mother said she couldn't bear to see him—but she couldn't bear to leave the room, either. She stood watching him, hypnotized and appalled, itching to sew it herself, and they talked at each other with vehemence. Then the inevitable accident happened: the needle came forcibly up through the waistcoat, it struck on the button, Father pushed at it harder, and it burst through the hole and stuck Father's finger.

He sprang up with a howl. To be impaled in this way was not only exasperating, it was an affront. He turned to me, as he strode about on the rug, holding onto his finger, and said wrathfully, "It was your mother."

"Why, Clare!" Mother cried.

"Talking every minute," Father shouted at her, "and distracting a man! How the devil can I sew on a button with this gibbering and buzz in my ears? Now see what you made me do!" he added suddenly. "Blood on my good waistcoat! Here! Take the damned thing. Give me a handkerchief to tie up my finger with. Where's the witch-hazel?"

FATHER AND THE
CRUSADER'S THIRD WIFE

One of the ways in which Father and Mother were as alike as two peas was in their love of having good times. When they went to a dance or a dinner where they enjoyed themselves, they were full of high spirits. They had a lot of gusto about it, and they came home refreshed.

But there was this great difference: Mother always wanted to go; Father never. Mother was eager, and she was sure in advance they would like it. She had a romantic idea, Father said, that all parties were pleasant. He knew better. He said he hated them. All of them. He refused to go anywhere. When Mother asked him about accepting this or that invitation, he said she could go if she liked, but he certainly wouldn't. He would settle down in his chair and say, "Thank God, *I* know enough to stay home."

But Mother couldn't go to a dance or a dinner without him. That would have been impossible in those days. It was almost unheard of. The result was that she accepted all invitations and didn't tell him until the time came to go, so that Father went out much more than he meant to; only he always made a scene first, of course, and had to be dragged. Every time he got into the carriage and drove off to their friends', he felt imposed upon and indignant, and Mother was almost worn out.

The surprising thing was that after all this, both of them had a good time. They both had immense stores of energy and resilience to draw on. Mother would alight from the carriage half-crying, but determined to enjoy herself, too; and Father, who could never stay cross for long, would begin to cheer up as soon as he went in the big, lighted doorway. By the time they were at table or in the ballroom, they were both full of fun.

"Aren't you ashamed of yourself," she would say, "making such a fuss about coming!"

But Father had forgotten the fuss by then, and would ask what on earth she was talking about.

When he sat next to some pretty woman at table, his eye would light up and he would feel interested and gallant. He had charm. Women liked him. It never did them any good to like him if the wine wasn't good, or if the principal dishes weren't cooked well. That made him morose. But when the host knew his business, Father was gay and expansive, without ever a thought of the raps Mother would give him on the head going home.

"Clare, you were so silly with that Miss Remsen! She was laughing at you all the time."

"What are you talking about now?" he would chuckle, trying to remember which was Miss Remsen. He was not good at names, and pretty women were much the same to him anyhow. He was attentive and courtly to them by instinct, and Mother could see they felt flattered, but no one would have been as startled as Father if this had made complications. He thought of his marriage as one of those things that were settled. If any woman had really tried to capture him, she would have had a hard time. He was fully occupied with his business and his friends at the club, and he was so completely wrapped up in Mother that she was the one his eye followed. He liked to have a pretty woman next to him, as he liked a cigar or a flower, but if either a flower or a cigar had made demands on him, he would have been most disturbed.

It thrilled Mother, at parties, to meet some distinguished and proud-looking man, especially if he made himself agreeable to her, for she greatly admired fine males. She was critical too, though; they had to be human to please her. She was swift at pricking balloons. If there were no one of this high type to fascinate her, she liked men who were jolly; quick-minded men who danced well or talked well. Only they mustn't make love to her. When they did, she was disappointed in them. She said they were idiots. She not only said so to others, she said so to them.

"Mercy on us, Johnny Baker," she'd say crossly, "don't be such a fool!"

Johnny Baker belonged to his wife, that was Mother's idea, and if he didn't know it, he was stupid. Mother hated stupidity. She seemed to go on the principle that every man belonged to some woman. A bachelor ought to be devoted to his mother or sister. A widower should keep on belonging to the wife he had lost.

This last belief was one that she often tried to implant in Father. He had every intention of outliving her, if he could, and she knew it. He said it was only his devotion to her that made him feel this way—he didn't see how she could get on without him, and he must stay alive to take care of her. Mother snorted at this benevolent attitude. She said she could get on perfectly well, but of course she'd die long before he did. And what worried her was how he'd behave himself when she was gone.

One day in an ancient chapel near Oxford, they were shown a tomb where a noble crusader was buried, with his effigy laid out on top. Mother was much impressed till the verger pointed to the figure beside him, of the lady who had been his third wife. Mother immediately struck at the tomb with her parasol, demanding, "Where's your first, you old thing!"

The verger was so shocked that he wouldn't show them the rest of the church; but Mother didn't want to see it anyway. She told the verger he ought to be ashamed of himself for exhibiting an old wretch like that, and she went out at once, feeling strongly that it was no place for Father.

FATHER AMONG THE
POTTED PALMS

Although Father enjoyed himself when Mother and he went to parties, the idea of giving a party in his own home seemed monstrous. The most he would consent to was to have a few old friends in to dinner. He said that when Mother went beyond that, she turned the whole place upside down. He said he declined to have his comfort "set at naught" in that manner.

Father put comfort first in his home life: he had plenty of adventure downtown. But Mother got tired of dining with nobody but his old friends all the time. She wanted to see different houses, new people. By temperament she was an explorer.

She knew that an explorer who got no invitations to explore sat at home. And the surest way to get invitations was to give them, and to all sorts of people, and turn Father's home upside down whether he liked it or not.

To forestall opposition, Mother's method was to invite one couple whom Father knew, so that when he looked around the table one or two of the faces would be familiar, but as to the others she experimented. If questioned by Father as to who'd be there, she said, "Why, the Bakers, and I hope a few others." This reassured him till the night of the dinner arrived. Then, when he came home and found potted palms in the hall, it was too late to stop her.

That dinner for "the Bakers and a few others" was a dinner of ten, and the principal guests were the Ormontons, whom Mother had been determined to invite ever since she had met them. She didn't really know what they were like yet, but they had looked most imposing.

One night just a week before the event, we heard a ring at the front door. It was about seven o'clock. We were just finishing our six-o'clock dinner. Mother had come in so late from the Horse Show that she hadn't bothered to dress; she had thrown off her frock on her bed and slipped into a wrapper. Bridget, the waitress, an awkward girl whose mouth dropped wide open in crises, went to answer the bell.

We heard her open the door. Then, in the silence, there was the sound of somebody going upstairs. We looked in surprise at one another. Only dinner guests ever went up automatically that way, expecting to take off their coats and wraps in some upper bedroom.

Mother leapt from her chair and ran out to the hall. She had guessed what was happening. Sure enough, there was Bridget, staring helplessly with her mouth gaping open, at two stately figures, the Ormontons, resplendently marching upstairs.

At the head of those stairs was Mother's bedroom, in the wildest disorder. Another moment and Mrs. Ormonton would have gone in there to take off her wraps. "Why, Mrs. Ormonton!" Mother called, in a panic. "Haven't you made a mistake?"

The march upward was halted. The two dignified figures looked solemnly over the banisters.

"It's *next* Tuesday that you're coming to dine!" Mother cried, clutching in dismay at her wrapper.

Mr. Ormonton stared disapprovingly at Mother a moment. Then, as he began to take in what had happened, he pursed his lips, his eyes popped, and he turned and scowled at his wife. She looked at him in fright and slumped slowly, like a soft tallow candle.

"*Next* Tuesday," Mother faintly repeated.

The Ormontons pulled themselves together and came slowly down.

They stood helplessly in the hall by the hatrack. As they had dismissed their carriage, they had no way to remove themselves from our home. A streetcar was impossible for an Ormonton in full evening dress. They would have to wait till a cab could be sent for, which would take at least half an hour and probably more.

If we could have offered them some impromptu little meal, it might have been welcome to both of them, but we boys had eaten every last scrap, and Mother couldn't think how to manage it. She didn't feel she knew them well enough to have that awful Bridget bring up some cold meat and a glass of milk and an old piece of pie. So they waited in their sumptuous clothes, cross and wretched and hungry. They had little or no sense of fun, even in their happiest moments, and they certainly did not feel light-hearted as they sat in our parlor. Mother had to make conversation, in her wrapper, till almost eight o'clock. Mr. Ormonton said nothing whatever. He felt too much wronged, too indignant. Father strolled in and offered him a cigar. It was stiffly declined.

A week later, when they again rang the bell, they were stiffer than ever. But by that time our easy-going household was completely transformed. Instead of Bridget and her elbows, a butler suavely opened the door. Large potted palms stood in the hall. The Ormontons felt more at home.

They could not have imagined how much work Mother's preparations had cost. To begin with, she had gone to a little shop she had found on Sixth Avenue, under the Elevated, a place where they sold delicious ice cream and French pastries and bonbons, which was run by a pleasant and enterprising young man named Louis Sherry. He had arranged to send over old John, a waiter, to be our butler *pro tem,* and a greasy and excitable young chef to take charge of our kitchen, and they had brought with them neat covered baskets which they wouldn't let us boys touch.

Old John and Mother had a great deal to do in the dining-room: getting out arsenals of silver to be laid at each place, putting leaves in the black-walnut table, filling vases with flowers, arranging little plates of salted almonds and chocolates, and I don't know what else. The heavy plush furniture in the parlor had to be rearranged, too, and piles of special plates taken down from the pantry top shelf, and an elaborately embroidered table-cloth and napkins got out of the linen closet. And after Mother had run around all day attending to these, and had laid out the right dress and slippers, and done things to her hair, she had ended by desperately tackling the worst job of all, which was to put her bedroom in order.

This room, in spite of Mother's random efforts, had an obstinate habit of never being as neat and pretty-looking as she wished it to be. On the contrary, it was always getting into a comfortable, higgledy-piggledy state. And every time Mother gave a dinner, she felt guiltily sure that the ladies who took off their wraps in it would have gimlet eyes. Everything, therefore, had to be put away out of sight. Her plan was to do this so neatly that any drawer which these prying creatures might open would be in beautiful order. But she never had time enough, so after the first two or three drawers had had their upper levels fixed up, things were pushed into the others any which way, and when she was through they were locked. Letters and pieces of string were hurried off the dressing-table, medicines and change off the mantel, stray bits of lace, pencils, veils, and old macaroons off the bureau. Some were jammed into cabinets that were already so full they could hardly be shut, some disappeared into hat-boxes or were poked up on dark closet shelves. Among these jumbled articles were many that would be urgently needed next week, but by that time even Mother couldn't remember where on earth she had put them, and she spent hours hunting hopelessly for a lost glove or key. When the bedroom was "picked up" at last, it had lost its old friendly air. A splendid spread lay on the bed smoothly. The bolster and pillows were covered as elaborately as if no one used them to sleep on. A big china kerosene lamp and some pink-shaded candles were lit. And Mother, all tired out, was being laced up the back in her tight-fitting gown.

Father had none of this work to do in his room. In fact he had no work at all. He dressed for dinner every night anyhow, and his room was always in order. Everything he owned had its place, and he never laid his clothes down at random. There were two drawers for his shirts, for example, another drawer for his socks, his shaving-kit was always on his English shaving-stand by the window. On his bureau were a pair of military hairbrushes, two combs, and a bottle of bay rum—nothing else. Each of his books had its own allotted place on his shelves. And on each shelf and in every drawer there was extra room. Nothing was crowded.

When he undressed to go to bed, he began by taking the things out of his pockets and putting them into a little drawer which he reserved for that purpose. He then hung his suit on its own regular hook in his closet and laid his underwear in the washbasket. He never left anything lying around on the chairs. He did these things so swiftly that he could dress or undress in ten minutes, and when he turned out the gas and opened his big window, his room was as trim as a general's.

On the night of the dinner, he came home at his usual hour, swore at the potted palms, and took John down to the cellar to get out the right wines. Then he went to his room; and as dinner was later than usual, he had a short nap. He got up a quarter of an hour or so before it was time for the guests to arrive, screwed in his studs, shaved and dressed, gave his white tie a sharp, exact twist, and peacefully went down to the parlor. Finding Mother there, adjusting a smoky lamp, he said he'd be damned if he'd stand it, having his comfort interfered with by a lot of people he did not wish to see. He added that if they didn't come on time, they needn't expect him to wait—he was hungry.

But the guests soon began clattering up to our door over the cobblestones in their broughams, and Father smiled at the men and shook hands warmly with the best-looking women, and got all their names mixed up, imperturbably, until John opened the great sliding doors of the little dining-room, and they went in to dinner.

As for the rest of the evening, it was just another dinner for Father, except that he had sherry and champagne instead of claret, and some dishes by a good chef. But Mother, looking critically around at her social material, and watching the service every minute, had to work to the last. No matter how formal and wooden her material was, it was her business to stir them to life and make the atmosphere jolly. She usually succeeded, she was so darting and gay, but on this high occasion some of the guests couldn't be made to unbend.

Father didn't notice that they were wooden, nor did he feel disappointed. With a good dinner and sound wines inside him, he could enjoy any climate. He also enjoyed talking to people about whatever came into his head, and he seldom bothered to observe if they listened or how they responded.

Bridget's duties were to stay in the pantry and help John and keep quiet. She stayed in the pantry all right, but she flunked on the rest of it. Each time that she dropped something, she made a loud, gasping sound. John went on about his business, ignoring this in a severe and magnificent manner, but nobody else was quite able to, except, of course, Father. To Mother's relief, he unconsciously saved the day for her by being too absorbed in his own conversation to hear these weird interruptions.

The climax came at dessert. By that time, Bridget was completely demoralized, and she so far forgot herself as to poke her face outside the screen and hiss some question hoarsely at John. An awful silence came over the table. But Father, who felt as astonished as anybody, took no pains to conceal it. He turned squarely around and demanded: "What the devil's that noise?"

Father's utter naturalness made even Mr. Ormonton smile. All formality melted away, to Mother's surprise and delight, and though Father had no idea he had caused it, a gay evening began.

FATHER HAS A BAD NIGHT

One winter morning when Father left the Riding Club on horse-back and rode through East Fifty-eighth Street, his horse fell with him. Not only did the stupid animal fall but he landed on Father's foot.

Father pulled his foot out from under, got the horse up, and went on to the Park for his ride. But he found later that one of his toes had been bent and that he couldn't straighten it out.

This was not only an inconvenience to Father, it was a sur-prise. He knew other men got smashed up in accidents, but he had assumed that that was because they were brittle. He wasn't. He was constructed in such a manner, he had supposed, that he couldn't be damaged. He still believed that this was the case. Yet one of his toes had got bent.

That toe never did straighten out and Father talked of it often. He felt that he had had a strange experience, one that was against Nature's laws, and he expected those who listened to his story to be deeply concerned and impressed. If they weren't, he repeated it.

We heard it at home hundreds of times, one year after another. "That's enough about your toe," Mother would cry. "Nobody cares about your toe, you know, Clare!"

But Father said that of course people did. He told all his friends at the club. "You know what happened to me? Why, one morning when the pavement was icy, that bay cob that Sam Babcock sold me fell on my toe—and he *bent* it! Never had such a thing happen to me all my life. Bent my toe! It's getting a corn on it now. Here. On top. My shoemaker says he can't fix it. There's nobody as stupid as a shoemaker, except that bay cob."

From this time on, although he still was contemptuous of dis-

183

the spare-room bed was by an open window facing the quiet back
yards, and as the neighbors, it seemed, had no cotton, they hadn't
much chance to rest.

The next day, Mother happened to stop in to see Mrs. Crane,
who lived a few doors away from us, and started to tell her about
my operation. But Mrs. Crane interrupted.

"Oh yes, Mrs. Day," she said. "My daughter and I knew
something had happened. It must have been terrible. We were
so sorry for him. We could hear him groaning all night. How very
hard it must have been for you. My daughter and I got a little
sleep toward morning, but I'm afraid you had none at all."

On her way home, Mother met another of the neighbors, Mrs.
Robbins, who lived on the other side of our block in the next
street, and whose rear bedrooms faced ours. Mrs. Robbins, too,
knew all about it.

"My room is in the front of the house," she said, "so I didn't
know what had happened until Mr. Robbins told me at breakfast. He talked of nothing else all this morning. He couldn't believe that I hadn't heard the—er—your poor son's dreadful
cries."

Mother waited that evening for Father to get home from his
office. The minute he came in, she pounced on him. "Oh,
Clare!" she said. "I am so ashamed of you! You get worse and
worse. I saw Mrs. Crane today and Mrs. Robbins, and they
told me what happened last night, and I don't believe any of the
neighbors got one wink of sleep."

"Well," Father answered, "neither did I."

"Yes, but Clare," Mother impatiently cried, seizing his coat
lapels and trying to shake him, "they thought it was Clarence
making those noises and all the time it was you!"

"I don't give a damn what they thought," Father said wearily.
"I had a bad night."

FATHER AND HIS OTHER SELVES

Father's attitude toward anybody who wasn't his kind used to puzzle me. It was so dictatorial. There was no live and let live about it. And to make it worse he had no compunctions about any wounds he inflicted; on the contrary, he felt that people should be grateful to him for teaching them better.

This was only one side of him, of course, as I realized better later, for I saw even more of him after I grew up than I had in my childhood. He was one of the jolliest and most companionable men I ever knew. He always seemed to have a good time when he went to the club. He liked most of the men whom he met there, and they felt that same way toward him. One or another of them walked home with him, usually, and stood talking with him by the front stoop. And when he rode with his friends in the Park or went for a sail on some yacht, or when he and his fellow-directors of some little railroad spent a week on a tour of inspection, they came back full of fun.

It was only with men of his own sort that he did this, however. They understood him and he them. They all had an air and a feeling, in those days, of enormous authority. When they disagreed, it was often quite violently, but that didn't matter. At bottom they thoroughly approved of and respected each other.

Toward people with whom he didn't get on well, though, he was imperious, and when they displeased or annoyed him, it made him snort like a bull.

I disapproved of this strongly when I was a boy. It seemed natural to me that any father should snort, more or less, about the behavior of his wife, or his children, or his relatives generally. It seemed natural, too, for a man to make his employees live exactly as he decreed. That sort of thing was so much in the air that I, for one, didn't question it. But Father didn't stop there; he expected everyone else to conform, even people he read about in the newspapers. Even historical characters. He never failed to denounce them indignantly when he found that they hadn't.

He felt the same way about persons he passed in the street. And sometimes in a horse-car he looked around at his fellow-passengers like a colonel distastefully reviewing a slatternly regiment. They didn't all have to be bankers or lawyers or clubmen—though if they were, all the better—but they did have to be neat and decent. And self-respecting. Like him. He would glare at men whose vests were unbuttoned, or whose neckties were loose, or whose general appearance was sloppy, as though they deserved hanging. He said he hated slovenly people. He said that they were "offensive."

"What difference does it make to you, Father?" I'd ask him. He didn't explain. I could have understood his quietly disliking them, for a sense of the fitness of things was strong in him; but why did he feel so much heat?

One day I came upon a magazine article which discussed this very matter. No ego ought to feel entirely separate, the writer explained. It should think of others as its own alter egos—differing forms of itself. This wasn't at all the way I looked at others. I expected nearly all of them to be different and I was surprised when they weren't. This magazine writer said that only unsocial persons felt that way. Well, at least this idea made Father's attitude understandable to me. If he was simply thinking of others as his own other selves, that might be why, when they didn't behave as such, he got in a passion about it.

Every morning Father sat in the big armchair in the dining-room window to look over his newspaper and see just what his alter egos had been up to since yesterday. If they hadn't been up to anything, he turned to the financial page or read one or two editorials—one or two being all he could stand, because he said they were wishy-washy. If, however, the Mayor had been faithless again to Father's ideals, or if Tammany Hall had done anything at all, good or bad, Father ringingly denounced these atrocities to us little boys and to Mother.

For a long time none of the rest of us joined in these political talks. This suited Father exactly. He didn't wish to be hindered, or even helped, when he was letting off steam. After a while, though, Mother began attending a class in current events, which an enterprising young woman, a Miss Edna Gulick, conducted on Tuesdays. Social, musical, and literary matters took up most of Miss Gulick's mind. But though she didn't go deeply into politics or industrial problems, merely darting about on the surface in a bright, sprightly way, she did this so skillfully, and made everything seem so clear to Mother, that the most baffling and intricate issues became childishly simple.

The day after one of these classes, just when Father was wholeheartedly bombarding President Benjamin Harrison and somebody named William McKinley for putting through a new tariff and trying their best to ruin the country, Mother boldly chimed in. She said she was sure that the President's idea was all right; he had only been a little unfortunate in the way he had put it.

Father laid down his paper in high displeasure. "What do *you* know about it?" he demanded.

"Miss Gulick says she has it on the best authority," Mother firmly declared. "She says the President prays to God for guidance, and that he is a very good-hearted man."

"The President," said Father, "is a nincompoop, and I strongly suspect he's a scalawag, and I wish to God you wouldn't talk on matters you don't know a damned thing about."

"I do too know about them," Mother exclaimed. "Miss Gulick says every intelligent woman should have some opinion—about this tariff thing, and capital and labor, and everything else."

"Well I'll be damned," Father said in amazement. "Who, may I ask, is Miss Gulick?"

"Why, she's that current-events person I told you about, and the tickets are a dollar each Tuesday," said Mother.

"Do you mean to tell me that a pack of idle-minded females pay a dollar apiece to hear another female gabble about the events of the day?" Father asked. "Listen to *me* if you want to know anything about the events of the day."

"But you get so excited, Clare dear, and you always talk so long and so loud that I never can see what you're getting at. About tariffs. And strikes."

"It is a citizen's duty," Father began, getting angrily into his overcoat, but Mother wouldn't be interrupted.

"Another reason that we all like Miss Gulick so much," she went on, "is that she says kindness is much more important than arguments. And she says that it makes her feel very sad when she reads about strikes, because capital and labor could easily learn to be nice to each other."

Father burst out of the house, banging the door, and finished buttoning his coat on the top step of our stoop. "I don't know what the world is coming to anyhow," I heard him exclaim to a few surprised passers-by on quiet Madison Avenue.

FATHER FINDS GUESTS
IN THE HOUSE

Father was a sociable man; he liked to sit and talk with us at home, or with his friends at the club. And in summer he permitted guests to stay with us out in the country, where there was plenty of room for them, and where he sometimes used to feel lonely. But in town he regarded any prolonged hospitality as a sign of weak natures. He felt that in town he must be stern with would-be house-guests or he'd be overrun with them. He had no objection to callers who dropped in for a cup of tea and got out, but when a guest came to our door with a handbag—or, still worse, a trunk—he said it was a damned imposition.

What complicated the matter was that nobody stayed with us usually except Mother's relatives. Father's relatives were well-regulated New Yorkers who stayed in their own homes, and he often told Mother that the sooner hers learned to, the better.

He had strong feelings about this and they always seemed to come out with a bang. When he got home for dinner and when Mother was obliged to confess that some of her relatives were concealed in the spare room, up on the third floor, those relatives were likely to wonder what was the matter downstairs. If Mother hadn't slammed the door, they would have heard indignant roars about locusts that ought to be sent back to Egypt instead of settling on Father.

Most of the guests had good consciences, however, and had been led to suppose Father loved them; and as they themselves were hospitable persons who would have welcomed him at their homes, they didn't suspect that those muffled outcries were occasioned by them. They merely felt sorry that poor Father was feeling upset about something. Mother encouraged them in this attitude; she said Father was worried about things and they must pretend not to notice. When Father glared speechlessly around the table at dinner, they felt sorrier for him than ever. Aunt Emma, who was a placid soul, once asked him if he had ever tried Dicer's Headache Lozenges, which were excellent in moments of depression and had also helped her anemia. Father nearly burst a blood vessel telling her that he was not anemic.

One of the things that Father especially detested about guests was the suddenness with which they arrived. So far as he knew, they invariably came without warning. The reason Mother never told him in advance was that he'd then have had two explosions —one when he was forbidding their coming, and one when they came.

Father made repeated attempts to acquaint Mother with his views about guests. This objectionable tribe, he explained to her, had two bad characteristics. One was that they didn't seem to know enough to go to hotels. New York was full of such structures, he pointed out, designed for the one special purpose of housing these nuisances. If they got tired of hotels, he said, they should be put aboard the next train at once, and shipped to some large, empty desert. If they wanted to roam, the damn gipsies, lend 'em a hand, keep 'em roaming.

But a still more annoying habit they had, he said, was that they wanted to be entertained, and every single one of them seemed to expect him to do it. Not content with disrupting the orderly routine of his household and ringing the bell every minute and sitting too long in his bathtub, they tried to make him go gallivanting off with them to a restaurant or give up his after-dinner cigar to see some long-winded play. He said to Mother, "I wish you to understand clearly that I am not a Swiss courier. I must decline to conduct groups of strangers around town at night. You can tell Emma that it is my desire to live here in peace, and that I do not intend to hold a perpetual Mardi Gras to please gaping villagers."

We didn't have visitors often, but still we did have a spare room. In this chamber was a little round fireplace, with a grate sticking out of it, surmounted by a white marble mantel. The mantel would have looked cold and tomblike if left to itself, but hanging from its edge there was a strip of red velvet about six inches deep, with a wavy gold border. On the mantel was a pink porcelain clock, trimmed with gilt, with a sweet-toned French bell. Two graceful though urnlike pink vases stood at the ends of the mantel, and on each side of the clock was a large Dresden figure. One was a curtseying shepherdess with a small waist, in a pink-and-green petticoat, and opposite her there danced a rosy shepherd, with one arm gone, playing away on a pipe.

The walls and carpet were dark. At each window were two sets of curtains, one lacy and white and one of thick silk brocade. The tiebacks consisted of elaborate loops with big tassels.

The principal pieces of furniture were a solid black mahogany bureau, tall and heavily carved, and a bed to match, so broad that it could have easily held several guests. Beside the bed stood a square black commode, with a white marble top.

This room, although somber, seemed waiting to be lived in; it had an air of dignified welcome. But when a guest started to investigate, he found that this was misleading. Except for the top of the bureau, there was really no place to put things. Every drawer was filled to bursting already with the overflow of other rooms. One of the two big closets was locked. In the other were ball dresses, an umbrella stand, piles of magazines, a small pair of steps, a job lot of discarded bonnets, and a painting of old Mr. Howe. After taking a good look at this closet, a guest generally gave up all hope of unpacking and resigned himself politely to camping out the best way he could.

His mind had little opportunity, however, to dwell on these small inconveniences, for he soon became engrossed by the drama of our family life. Our disconcerting inability to conceal any of our emotions absorbed him.

I never supposed that our daily lives were different from anyone else's until I went off on visits myself. At Jeff Barry's home, when I saw his dignified old parents being formally polite to each other, I thought they were holding themselves tightly in, and I used to wonder which of them would blow up first. I was relieved yet depressed when they didn't. They were so gentle and had such quiet ways that they seemed to me lifeless.

On a visit to the McGillians, I was shocked to discover that a married pair could be mean to each other. Even their children made sarcastic and biting remarks, as though they were trying to hurt one another in what I thought an underhand way. All our family got hurt often enough, but at least it wasn't deliberate. Our collisions were impulsive and open. We all had red hair and got angry in a second, but in a minute or two it was over.

Another family whose customs seemed strange to me was Johnny Clark's. Professor Clark, Johnny's father, when he was annoyed wouldn't speak. Around the first of the month, when the bills came in, he would sit without saying a word all through dinner, looking down at his plate. After we boys left the room, we heard Mrs. Clark beg him to tell her what she was to do. She said she was willing to live in a tent and spend nothing if he would only be pleasant. Mr. Clark listened to her in silence and then went off to his study.

This seemed to me gruesome. In our household, things got pretty rough at times but at least we had no black gloom. Our home life was stormy but spirited. It always had tang. When Father was unhappy, he said so. He poured out his grief with such vigor that it soon cleared the air.

If he had ever had any meannesses in him, he might have tried to repress them. But he was a thoroughly good-hearted and warm-blooded man, and he saw no reason for hiding his feelings. They were too strong to hide anyway.

One day while Father was in his office downtown, Auntie Gussie and Cousin Flossie arrived. Mother immediately began planning to take them to dine at the Waldorf, a much-talked-of new hotel at Fifth Avenue and Thirty-third Street, which she very much wanted to see. She knew Father mightn't like the idea, but he would enjoy himself after he got there, and she thought she could manage him.

When he came in, she went to his bedroom to break the good

news to him that instead of dining at home he was to go off on
a gay little party. She meant to do this diplomatically. But she
wasn't an adept at coaxing or inveigling a man, and even if she
had been, Father was not at all easy to coax. Whenever she was
planning to manage him, the very tone of her voice put him on
guard; it had an impatient note, as though really the only plan
she could think of was to wish he was manageable. So on this
occasion, when she tried to get him in a good mood, he promptly
got in a bad one. He looked suspiciously at Mother and said,
"I don't feel well."

"You need a little change," Mother said. "That'll make you
feel better. Besides, Gussie's here and she wants to dine with us
tonight at the Waldorf."

Father hated surprise attacks of this kind. No matter how
placid he might be, he instantly got hot when one came. In less
than a second he was rending the Waldorf asunder and saying
what he thought of anybody who wanted to dine there.

But Mother was fully prepared to see him take it hard at the
start. She paid no attention to his vehement refusals. She said
brightly that the Waldorf was lovely and that it would do him
good to go out. There was no dinner at home for him anyway, so
what else was there to do?

When Father took in the situation, he undressed and put on his
nightshirt. He shouted angrily at Mother that he had a sick headache. It made no difference to him whether there was any dinner
or not. He couldn't touch a mouthful of food, he declared. Food
be damned. What he needed was rest. After tottering around,
putting his clothes away, he darkened his room. He climbed into
bed. He pulled up the sheets, and he let out his breath in deep
groans.

These startling blasts, which came at regular intervals,
alarmed Auntie Gussie. But when she hurried down to help,
Mother seemed annoyed and shooed her back up.

The next thing she knew, Mother impatiently called up to her
that she was waiting. She had got tired of scolding Father and
trying to make him get out of bed, and had made up her mind to

dine at the Waldorf without him. She and Auntie Gussie and Flossie marched off by themselves. But they had to come back almost immediately because Mother didn't have enough money, and when she rushed into Father's sick-room and lit the gas again and made him get up and give her ten dollars, his roars of pain were terrific.

After they went out, his groans lessened in volume and were presently succeeded by snores. Father had a good nap. When he woke up, he felt happier. He said his headache was gone. He came downstairs in his dressing-gown and slippers, and sent for some bread and milk. He ate several huge bowlfuls of it with gusto, peacefully smoked a cigar, and was back in his bed again, reading, when Mother came home.

FATHER AND HIS PET RUG

Father liked spending his summers in the country, once he had got used to it, but it introduced two major earthquakes each year into his life. One when he moved out of town in the spring, and one in the fall when he moved back. If there was one thing Father hated it was packing. It seemed a huddled, irregular affair to a man with his orderly mind. For a week or more before it was time to begin he was upset by the prospect. He had only a few drawers full of clothes to empty into a trunk, but it had to be done in a certain particular way. No one else could attend to it for him—no one else could do the thing properly. All that Mother could do was to have his trunk brought to his room. When it had been laid in a corner, gaping at him, his groaning began. He walked around, first putting his shirts in, then his clothes and his underwear, then burrowing under and taking some out again to go in the suitcase, then deciding that after all he would not take part of what he had packed. During all such perplexities he communed with himself, not in silence.

The first sounds that used to come from his room were low groans of self-pity. Later on, as the task he was struggling with became more and more complicated, he could be heard stamping about, and denouncing his garments. If we looked in his door we would see him in the middle of the room with a bathrobe, which had already been packed twice in the suitcase and once in the trunk, and which was now being put back in the trunk again because the suitcase was crowded. Later it would once more go back in the suitcase so as to be where he could get at it. His face was red and angry, and he was earnestly saying, "Damnation!"

Long before any of this began Mother had already started her end of it. Father packed only his own clothes. She packed everything else: except that she had someone to help her, of course, with the heavy things. In the fall, for instance, a man named Jerome sometimes went up to the country to do this. He was a taciturn, preoccupied colored man, an expert at moving, who worked so well and quickly that he kept getting ahead of his schedule. It was distracting to Mother to plan out enough things to keep Jerome busy. It was also distracting to see him sit idle. He was paid by the day.

But the principal problem that Mother had to attend to was Father. He said that he didn't really mind moving but that he did object to the fuss. As to rugs, for instance, he refused to have any at all put away until after he and all his belongings had been moved from the house. This seemed unreasonable to me—I said he ought to allow them to make a beginning and put a few away, surely. He would admit, privately, that this was true perhaps, but here was the trouble: if he once let Mother get started she would go much too far. "When your mother is closing up a house," he said, "she gets too absorbed in it. She is apt to forget my comfort entirely—and also her own. I have found by experience that if I yield an inch in this matter the place is all torn up." He added that he had to insist upon absolute order, simply because the alternative was absolute chaos. Furthermore, why shouldn't the process be orderly if it were skillfully handled? If it wasn't, it was no fault of his, and he declined to be made to suffer for it.

Mother's side of it was that it was impossible to move out imperceptibly. "Things naturally get upset a little, Clare dear, when you're making a change. If they get upset too much I can't help it; and I do wish you would stop bothering me."

One result of this difference was a war about the rugs every fall. Two or three weeks before they left, Mother always had the large rug in the hall taken up—there was no need of *two* rugs in the hall, she told Father.

"I won't have it, damn it, you're making the place a barracks," he said.

"But we're *moving*," Mother expostulated; "we must get the house closed."

"Close it properly then! Do things suitably, without this cursed helter-skelter." He retreated into the library where he could sit by a fire, while Mother went in and out of cold rooms and halls with her shawl on.

The library had two large heavy pieces of furniture in it—a grand piano, and a huge desklike table piled with papers and books. This table filled the center of the room and stood square on a rug. It was hard work to lift that heavy table to get the rug out from under it. Until this was done, every year, Mother kept thinking about it at night. Strictly speaking, it wasn't necessary to have that rug put away much beforehand, but she wanted to get it over and done with so that she could sleep. But Father was particularly dependent on this rug because he liked to sit in the library; he was always determined that it shouldn't be touched till he left.

He couldn't, however, remain on guard continuously. He sometimes had to go out. In fact he was maneuvered into going out, though this he never quite learned. In the late afternoon when he supposed the day's activities over, he would come out of the library and venture to go off in the motor. Not far, just to get the evening paper, which was a very short trip. His mind was quiet: he assumed that nothing much could be done in his absence. But just as he was leaving he would be given some errand to do—some provisions to buy in the next town beyond, or a book to leave at some friend's. Or if this might make him suspicious, nothing would be said as he left, but the chauffeur would be given instructions what to say when he had bought Father's paper.

"There are some flowers in the car, sir, that Mrs. Day . . ."

Father looked up from his paper, and looked threateningly over his glasses. "What's all this?" he said. *"What?"*

The chauffeur repeated mildly "—that Mrs. Day wishes left at the church."

"Damn the church," Father answered, going back to the

Mother cease firing. Yet now after he had lowered his temperature again back to normal, and settled down to enjoy the fruits of his victory, namely his own big square rug, here was Jerome bringing him instead a long narrow hairy monstrosity.

"What's that?" he demanded.

Jerome limply exhibited the monstrosity, feeling hopeless inside, like a pessimistic salesman with no confidence in his own goods.

"What are you bringing that thing in here for?"

"Yessir, Mr. Day. Mrs. Day says put it under your feet."

Father started to turn loose his batteries all over again. But his guns had gone cold. He felt plenty of disgust and exasperation, but not quite enough fury. He fired what he had at Jerome, who stood up to it silently; and he kicked the offending white fur rug, and said he wouldn't have it. But something in the air now seemed to tell him, in his turn, he had lost. Even Jerome felt this, and put the rug under his feet, "temporary," leaving Father trying to read his paper again, indignant and bitter. He particularly disliked this white rug. He remembered it now from last year.

Mother went back to the linen. The house became quiet. The only sounds were thuds in the laundry yard, where Jerome was at work, beating and sweeping his booty, concealed by the hedge.

By the library fire Father was turning over the page of his paper, and glaring at the white rug, and saying to himself loudly, "I hate it!" He kicked at the intruder. "Damn woolly thing. I want my own rug."

FATHER AND THE FRENCH COURT

Except in his very last years, when he began to get shaky, Father wasn't bored in his old age, like some men. He kept up his billiards, enjoying the hard shots, until his eye grew less true; and he always found it absorbing to try to beat himself at solitaire. He enjoyed his drives until automobiles came and ruined the roads with their crowding. He enjoyed having a go at the morning paper, in a thoroughly combative spirit. Every time the President said or did anything which got on the front page, Father either commended him—in surprise—for having some backbone for once, or else said he was an infernal scoundrel and ought to be kicked out of office. "And I'd like to go down there and kick him out myself," he'd add fiercely. This was especially the case in President Wilson's two terms. There was something about Woodrow Wilson that made Father boil.

His dentist had made a bridge for him, at this time, to replace a lost tooth in front. Father soon took it back. "What's wrong, Mr. Day?" Dr. Wyant said. "Is the occlusion imperfect?"

"Why, your thing won't stay in; that's what's wrong with it," Father replied.

Dr. Wyant was puzzled. "You mean that the denture seems to work loose when you are at table?"

"No," said Father, "it stays in when I eat, and it usually stays in when I talk, but when I read my paper in the morning, and say what I think of that man Wilson, your thing pops right out."

So life wasn't boring in his old age to Father. He read more books then, too; particularly books about past and current political clashes. In these he always took sides. When his side won, he wanted their victory to be decisive; but if the other side won, they needn't hope to inflict a decisive defeat. The harder they pressed

One point I've left out is that each volume had the owner's monogram on it. This had made the set seem quite de luxe when the agent hypnotized Mother. But even then Mother had been doubtful about the French Court; she hadn't felt sure they were nice, though she had hoped for the best, and she thought it would be safer not to have her own monogram on them. So she had had the agent use Father's. This afterward seemed to prove she really had meant them to be a gift from the start. Father didn't believe it for a moment. Yet there was the evidence.

"I can't make Vinnie out," I heard him mutter, staring hard at the monogram.

They had been married for almost fifty years.

FATHER PLANS TO GET OUT

One evening when Father and Mother and I were in the library talking, a trained nurse came in to take Mother's blood pressure, as the doctor had ordered. This was a new thing in Mother's life. It alarmed her. She turned—as she always did when she was in any trouble—to Father.

"Clare," she said urgently to him, "you must have yours taken too."

Father scowled at the nurse. Blood pressure was something which he had been hearing more about than he liked. He had just passed his seventieth birthday, many of his old friends had died, and when he and a few other survivors met at the funerals that came often now, Father had seen some of them shaking their heads and whispering things about "blood pressure." What angered Father about it was that it seemed able to kill healthy men—men who he had felt sure would last for the next twenty years. Like himself. He'd talk at the club with one of them in the evening, after a few games of billiards, and the next week he'd pick up the paper and see that that man had died.

Father said he wouldn't mind if people died only once in a while, as they used to. He said we all had to die, he supposed. But he didn't know what the matter was nowadays. Somebody died every month. And it never was a wizened old walnut, like John Elderkin, it was always some sound, healthy man. No excuse for it. When he asked his friends at the club to explain it, he never got a clear answer. All they could talk of down there was blood pressure.

He said he was beginning to hate all these funerals. They were getting to be disturbing and unpleasant things to attend. He told General Anderson he didn't see why they kept going to them.

One Sunday when she herself was past seventy, and when Father in spite of his blood pressure and everything else was nearly eighty, she asked him if he wouldn't like to drive out with her to Woodlawn. She hadn't any flowers to take, but she had happened to think of that chair, though she didn't say so to Father. She merely said that it was a beautiful day and that it would do him good to go out.

Father refused. Positively. He winked robustly at me and said to Mother, "I'll be going there soon enough, damn it."

Mother said that he ought to come because one of the headstones had settled and she wanted him to tell her whether he didn't think it needed attention.

Father asked whose headstone it was, and when Mother told him he said: "I don't care how much it's settled. I don't want to be buried with any of that infernal crowd anyhow."

Mother of course knew how he felt about some of the family, but she said that he wouldn't mind such things when it was all over.

Father said yes he would. He became so incensed, thinking of it, that he declared he was going to buy a new plot in the cemetery, a plot all for himself. "And I'll buy one on a corner," he added triumphantly, "where I can get out!"

Mother looked at him, startled but admiring, and whispered to me, "I almost believe he could do it."

LIFE WITH
MOTHER

NOTE

Most of the chapters of this book were published before Clarence's death, but some were still in manuscript. These had to be sorted carefully because he had a habit of writing on whatever scrap of paper was handy—backs of envelopes, tax memoranda, or small pads of paper which he could hold in his hands on days when they were too lame for the big ones.

We talked daily about his father and mother and I knew perfectly the material he had in mind to use. Then I found, as I read and sorted the manuscripts, not only had he told it to me, but that he had written it down. Clarence had done all but the last chores involved in preparing a manuscript for a typist. All that remained to be done was the mechanical job of piecing together the incidents so that they could be copied. His work on his father and mother was finished.

There was one exception: Mother's last home was so characteristic of her and meant so much to her that, following notes, and copying from Clarence's diary, I inserted a description of her last days.

When he was alive Clarence used to speak of what the interest of his friends, his brother George Parmly Day and his wife, and Mr. Knopf and his staff had meant to him. It would not be fair to publish this book without thanking them for their continuing kindness; and also thanking two of his friends especially:

213

Mrs. Alice Duer Miller and Mrs. Katharine S. White, for their ever-ready and helpful criticism.

KATHARINE B. DAY

June 1937

MOTHER READS MY
ARTICLE TO FATHER

There has been some discussion in the Day family, among its members and friends, of the things that I say about Father and Mother. One of their objections is that in several places I haven't been accurate. I have tried to be, but memories are sometimes inexact, and mine is no exception.

However, these pieces have been subjected to a great deal of scrutiny, helpful and otherwise, from members of the family who have sometimes remembered things differently. Cousin Julia for instance insists that Mother's musicales occurred in the evening, whereas I have described one as taking place in the late afternoon. I feel sure that in this case I am right, for we used to write each other long letters about family doings and these have given me contemporary accounts of the scenes I've described. Other scenes have come down through the years as family anecdotes. Since I was an actor in most of them they have remained dramatically printed on my mind. Besides, any memories of two such persons as Father and Mother are bound to be vivid.

The other family objection is that in printing these stories I have not been decently reticent. My feeling was that these two persons were so utterly themselves, so completely natural and true, that the only good way to tell about them was to paint them just as they were.

The first article I printed about them was written one night when I needed an extra paragraph for a column which I was occasionally writing, that year, for the literary supplement of the New York *Evening Post*.

On a visit to Father and Mother one summer I found that they had a new dog. He was leading a happy and interesting life with them, but a somewhat bewildered one too. I had made a note in my diary of the following instance:

My father is fond of dogs. Likes to train them. His method is this: He says to the new dog, "Good Jackie," or whatever the name is. The dog wags his tail. "Come here," says my father; "come here, boy." The dog looks at him doubtfully. My father, who hasn't a great deal of patience, raises his voice: "Come! Come here, sir!"

The dog grows alarmed and tries to get out.

My father advances upon him, repeating, "Come here!" with increasing annoyance and sternness.

"I wish you'd let Jackie alone," says my mother. "He doesn't know what you want of him."

"Pooh! Of course he does," declares my father. "He knows damn well. Come *here,* sir!" And he drags the new dog from under the sofa.

"Sit up," he instructs him. The dog is utterly limp. "Sit up. Come! Sit up." He shakes his finger at him. "Sit up, sir!"

"Oh, please don't," says my mother. "How *can* you expect the poor thing to sit up when he doesn't know a word that you're saying!"

"Will you let me alone?" shouts my father. "Sit *up,* sir! Sit *up!*"

My mother goes to the door. "I'll not stay here and see that dog frightened to death."

"Frightened!" my father says, testily. "What nonsense! I know dogs. They all like me."

The dog sees the door being opened and suddenly bolts.

My father grabs fiercely at him. In vain. "Confound it!" he says, in a passion. "Now see what you've done! You've spoiled my whole plan." He stamps.

"You could never—" my mother begins.

"I COULD!" roars my father. "But I can't do a thing if I'm interfered with. Where's that dog gone? JACKIE! Here, Jackie! Come here, sir!"

I copied this fragment out of my diary, tucked it in as a filler, and when it appeared I showed it to Mother.

"I remember that day," she said. "That's just the way he always treats dogs." She hurried off with the clipping to where Father was, in the library. "Here, Clare," she said triumphantly, "read this!"

Father read it in his usual slow, careful, methodical way, taking note of each word. He looked up at Mother with a smile of satisfaction and sympathy. "I hope you'll behave yourself after this," he chuckled, "that's just how you kept interfering with my training that dog."

This emboldened me to try my hand at describing a few other incidents of our family life, scenes which I felt were too good to remain buried forever. They came out in *Harper's*. Every time one appeared it became a subject of debate between Father and Mother. For some reason or other, perhaps because they were without self-consciousness, the publicity seemed to be of small or no concern to them, so long as each felt I had been strictly accurate and presented his or her side so clearly that the other should blush. Neither of them ever did blush, however. They got so provoked at each other once or twice, because of this, that they went back and re-fought the whole battle.

These sketches were read by other persons, friends of theirs—including some who had felt rather buffeted, when they had been our guests, by the sudden indoor squalls or tornadoes that characterized our family life. They told me that these stray fragments had made them understand Father better.

Strangers wrote to me that this or that member of their own families was very much like Father. The effect upon most of these readers was to enroll them as Father's friends.

So a few years after Father and Mother died I began again describing old scenes.

These characters may or may not be Father and Mother. All I can say is that they are Father and Mother as I saw them.

MOTHER AND FATHER MEET

Father, although spirited and jolly, was a clear-eyed and careful young man. He was methodical about arranging his life, step by step. He did things one at a time.

Until he got married he continued to live with his parents. He ate out a good deal, but he didn't approve of living in lodgings—it would have made him feel lonely—and he saw no reason to set up a home of his own until he had a wife to put in it.

He was a self-reliant young man however. He had made his own way from the start. It wasn't until he was twenty-one and had had nearly seven years' business experience that he asked any favors of Grandpa, and all he then asked for was a loan of three thousand dollars (at six per cent) to buy a seat on the Stock Exchange. This was in 1866. He and another young man, Fisher Johnson, formed a firm of their own, and by the time Father was twenty-five he was becoming well-seasoned. He had gone through the panic of '69 and Black Friday, and had begun to make money. He then started in to arrange the other sides of his life.

One of the first things he did was to throw out the furniture that his parents had put in his bedroom, and buy and install a set to his liking—a solid brown walnut bed and bureau, chiffonier, chairs and table that he used for the next forty years. This set also included a carved upright desk with places for his files and account books.

His next step was to buy a little clavier keyboard and learn finger-exercises. When he had exercised his fingers enough to warrant it, he bought a piano and hired an old German musician to teach him how to play.

What with Father's intolerance of the old family furniture, and his criticisms of old family ways, and his pounding determinedly night after night on his piano, Grandpa began to get restive. But Grandma, to whom Grandpa was silently but deeply devoted, interceded for Father every time things came to a head and managed from one day to another to smooth Grandpa down.

Grandpa tried to be patient, on the theory that his son would soon marry. Father seemed to be planning to propose to a cousin of his who lived in West Springfield. They must have had some understanding between them for he gave her a ring and a watch. But they soon had a quarrel. They decided they had made a mistake, and the ring was returned.

Disappointing as this was to Grandpa it did not interrupt Father's program; it merely changed a little the order of the steps he was planning. He joined a club and went there regularly to see other men and play billiards. He disliked to visit ordinary billiard parlors. He had made up his mind they were low. As to drinking, he took wine with his dinner, and beer or ale with his lunch, but he didn't drink at bars or between meals because that was a poor way to do it.

In 1869 he found that he could get away for a few months from business and he thereupon treated himself to a vacation abroad. He had several things to attend to, in Europe. He went to the best watchmaker in Switzerland and selected a watch so much to his taste that he wore it for the rest of his life. It was a solid, good-looking gold watch with a cover that Father had to snap open, and it had to be wound with a key. When I was a young man it seemed out of date, but it kept perfect time.

After getting just the right watch, he went to London to get proper clothes. The one place that you could rely on to know all about clothes was Poole's. Father ordered only enough clothes at Poole's for his immediate needs, but he left them his measurements, and thus felt this whole matter satisfactorily settled and off his mind, like his watch and his furniture.

From that time on, Poole sent him samples of cloths every year, and Father ordered a suit or an overcoat or whatever he needed. He took good care of his clothes, and he never had many at once, but they had to be right. The only trouble was that in later years, when he put on more weight and when he went to England less frequently, Poole's clothes didn't fit. A sturdy well-made box would arrive, through the Customs, and underneath all the layers of tissue paper would be a handsome dress-suit. Upon trying to force himself into it, Father didn't feel comfortable—the damn thing wouldn't button. He would thereupon get into a cab with this suit and go to his Fifth Avenue tailor, a most supercilious man, to whom Father never gave any business except repairs or refittings. He would unwillingly alter Poole's things, as directed, at the same time pointing out to Father—without any effect— that he would do much better to buy his clothes in New York in the first place. In reply, Father would admonish the tailor to make a better job of the alterations than he had last time, and he would add that he would be glad to buy his things in New York as soon as he could find any tailor here who knew how to make clothes.

Each time he went abroad, he would revisit Poole and adjure him to get his measurements right; and after that, at least for a year or two, there would be a season of peace, when everything that arrived fitted him perfectly, and when the Fifth Avenue tailor was given no work to do except to clean and repair Poole's new masterpieces. But after a while Father would gain a few pounds again. This was always an unwelcome surprise and he disliked to admit to himself it was true. Although he never skimped himself on his food, he thought that he ate very little. So whenever new difficulties came upon him, trying to button Poole's clothes, he would never send Poole any new measure- ments—he didn't see how he could have changed. At the most he would mention, when he wrote, that the clothes shouldn't be so damned tight. This worried Poole, who hated to guess as to where and how to make changes.

Father came back from his first trip to Europe with his watch and his good clothes from Poole, like a Columbus who had dis- covered a pleasant and useful new world. He had taken his ease in its cities, he had enjoyed the orderly loveliness of The Hague and the solid richness of London, and everywhere he had seen

what taste and time could do for homes in the country. He had
no wish to live among Europeans for he looked down on them,
somehow, but he respected them too for the contributions they
had made to his comfort. He was especially charmed with their
cookery, their wines and their manners.

The next year, 1870, when he was twenty-five, he went over
again. He wanted to see more of Europe. He also wanted some
shirts.

Sailings in those days were early. Father arrived at the dock
at seven in the morning, and looked over the ship. It was the
St. Laurent of the French Line, an iron vessel of three thousand
tons, painted a soft gray and green, and equipped with eight life
boats. A liner of nine or ten thousand tons is considered tiny
today, and most of them are from twenty up, but the *St. Laurent*
seemed stately to Father, with her tall masts and white sails. She
was rigged as a bark but she had engines too of course. They
were of over nine hundred horsepower. Also, *"grand innovation
pour l'époque,"* she was one of the new type of ships equipped
with a little iron propeller instead of side paddle-wheels.

There was a great crowd on the dock, or what seemed like one
in 1870, for this splendid ship had accommodations for two
hundred first-cabin passengers. As Father made his way on board,
past the bulky flounces and skirts of the ladies, he saw a man he
had met on the Stock Exchange, Alden B. Stockwell. Red mustache, bushy flowing red whiskers, ten years older than Father—
a dignified and powerful man who had come to New York from
Ohio. Alden Stockwell was saying goodbye to his brother, Levi,
and to their little sister, who was seventeen but who still wore
her hair in a red braid down her back. Girls were younger at
seventeen then than now. They were kept in school until the very
last minute, when they suddenly "came out" as young ladies.
Father was introduced to Levi Stockwell and this schoolgirl, his
future wife, and the *St. Laurent* sailed.

Levi got seats for the three of them together at table, so that
his little sister wouldn't have to sit next to some stranger. This
was an exceedingly agreeable arrangement for a sociable young

man like Father, who liked company but who was too formal to
pick up acquaintances.

Everybody was formal. "Even upon a ship, men preserve the
habits of society," a Frenchman of the seventies wrote. "They
are careful of their dress, their manners, their conversation, the
effect they may produce upon others; each strives to assume his
most *distingué* air. The ladies, who, thanks to the privileges which
custom readily grants them, are always impenetrable even to
those who are their acquaintances, become even more impenetrable on a voyage, among the wraps, the shawls, the thick veils
which transform them into traveling sphinxes."

There were a number of South American passengers on board
the *St. Laurent,* dark and talkative men who couldn't speak English. They chattered on deck day and night, volubly and rapidly,
and sometimes they woke Father up. It annoyed him. He told
Levi Stockwell, he told everybody he met, what an infernal
nuisance these Spaniards were getting to be.

Levi said nothing, but the next morning he got up very early.
The decks were deserted. He took up his stand just outside the
open porthole of Father's cabin, and putting his mouth as close
to it as he dared he rapidly repeated all the Spanish words that
he could think of. There were less than a dozen but he muttered
them over and over. The effect was one of a bevy of Spaniards
engaged in an endless dispute.

Levi, who was keeping his ear cocked, soon heard sounds inside
Father's cabin, where a sleepy young man was loudly saying
"Damn" to himself, in his berth. Levi's Spanish instantly became
low and soothing. Father's mutterings stopped. But after he had
had time to go back to sleep, the Spanish voices again grew excited, and they soon became so noisy and urgent that Father
sprang out of bed.

"I swear those fellows gabble all night," he said to little Miss
Stockwell at breakfast.

Strange to say, this Mr. Day had a letter of introduction to
Dr. George Parmly of Paris, who was one of the Stockwell family's own cousins and the one Mother later loved best. But as to

whether she liked this Mr. Day, she seemed far from sure. One day he called to the waiter: "Here, bring that back, I want some more—that is *good*." Mother told him, "There are other people here besides you!" "He makes me so mad," she wrote her mother.

Young Mr. Day didn't mind that in the least. He found this schoolgirl great fun. He promenaded the deck with her on breezy days, with her veils flying and her skirts billowing out, and on foggy days he placed her chair where the cordage and yards wouldn't drip on her. He brought her hot cups of tea. And when the weather grew rough and she was too ill to stir, he and Levi took turns carrying her up on deck for a breath of fresh air.

The air wasn't good down below. Even that Frenchman, when he wrote of his travels, spoke about the closed portholes. At night, he said, "the atmosphere below is warm and heavy, and silence reigns, only broken by the regular breathing of the sleepers."

The *St. Laurent* made eleven or twelve knots in good weather but only about six in storms, and by the time she reached port Father had definitely attached himself to the two Stockwells. Flowers and trees were in bloom when they landed. They went to spend May in Paris. And in between seeing sights with his new friends Father did what he'd come for, he went to Jourdain et Brown's shop in the Rue Halévy and had himself measured for shirts. He got his shirts, socks and handkerchiefs from them most of the rest of his life. The handkerchiefs were always plain white with white monograms on them, but the French socks were sometimes very gay and lively in color for Father, who was in all other respects most conservative in his manner of dressing. I think he permitted himself to wear them because he thought they were hidden.

As with his clothes, Father had troubles with his shirts in later life, for he began to get thick in the neck, and he had to stretch his throat violently, to get his French shirts to button. They were stiff white shirts, made open-front, and with stiff standing collars attached, and he got very red in the face getting into them, dressing for dinner at night. They were made in such a way, as was then the custom, that he had to pull them on over his head;

he would thrust his arms out through the sleeves and come bursting out at the top. The cuffs were stiff of course, and had rounded corners. At times, when the fashion changed, cuffs would be made with square corners for years, but not Father's. His cuffs had originally been rounded, and rounded they stayed. Also, on every one of his shirts, all his life, there was a little starched tab with a buttonhole in it, in front, at the waist-line. The original purpose of these was to hold up a man's drawers, but Father never used them for that, or for anything else. Yet, late in his life, when he was finally driven to order some shirts in New York, and when Kaskel objected to putting tabs on, asking what they were for, Father said roundly that he didn't happen to remember, but he wanted them put on just the same.

In his old age his sons used to urge him to wear soft shirts and be comfortable, at least in the country in summer. He finally consented to try one. But before putting it on he examined this outlandish thing with a frown, and went down to breakfast very slowly in it, feeling (he said) indecent. By lunch-time he had gone back upstairs again, and put on a stiff one.

On the night that Father came back from his first trip to Jourdain et Brown's, when he went to dinner, Levi refused to shake hands with him. Levi was carefully holding on to his right hand as though it were some precious object. He would allow no one to touch it. He could never use it to shake hands with common people again, he declared, or with anyone else except monarchs, because that hand had been shaken that very afternoon by the Emperor. Some fellow-officer had introduced Levi to the court at the races.

Two months later war had suddenly broken out, the Battle of Sedan had been fought, and the Emperor was being led away as a prisoner in the hands of the Germans. By the following January the Parisians were eating cats, eating horses, and hungrily paying a franc apiece even for rats.

But nobody dreamed of these terrible things in Paris that spring. Levi Stockwell hurried around attending to the matters of business in which his brother Alden was interested, and their little red-headed sister went out walking with young Mr. Day. He and she visited the galleries and cathedrals together, they drove together to pay their respects to good Dr. George Parmly, and just as those new shirts were ready and he was preparing to leave, young Mr. Day began to discover that he had fallen in love.

FATHER VISITS THE WAR

Mother was only eight years old in April 1861, when the Civil War started, but all her four brothers were older, and two of them went to the front. Brutus Stockwell, the youngest, was away at school, in France. Alden, the eldest, was tied up in business in Cleveland, where the first ship-loads of ore had begun to arrive from the Great Lakes. But Levi got a commission in the navy and served under Farragut, and Norris was one of the youngest captains of infantry to march with Sherman through Georgia. All four brothers were lively by nature—athletic, red-headed men.

The Stockwells lived in Ohio, the Days in New York, and in the sixties the two families never had heard of each other. Physically they were rather alike. Father was athletic and lively, and he had red hair too, but he was only sixteen when the war began and Grandpa didn't want him to go. Grandpa, though he had voted for Lincoln, had hoped that war wouldn't come, and when it did come he was disgusted—but Grandpa was fifty. Father wasn't disgusted, he was interested and pleased. He was working downtown in New York, in Gwynne & Day's office, the firm in which his elder brother was the junior partner. In the evenings when he came home from business he sat by the lamp in his bedroom and made elaborate drawings of soldiers in one of his schoolboy notebooks. I found it among his papers years afterward —a thick, square, well-made old blank-book, full of sums in arithmetic, and clippings from Civil War newspapers, and drawings by Father of cannon and bearded Zouaves.

Father's patriotism however was tempered with humor, and he seems to have been extraordinarily tickled by the fun Grandpa made of "top-lofty" patriots. At any rate he cut out many of the most biting articles that Grandpa kept publishing, and pasted them in that fat blank-book, alongside his own warlike drawings.

When Father was seventeen he decided to join the old Seventh Regiment. It was characteristic of him to look over the ground before he did anything and then do it in what he considered the very best way, and the Seventh was generally regarded as the best in the country. Its ranks were full, he found at the armory, but vacancies occurred now and then, because, as there was a shortage of officers in the new armies, the older members of the Seventh, even the privates, were in demand for these jobs. It was about the nearest thing that they had, in the sixties, to an officers' training corps. Father put his name down on the waiting list and went back to his office.

Half the best young men in New York wanted to get into the Seventh. Even the newspapers in London had spoken admiringly of the "world-renowned Seventh Regiment." And when President Buchanan made a speech to them, before the election of Lincoln, he had felt so moved that he said, "The stout, hardy, noble and defiant look which you exhibit shows that in the day and hour of battle you would be at the very front."

The Seventh had tried to get to the very front when the war started. It had sprung to arms and gone to the defense of Washington as soon as Sumter was fired on. A week later, however, when all real danger to the city was over and plenty of other troops had arrived, the Seventh felt that its object had been accomplished and that it might as well go back home.

At this point the government asked it to enlist for three months in the army. This didn't seem fair to the Seventh. They had been distinctly assured, when they started, that they would only be away for two weeks. They at once held a meeting, however, and voted on this. They decided to enlist as a body, and to serve thirty days.

When this thirty-day period was over, the men entrained and came home. "The lower classes" made unpleasant remarks about their return, but the regiment was welcomed all the more warmly by all the best citizens.

In 1862 when Stonewall Jackson burst into the Shenandoah Valley, and it looked as though he might capture Washington, the government requested the Seventh to help out again. By this time Father had been elected a member. He got a leave of absence from Gwynne & Day and went off, as a private in Company D.

Unfortunately, at least from Father's point of view, Stonewall Jackson subsided, and instead of seeing action in the field the Seventh was put into barracks near Baltimore. And as though this wasn't bad enough the Secretary of War then requested the regiment, instead of enlisting for thirty days this time, to stay for three months.

Nobody liked the prospect of sitting there for three months in barracks. Father wrote to his mother that his company had been sent to Mt. Clare Station where they slept in the open, and as it was damp and cold he added, "I wish you would send me a colored night-cap and some segars."

It wasn't certain whether the regiment would be willing to stay on or not. "I don't think I could stay," Father wrote, "on account of my business, for I don't think Gwynne and Day could very well spare me for as long as that."

(He was seventeen, going on eighteen, and here he was already talking this way and smoking "segars.")

In his next letter he sounds somewhat younger.

"I hope it will be over with soon," he wrote, "as I shall not stay more than a month, but that is not saying I'm homesick for I can get along very well.

"I received your box of things yesterday. The cake &c was very much appreciated in 'our mess' and also the lemons, with which I made some lemonade last night and it tasted first rate as I was very thirsty and the water is not very good, being limey, which is not grammatically correct but still will express what I wish to say. About 12 o'clock night before last it commenced raining and rained all day yesterday in perfect torrents, and most of last night. My tent got pretty well water soaked and commenced leaking, and in an hour or so the floor was as wet as thunder and we had to huddle all together to keep dry, and even in that manner we got very damp. I tell you, Mother, boards are a perfect luxury, at least I thought so when we got our board floor up last Sunday, after sleeping two or three nights in wet straw.

"We have our tent fitted up very nicely; at the end opposite the door is a musket rack with a shelf on top, then there are two bunks on each side and one directly in front, in which I sleep. The bunks by the by consist of a knapsack for a pillow and a blanket spread out on the floor. From the top of the tent we have suspended two shelves one under the other on which we put our dishes, and in the center we have a table, all of which we made ourselves so we think a great deal of them on that account.

"I wish you would send some lemons, oranges, ginger snaps, cake, and if possible a nice pie, which last luxury I have not seen since leaving N. Y., also some segars as I have but two left, and some sugar. The sugar I would prefer to be ordinary brown sugar rather than the kind you sent before. Those shoes are splendid being large and easy.

"Hoping to hear from home soon

"I am

"Your Aff^t Son."

On June 19th he wrote from Mt. Clare Station, "We are to be sworn in this afternoon." And lower down he added:

"Four hours later.

"We are Sworn in and I am now nothing but a 'volunteer' and a 'mudsill.' Our company being on detached duty was sworn in by itself, the reg^t being sworn in at the fort.

"There was but one man in our company who backed out and that was Brundage.

"Those members who remained at home will be referred to the Adjutant General of the State of N. Y. and will be dealt with according to the law."

As they had agreed to enlist for three months, Father added: "I suppose I have lost my situation at G & D's. Well, it is my

sacrifice in this war; but I don't think they are very patriotic because most all the other houses who have clerks in this reg^t are
saving their places for them and continuing their salaries. In
regard to my washing I get that done by women who come to
the Fort for it. I get down to the city once in a while and take
a good bath and eat a good dinner and all together I manage to
get along very well. Our rations are very short sometimes and
occasionally we have only bread and tea for supper.

"Today I was down to the house of Winans the Secesh with
a member of our company who is intimately acquainted with
them. His family (Winans') are Union but he is Secesh. While
there I had some very nice cherries—invited to come again.
Hoping to hear from you very soon as letters from home no
matter how short are a very great source of gratification,

"I am, Your Aff^t Son."

Three days later his company got back to its barracks, and he
found that box of things waiting. But

"I was very much disappointed on opening the box to find the
pies all mouldy," he wrote, "and after eating one or two of them
on top and coming to the 3d or fourth I couldn't go them and
even the very niggers would not eat them and I had to throw
them away.

"In regard to the segars Father sent they were very acceptable
indeed. I guess I shan't sell any of them as I have plenty of room
in my knapsack." (Apparently cigars were not shared as freely
as cigarettes are today.)

"I have great trouble in keeping my dishes. I have none of
them left except my plate that I brought away from N. Y. I
have lost two or three sets of knives forks and spoons and one
cup; at present I am using a knife without a handle, and a fork
with the tines broken half off.

"The pail which you sent the pies in comes very usefull indeed,
but I wish you had sent a whole saucer instead of that broken
one."

"Fort Federal Hill
"Baltimore July 15/62

"Dear Mother

"It is very hot indeed to day and was yesterday.

"Yesterday we had a long battalion Drill and the Lt Col only stopped when one of the 8th Co was sun struck and several in the different companies dropped from the heat. I did not go on drill and would not on such a hot day and I expected to be put on guard to day as a punishment but was not however as there were too many of my opinion. Colonel Lefferts is absent and Lt Col Price is in command and I think over uses his power which I infer from the drill of yesterday because if the Col had been here he would not have had any drill at all on such a scorching day.

"Those pickles you sent were very good indeed and came very nice with dinner.

"Some one stole most all my cakes and those crullers and cookies you sent and I did not get more than twenty of the whole lot and that had to go among four of us."

Father's next letter was about Lieutenant-Colonel Price, who, according to a contemporary record, was an obstinate little man with a shrill voice. He had been born in London, he was precise in his habits and quick and erect in his movements, he wore a chin beard with no mustache, and he was in the real-estate business.

"The boys are down on him," Father wrote. "He either mistakes the men he has to deal with or else wishes to show his power; but he will have to be pretty sharp to get ahead of the boys. To night he sent out some prisoners that were detained in the guard house, for some petty offences, to haul down the flag at retreat; they hauled down flag, rope, and everything, the consequence is that it will take about half a day to fix it up again and unless the boys have a mind to they wont put it up as they can't force any man to climb up such a high pole as that and endanger his life." (Not in wartime!)

"P.S.," Father added. "Last night, the boys collected around the Colonel's quarters and sung sonnets on Lieut Col Price which were not very complimentary to him. I just received Father's letter Ask him to send me Pickwick Abroad or some good novel in paper covers."

"Aug. 16/62

"Dear Father

"I received your letter to day enclosing $4 Baltimore money.

"Yesterday I was on guard and I hope it will be the last time. Another steamboat load of wounded soldiers came up from Ft Munroe. If the Irish attempt any riot in N. Y. after a fair and impartial draft I think they had better send the whole crowd of those concerned in the riot off to the war, whether they have been drafted or not.

"P.S. Instead of the Waverly send the Sunday Times and please send it Monday."

A week or two later the regiment's three months were over, and it came back to New York, and again it was welcomed with cheers, although not quite so warmly.

In later years, when Mother came across these old letters of Father's, she spoke in quite a critical tone about them, much to his surprise. "Was that all you did, Clare?" she asked him, at dinner one evening. "Didn't they call out the Seventh again?"

Father said yes, the Seventh went South for about a month in 1863, but he and a lot of others had known better that time than to start, until they saw whether the regiment was going to barracks or battle. Wouldn't be worth their while to go, their idea was, unless there was a chance to see action, and when it turned out to be those same old Baltimore barracks, all these members stayed home.

Mother said that her brothers hadn't been home except when they got a furlough, and that even after Levi was captured he had got out of prison and gone back to his ship.

Father replied that as for Levi and Norris, there was no reason why they shouldn't serve—they had had nothing else to do, probably. As for himself, not only had he been busy at the office but he had used common sense, and he had formed a poor opinion while in barracks of the way in which wars were run. He said that Mother was only a woman and knew nothing about it, and furthermore that nothing would have induced him to serve for four years unless they had let him take charge of things and run the damned war himself.

Mother said she still couldn't understand what the Seventh kept coming home for. "Why didn't they stay down there and fight?"

As there didn't seem to be any answer to this that would satisfy her, Father closed the discussion by saying that so far as he was concerned he was not a French peasant. He said that he was an American, and he didn't intend to serve as a pawn to be moved around a chess-board by anybody. He admired the farmers of Lexington and Concord, he said, who had swarmed out like a nestful of hornets, done their work and gone home, and he had done exactly the same at the first opportunity. He seemed to feel satisfied that he had made a very good hornet.

FATHER'S METHODS OF COURTSHIP

It took Father three years to propose, Mother once told me. In the first place he needed time to feel sure that he was in love. He had made one mistake before he ever met Mother, and one was enough. Secondly, Mother was still a pupil at Miss Haines' School in Gramercy Park. He couldn't marry a schoolgirl. The other difficulty was that she was rich, or at least she was the sister of one of the richest men he knew down on Wall Street. Alden Stockwell had a yacht and drove a four-in-hand. He engaged a private car when he traveled. He had a house on Murray Hill in New York and another in Mayfair in London. Father called him a nabob.

Father was a prudent young man and his objection to marrying the sister of a nabob was due to his belief that she would expect him to provide for her more luxuriously than he possibly could, or, in fact, than he had any intention whatever of doing.

Meanwhile Mother was being courted by other beaux, even before she left school. She had had six proposals of marriage by the time she was twenty. One was from an elderly man who had known her as a child in Painesville, Ohio. Another was from her Sunday School teacher at a church in New York. Others still were from polite young New Yorkers who were fascinating but who frightened her by getting drunk, and one was from a wise and handsome foreigner, a Turco-Italian, whom she felt attached to and trusted, but with whom, as he saw for himself, she really wasn't in love.

She wasn't in love with Father either, she thought. He didn't behave right at all. As a little girl she had sat on the step by Grandma's white picket gate and stared down the road and wished that a carriage would come dashing up for her and whisk her away. That wasn't at all the kind of thing, she thought, that a young man like Father would do.

All her beaux except Father had offered her beautiful presents —so beautiful that they were sometimes returned, they were too much to accept. They had all sent her flowers. It had never occurred to Father, apparently, to offer her anything.

She didn't know what to make of the man. He was too independent. Another provoking thing about him was that he didn't even pay her nice compliments. Yet somehow he had a kind of realness for her that those other men lacked.

Early in 1873 something terrible happened. Her brother Alden had got into a financial contest with Mr. Jay Gould, and all of a sudden Alden had found himself outflanked and defeated. His losses ran into millions. He still had his home and his yacht but his whole position was dangerous.

He had been making elaborate plans for Mother's coming-out party. She was his only sister and he was a widower. In spite of his losses he generously went ahead with his program.

It was a bitter cold night when the guests came, and Alden was a desperate man. But he was also a proud one. His beautiful home was festooned with roses till it was one mass of flowers, two orchestras played, the conservatory was filled with bright lanterns and trays of jeweled favors were provided as souvenirs for the dancers. Not so very long afterward a sheriff sat smoking in the hall where the orchestra had played the Blue Danube Waltz, the servants were hurrying to leave, joking over the bundles of things they had pilfered, and tradesmen were attaching the paintings and the chests of silver and plate. When that day came Mother sat at the window upstairs and saw her own little ponies with their silver-mounted harness led away with her phaeton.

But Alden although he had been mortally wounded, financially, was too strongly entrenched to topple over at once. His affairs and his assets were ramified. His ruin took time. Meanwhile, when the spring came, Mother was put on the train to

Ohio, leaving behind her a brother who no longer smiled and who hardly spoke but who would not acknowledge defeat.

It was at this stage of affairs that Father asked Mother to marry him.

When Great-Aunt Lavinia heard the news she wrote to Grandma at once strongly advising that she make Mother marry. "The Days are not rich," she said, "but they have always lived very comfortably." But Mother wasn't sure whether she was in love or not. She didn't know what to do.

There was one thing she could do however, she could tell Father to come out to Painesville. This was a test she had imposed on each of her suitors before taking them seriously, and it had been quite a help to her, and perhaps to them too. She felt that before she made up her mind to spend her life with a man, he and she had better see each other in her old family home.

Mother had grown up in Painesville. It had been settled by Vermonters and other New Englanders who had traveled in covered wagons to get there, late in the seventeen-hundreds. Its quiet, broad, shady streets, its brick sidewalks, its white Colonial houses surrounded by trees, each with its own front lawn and garden inside of a white picket fence, made it one of the loveliest towns in the Western Reserve. But lovely as it was, in its own way, its standards of comfort were simple.

The last previous suitor before Father who had come out to Painesville was a fashionable young man from New York who was wholly unused to small towns. He was dismayed by the service, the customs, and the limited fare of the town's one hotel. He was unprepared to have people stop and stare at him as he walked down the street. Being a mercurial youth he had become so depressed by all this that he had got drunk, very drunk, in an effort to cheer himself up. This became known, like everything else in Painesville, and it had created a scandal.

When he was sober again and realized what a sensation he'd caused he apologized to Grandma and Mother for having "disgraced" them. Grandma said he had better apologize to himself for he hadn't disgraced her and couldn't. He took the next train back to New York and immediately got drunk again.

Mother didn't quite dare to marry a victim of drink but she always kept a tender spot in her heart for this bewildered young man. She followed his later career half-maternally, and she even kept track of his children. His weakness for drink turned out to be permanent, but it was more or less harmless too. He was so gay and sociable by nature that everyone liked him. His only trouble was that he was easily discouraged, and that he had no head for liquor.

When Father arrived in Painesville he behaved very differently from any of his predecessors. Whatever their private opinions of Painesville had been they had been much too guarded to express them. Father expressed his at once. He told Mother and he told Grandpa and Grandma Stockwell just what he thought of it. He said it was "a damned hole."

The decent people of Painesville regarded it as needlessly profane to say damn, but in other respects they had no great objection to Father's frankness. In fact, it amused them. He seemed to be a clean, energetic, likable-looking young fellow, and all the time that he was in Painesville he did not "touch a drop." He told Mother that this was merely because there was nothing in the place fit to drink, but the rest of the town didn't know this, and his sobriety and vigor impressed them. It even impressed Grandma a little. She and Father didn't get on well—then or later—but she had nothing against him, she said.

He said he wouldn't leave until Mother had promised to marry him, and he urged her to hurry. In his next sentence she found that although part of this was ardor, the rest was impatience—he wanted to get out of Painesville. He said he should think that she'd want to get out of there too.

They were married in New York in June. It was a small quiet wedding—only about a dozen of the family were present. It was held in Alden's big house. Alden was grave. He hadn't taken to Father. Immediately after the ceremony the young bride and groom sailed for France.

It had all been so sudden, just at the last, that Mother felt shaken up. The weather was rough. She took to her berth and she stayed there; and when Father offered to bring her anything to eat she begged him not to, and moaned.

Father could not understand this. He had an excellent appetite himself and he found the weather exhilarating. He urged Mother to get up on deck. She'd be all right in an hour or two, he assured her, if she'd "make an effort." When this had no effect he went off and filled his lungs with sea air and ate three hearty meals a day and felt very sorry for Mother. He kept trying to think of something that he could do for her to make her well again. One afternoon, ruddy and glowing, he opened their cabin door.

"Vinnie?" he said. "Aren't you feeling better yet? I wish you'd been with me at lunch."

No answer.

"I had two helpings of salmon," he added, to tempt her, "and the sauce Tartare was delicious."

A vivid but most unwelcome picture sprang up in Mother's mind of that thick, too thick and greenish sauce oozing over a plate. She pulled herself together and begged him faintly, "Don't talk to me, darling, just now."

He returned to the upper deck, mystified, and smoked a cigar.

It was nearly a year, Mother once told me, before she could bear to eat salmon, with or without sauce Tartare.

Neither of them had been in Paris since the German armies had come and gone again. They found it was crowded. The Shah of Persia and his glittering court were the guests of the government, a whole hotel had been reserved for their use, and the city was being given over to illuminations and fêtes. (That hotel had to be specially fumigated afterward, Father used to observe, when Mother was describing the splendor of Paris that season.) Every now and then, as they were walking along, there was the sound of galloping horses and the Shah's outriders dashed down the street, followed by the Shah himself in his great open carriage and the music of trumpets. Mother was thrilled. But Father said it would take more than a Shah to thrill him. He said the Shah was a nuisance.

One night when there was to be a grand display of fireworks in the Bois, Mother insisted on going, so after dinner they drove out there in their evening clothes, and both of them enjoyed it immensely until it came time to go back and they found that they could not get a carriage. Even then it was all right at first, walking along the Champs Élysées, but Mother's evening slippers were so thin, and their hotel, the Grand Hôtel de l'Athénée, was so far away, that Father had to keep stopping to let Mother rest, and at last when the slippers had given out completely and he found that she was trying to keep up with him in her stocking feet he had to carry her. Mother was so tired by this time that she willingly let him, hoping he would feel that bearing his young bride in his arms was romantic, and possibly he might have thought so if the distance had only been less. But as he went on and on she didn't get any lighter and Father began to remember that he hadn't wanted to come. He felt sorry for Mother and he loved her, but he could not keep wholly still, and as he staggered on, stray passers-by heard him denouncing the Shah.

It was to be over twenty years before they ever went to Europe again. When they got back late in the summer and Mother went on for a visit to Newport, where Alden, who was braving things out to the last, had taken a house for the season, a telegram from Father suddenly summoned Mother back to New York. The great panic of 1873 had started, the post-war prosperity of America was crashing in ruins, nobody knew or could guess what was coming, and he wanted her there at his side.

GRANDPA ASSISTS AT A SÉANCE

It was a frosty Sunday in November, and Father and Mother were taking me to Grandpa Day's for a one-o'clock dinner. As we sat in the horse-car, Mother was talking about Grandma's interest in spirit messages. She said it seemed to crop up again every few years. Father pished violently and said that Grandpa ought not to allow it.

At dinner, Grandma managed to feed me so much that Father said I would burst. Even Grandpa, who seldom bothered to interfere in such matters, laid down his knife and fork and told us about his Aunt Martin, whose idea of bringing up a boy was to watch him at table and "pop a doughnut in his mouth every time the boy gaped." I asked him earnestly where Aunt Martin lived. They all laughed except Grandma, who whispered to me, "There isn't any such person, dear," and gave me some more pumpkin pie.

After dinner, we sat around the coal fire. It took the chill off the high-ceilinged room, and its red, steady glow felt delicious to me as I curled up on the carpet. The wind slapped the vines against the tall windows. Grandma and Father talked quietly together, and Father patted her shoulder affectionately and told her about all his plans.

When he had finished, Grandma started to talk about spiritualism. Mother caught her eye and pointed at me and shook her head, but Grandma went mildly on. She wouldn't speak of any experiences, she told Mother reassuringly. She just wanted to say how happy it had made Mrs. Perkins.

In a moment or two, Father stood up. The goodbyes began, and we soon were on our way home, walking up the long Madison Avenue hill.

There was a good deal of excited arguing in those years about whether spirits could talk to us. Grandma, of course, didn't argue, but she felt quite sure it was true. Her only daughter, little Mary Day, had died very young, and when spiritualistic mediums said that the dead were not only alive but eager to speak to the living, it made Grandma feel life was beautiful.

Naturally, she sometimes desired to share this belief. She knew enough not to try to share it with Grandpa or with her grown-up sons, but one time when two of Uncle Hal's children were staying with her, Grandma told Will, the elder, about how the spirits watched over us. She felt that it was a sweet and comfortable thought to put in his mind. Will didn't take it that way. He was not romantic about things, he was a matter-of-fact, careful boy, six years old, and when he was told that spirits were floating around him, even when he was in bed at night, he felt very uneasy. One evening in particular, Grandma took Will into her shadowy bedroom, where her friend old Mrs. Caister was sitting sewing, under the dim little gas-jet, and read aloud many strange happenings from a spiritualistic magazine, the *Banner of Light*. This upset Will so much that when he went to bed he made Mrs. Caister stay with him and sit on the stairs just outside his door until he was asleep.

Grandma was so serene and quiet minded herself that she sometimes forgot others weren't. She didn't tell Will's sister, Ella, about the spirits—Ella was only three—but she told her about Jack the Giant Killer so vividly that Ella began having nightmares.

With all her serenity Grandma was shy in some ways, or reserved, and in spite of her interest in spiritualism she didn't quite like to go to a medium. She was so trusting, too, that it seemed needless. She felt that if a few of her old friends and herself sat around a table in silence, and after a while began asking questions, some friendly spirit would probably come in the room and get under that table, and rap a few replies on it for them. One rap for yes, two for no.

She decided that the best time and place were in the afternoon

in the dining-room, where she had just the right table. The only
trouble was that that was where Grandpa took his afternoon
naps, on a small leather sofa. When she spoke to him about it,
however, and told him her plans, he was quite accommodating
for once. He didn't offer to move out—he liked that special sofa
—but he said it was a large room and if they didn't talk too loud
she and her friends wouldn't disturb him. So a day was set for
their séance.

The ladies arrived one by one, in their long capes or India
shawls, and their ribbony bonnets, and stood talking with
Grandma and Mrs. Caister in the hall a few minutes. Then they
came softly into the dining-room. Grandpa's sofa was over in the
far corner, and there he lay, with his handkerchief over his face,
gently snoring.

The ladies sat down at the table. The pleasant old room was
quiet. Outside the tall windows were the shady green leaves of
the ivy. Esther was singing in the back yard as she hung up the
wash.

After a while, when the ladies had got used to sitting there, and
felt reassured by Mr. Day's peaceful snores on the sofa, one of
them whispered a question to the spirits. She waited and waited
for an answer, but the table was silent. Another lady tried, and
then another. They had no success.

Then, while they were whispering to each other about it,
they all heard a faint rap. Mrs. Adams was so frightened she
wanted to run from the room. Some of the others were hungrily
curious. They all were excited. Mrs. Perkins said "Sh-h-h," and
asked the table whether her sister had been sorry to die. The table
was still. They looked disappointedly at each other. Mrs. Perkins
frowned and asked the same thing again. After a long minute of
silence, they heard two feeble raps.

From this on, they could hardly contain themselves. Questions
were fired at the table helter-skelter, the raps got louder and
louder, and more imperious. The only disturbing feature was
that they couldn't quite understand some of the tidings they got.

Old Miss Dykeman had a question to put to her Uncle Jack. He had been a hearty old reprobate who had led his wife quite a life, and after they both died Miss Dykeman used to wonder about his probable fate. "Uncle Jack, are you happy?" she sadly whispered.

The table rapped a loud "Yes."

The ladies made little murmurs of surprise. Miss Dykeman looked incredulous.

"Try his wife," said Mrs. Perkins.

Miss Dykeman got out her smelling salts. "Are you in heaven, Aunt Minna?" she asked.

According to the table, Aunt Minna was in heaven, yes, and was very happy indeed, but in reply to another chance question she said Uncle Jack wasn't there.

"But he said he was happy," Mrs. Perkins snorted. "Ask him again."

Uncle Jack again announced with a bang that he was perfectly happy. Mrs. Perkins asked him point-blank if he was in hell. He said yes to that too. This led to so much discussion among the ladies that that particular séance broke up.

At the next, they got no answers at all. The conditions had seemed better that day, because they had come early, and when Grandpa appeared he found they had moved his sofa into the next room. But though they kept their hands a long time on the table, there wasn't even one rap.

The following week, however, more than made up for this failure. Mrs. Adams and Miss Dykeman had given up, and Mrs. Beecher was invited instead. Grandma had asked Grandpa in advance to move into the parlor once more, for his nap, and he said that he would be glad to if that Mrs. Beecher was coming. She was a hard-eyed old lady who was very proud of her family. When she at last condescended to ask the table about them on this occasion, however, after listening for a long time to the happy raps about other persons, she found to her horror that practically all her own departed dear ones had gone to the wrong place.

Then, one Sunday, Uncle Hal brought Will and Ella to dinner, and Grandma told him he needn't disbelieve any longer that people "on the other side" sent us messages, because she and her friends had received some on that very table. Uncle Hal looked at the table, but said he still didn't believe it.

Grandma offered to show him how simple and easy it was. They drew up their chairs, Will and Ella and all, and sat down. Uncle Hal looked under the table first. He couldn't see anything, but he kept peering around underneath, breathing heavily because he was stout. He didn't suspect Grandma, of course, but he knew what Grandpa was like.

Grandma waited patiently. Uncle Hal had to give up. He frowned in silence, perplexed and still suspicious. The others put their hands on the table. He put his there, too. Then his eye caught sight of a thread on the carpet. He got down on his hands and knees again and discovered that this thread ran up behind one of the legs and then along the under side of the table to the center, where a finger of a kid glove was hanging. There was a small leaden weight inside this finger, and any pull on the thread made it rap.

Uncle Hal chuckled and pursued the other end of the thread. It led under the sliding doors into the parlor. He opened them and went in, thread in hand. Grandpa looked up at him disgustedly. "That's it, Hal," he growled. "Now you've done it. Spoiled the whole thing."

He stopped speaking, abruptly. He saw Grandma coming in through the doorway.

Grandma didn't say anything. She took spiritualism very seriously, but her kind of serenity was founded on great good will to everyone. She turned to where Grandpa lay on his sofa, chagrined and a little bit sheepish, and surveyed him a moment. He raised his eyes to hers, and they presently exchanged an affectionate smile. Then he slowly heaved himself up and threw his thread in the fire.

MOTHER SHOWS US OFF

Mother was sure that her four boys were the best little boys in New York. Other people didn't always agree with her, but usually she didn't know it. Little May Lewis who lived around the corner in Forty-eighth Street, for instance, had a nurse who used to warn her to keep away from those red-headed Day boys. If Mother had ever heard of this she wouldn't have waited a second, she'd have pinned a big hat on her own wavy red hair right away, and grabbed up her muff and her gloves, and gone racing around to the Lewises to tell them that their nurse was quite wrong, and that her boys never did anything they shouldn't, or gave her a moment's uneasiness. And she'd have burst in upon them so impetuously, in her haste to defend us, and spoken so fast and so vehemently, that it would have been impossible for any of them to calm her down. In fact, when polite persons attempted to do this, so as to smooth over an awkward situation, it added to Mother's annoyance. She felt that they were trying to get away from the point she was making. She said they were "just talking nonsense." But nobody ever had time enough anyhow to calm Mother down. She would rush to our defense, stun the enemy, and hurry straight out.

Not that May Lewis's nurse was our enemy, she was merely more realistic than Mother, and she probably had seen enough of the way that we played on the streets to know that a little girl had better go and play somewhere else. Mother's firm belief, however, was that we never really meant to be rough, and that anyway we were privileged characters because we were boys. All males, Mother instinctively felt, were a special kind of creation. They owed certain duties to women and girls, but they also had certain rights.

I used to feel that it was kind of inconvenient to have her be so very proud of us. Somehow it seemed to make it obligatory on us not to disappoint Mother—or at least not to fail her any oftener than we could help. But it also implanted in us such a high opinion of ourselves, as good boys, that when we did get into trouble it appeared to us to be accidental. Accidental and therefore excusable. We were ready to be sincerely repentant but we didn't expect to be punished.

Father's attitude was different from Mother's. He often remarked, "I know boys." His standards of behavior for children were as high as hers were, or higher, and he was only too ready to believe that we hadn't lived up to them. At such times it did us very little good to explain that we had got into this or that scrape "by accident." "Of course it was 'by accident,' " he would impatiently roar, as though it was unthinkable that any boy could mean to defy him, "but it's your business to see to it that accidents of this sort don't happen. And a spanking will probably assist you to bear that in mind."

"Oh, not this time, Clare," Mother begged him one Saturday, when he was saying this to me. "Clarence didn't really mean to knock off the cabman's hat with his little snowball." I fully agreed with her. I had hoped to do it, but when I succeeded I had been immensely surprised—so surprised that I hadn't been quick enough to make good my retreat. Also I hadn't known that Father was inside the cab. I didn't feel more than half guilty. But Father said again, "I know boys," and proceeded to give me a spanking.

When he had finished he went down to the club for an afternoon game of billiards, and as the snow had now turned to rain I went up to the nursery. It was Delia's afternoon out—she was Harold's nurse—so Mother told us three older boys to let Harold play with us, and see that he didn't get hurt.

There was always some unfinished game going on in the nursery. We kept our wooden blocks and marbles and our lead soldiers there, and the wars they were in never stopped. In a very few minutes we were so busy that I had forgotten my spanking. Harold, being too small to fight, had been put up on the bed. He held a piece of an old curtain rod up to his eye, as a spy-glass, and with this he swept the horizon and chanted to himself "Ship ahoy!" We others were laying in a supply of ammunition for a battle at sea.

We had invented a man called Captain Sinkem, a lean priva-teer, and he had been ravaging the wooden-block coasts of the nursery for days. He had originally belonged to a lead soldier regiment of Turkish Zouaves. His face had been battered in long ago, giving him a sinister look, and his baggy red trousers added to his piratical air. His ships had been made by ourselves out of old *Youth's Companions,* on the model of the famous Civil War ironclad *Merrimac.* There was a picture of her in our story-books, looking evil and strong, with sloping bulwarks, a thick covered top, and a ram at her bow. Her simple triangular shape made her easy to copy, at least in our hasty style. We could build an iron-clad in ten minutes. Some numbers of the *Youth's Companion* were thicker than others, but even the thin ones, when folded up, made pretty good warships, and ships that had hulls of many layers were almost impregnable. It was no wonder that Captain Sinkem had done a lot of ravaging in them. He had ravaged one coast so hard that he had bumped it all out of shape.

We always played fair in our games between good men and bad, though it really was much more exciting when the wicked man won. Of course he had to be conquered in the end and die a horrible death, but somehow a game began to get dull as soon as the good man had triumphed.

In this particular game, after vigorously acting for Sinkem, we had manned the forts and fired all our marbles at his ships. But in vain. They had merely bounced off the thick paper bulwarks. At each bounce Captain Sinkem and his pirates had cheered wildly inside.

Now however a new character, Admiral Harry Broadside, had built some ironclads too, and with these he had fended off Sinkem's ships. This was all very well as far as it went but it didn't content Admiral Harry. He was an officer of our little lead

Life Guards, and he was dressed in jack-boots and white pants and a tall bearskin hat, and his martial ambitions were correspondingly haughty and fierce. His one idea was how to destroy Sinkem's fleet altogether.

What he needed for this was new ammunition of a more deadly type. We suddenly remembered a box of old rocks, which we had been told not to play with. Mother loved to have us have a good time, and she never interfered with our fun, but she had warned us that if we threw those awful rocks at our soldiers we'd hurt ourselves with them. And Father had said indignantly that they were his old geology specimens, and that they weren't meant to be thrown around at all. He said that we ought to study them. He had collected them one at a time, in his boyhood, he told us, some of them from way up in Harlem, and some in the hills where the City afterward built Central Park, and he described how he had scrambled down gullies and dug in the slopes, and where he had found the purplish chunk of pudding stone and the silvery mica, and the commonplace-looking lumps of feldspar and hornstone and quartz.

If we had listened to him we might have learned something about the earth after all, to add to our school education, which was concerned almost solely with the history and the tongues of mankind. And as the history of mankind, in our school books, consisted chiefly of wars, all we wanted to use Father's specimens for was ammunition.

We got the box down from the closet and divided the rocks into piles. Now we could have a fine battle. The only crews we had to man our vessels were our lead soldiers of course, and they certainly made peculiar-looking sailors, but they were better than nothing. We marched them aboard in their helmets and plumes and red jackets. Harold tried to get off the bed to help us but we forcibly put him back on, and gave him a trumpet to console him and made him Ship's Bugler. He tooted a shrill croaky blast and the fleets put to sea—that is to say Admiral Broadside's vessels sailed away from the fireplace and Captain Sinkem's came out from under the bed and dashed around the floor rapidly, each fleet blowing sirens and loud warning blasts at the enemy, and the two opposing commanders shouting sneers and taunts and threats at each other. Then amid cheers and roars from the crews, and yells of "Boom!" with each shot we stood off and threw Father's rocks as hard as we could at the ironclads.

They did far more damage than our marbles. Two ships were knocked over. The thin ones soon began to look battered. Harry Broadside's big flagship, the *Disdain,* had only a few rips and dents, but Sinkem's was covered with scars. It looked as though he was now faced with death and destruction at last. I called upon him to surrender—I was acting for Admiral Harry—and George, who was acting for the Captain, began to look worried. He picked up the pudding stone rock, which was especially jagged, and hurled it despairingly at my flagship. It struck square on a gap in a crease which had been loosened already, and the next moment the *Disdain* opened up and spilled her crew into the sea.

In the midst of the terrific excitement that this bull's eye created, while George was dancing around and shouting, "Surrender! Surrender yourself!" and while poor Admiral Harry was trying to swim to some other vessel, we became aware that Bridget the waitress was there in the room.

"Your mother wants you," she said.

"Oh Bridget! Not *now?* She doesn't want us this very minute!"

"Yes, this very minute, and ten minutes before this by rights," Bridget said. "Haven't I been standing here telling you so at the top of me voice, and you boys racketty-banging around on the floor with them rocks, and screeching as if you'd have yourselves killed without the police in to quiet you!"

We knew we had done wrong to take Father's rocks out of the closet. Now we'd get into trouble. We pulled Harold off the bed in silence and started downstairs.

"Alanna machree! Would ye look at ye's!" Bridget expostulated. "Wash them dirty hands first. You can't go in the parlor like that. Come ye here, Har'l, till I run the comb through your hair before you go down to the quality."

"The parlor?" we shouted. "Then it's callers!"

"Sairtainly it's callers," said Bridget. "A lady with a grand, shiny bird in her hat, you'd think it was a duck by the size of it, and her old uncle with her."

We were immensely relieved. If it had been an order to stop throwing the rocks, that would have been a calamity; but callers, though of course they were a nuisance, would only take a few minutes.

It must be a terrible thing for modern children when a caller arrives, and when they have to sit down in the sitting-room and be introduced, and the visitor tries to make conversation and they are supposed to be social. There was never anything as artificial as that in the eighties. Not in our home at least. Children were children, and grown-ups were grown-ups, and the two weren't expected to mix. We boys liked our uncles and aunts and a few old family friends, but we looked upon other grown-ups as foreigners. And they felt that same way toward us.

There was nothing to regret about this that I can see. Quite the contrary. The Victorians had too much common sense to converse with children as though they were human beings. If Mother had had a little daughter she might have wished her to be social, but she didn't really expect that of us. She understood little boys.

On the other hand she did want her friends to have a look at us sometimes. She wanted to show us off to them and let them see what we were like. So when we were sent for, we generally had to speak pieces.

Mother had had to speak pieces herself in her childhood. It was the conventional thing to do in a parlor. It was like shaking hands. What the feelings of the visitors were about it I do not know, but it somehow solved the problem of how to get children in and then out again. Mother had recited so well at her school that she had been given a book as a prize, *"Legends of the Madonna,* by Mrs. Jameson."* (It had been presented to her "for perfect recitations in poetry, with the affectionate wishes of H. B. Haines, 10 Gramercy Park, 1870.") It was a nice-looking little volume, published by Ticknor and Fields, but when I looked

it over it seemed rather soulful and dull, and judging by its very
new appearance Mother never had read it.

George didn't like speaking pieces. He looked worried as we
started downstairs. I didn't mind because it never took long and
we were always allowed to go afterward. We slid down the
banisters and landed in a bunch in the hall.

The parlor was a long narrow room. It was full of plush
chairs and ottomans and vases and roomy glass cabinets—a good
room for boys to keep out of. We opened the sliding doors and
shoved and pushed each other against the dark curtains, struggling to see which of us could achieve safety by going in last. Any
boy who wasn't last usually got tweaked from behind as he entered. This made him fairly spring into the room, which was apt
to flatter the callers.

This afternoon one of us must have pinched Harold a trifle too
hard. He not only leapt convulsively through the curtains but
went in with a shriek. "Hush darling," said Mother, "this is
Miss Wilkinson. Say how-do-you-do to her." We lined up in a
row and were all introduced one by one, and—prompted by
Mother—we told Miss Wilkinson our names and our ages.

Remembering what Bridget had said I stared at the bird in
Miss Wilkinson's hat. There were no birds around in the streets
except sparrows in winter, but ladies' hats more than made up
for it. I had never seen a blue jay in the open, or a bobwhite or
a swallow, but I saw plenty of them on ladies. Miss Wilkinson's
specimen was even more interesting. He was a large bird with
prominent eyes, and a ruby red breast like a robin's. His long
wings stood stiffly out and his attitude was that of flight—he
looked as though he was about to swoop at the carpet and snatch
up a fish—yet in spite of all this he was reposing in a pink curlicue
nest, made of some light filmy stuff, such as chiffon. I wondered
if there were eggs in it. It would have been hard to find out,
for the nest constituted the crown of Miss Wilkinson's hat, and
the heads of several gold hat-pins projected from each side
and in front. Sticking out in the air, opposite to the heads,
were the pins' sharp, gleaming points, one of them so long that

I thought it might skewer George in the eye. He was nearest.

"Clarence will speak his piece first," Mother said. She looked at me encouragingly and I saw her lips form the first words. I took a long breath and plunged in.

> "On Linden, when the sun was low,
> All bloodless lay the untrodden snow;
> And dark as winter was the flow
> Of Iser, rolling rapidly."

In retrospect this selection of mine seems grewsome, but I never thought of it that way. I had chosen it because there was a picture in the book of bearded soldiers in helmets, with black, flowing plumes, marching at night through the snow, waving their sabers, blowing trumpets, and lighting their way with flaming torches, very splendid and ominous.

> "Then shook the hills with thunder riven;
> Then rushed the steeds to battle driven,
> And, louder than the bolts of heaven,
> Far flashed the red artillery."

All up and down Madison Avenue and in the side-streets, other little boys of the eighties were either reciting poems about battles or playing with their toy soldiers—even Willie Smith who lived on the corner and who was much the fattest and most phlegmatic boy whom we knew. Wars seemed to be done with in those days, except small ones in far-away places which didn't half count, and we thought of them only as romantic affairs, like Ivanhoe's tournaments.

The nearer I came to the doleful end of Hohenlinden the more cheerful I got. Mother was forming each word for me too. I recited the final stanza contentedly:

> "Few, few shall part where many meet!
> The snow shall be their winding sheet;
> And every turf beneath their feet
> Shall be a soldier's sepulchre."

Miss Wilkinson's uncle stroked his mustache and said "Excellent, excellent," but Mother shook her head at him, saying "Sh —sh," and motioning for George to speak next. His favorite was the Charge of the Light Brigade. Unfortunately however he couldn't pronounce the letter L properly. When it came at the beginning of a word he always said J instead. This rather changed Tennyson's opening and amazed Miss Wilkinson's uncle, for George looked earnestly at him with his honest blue eyes and began:

> "Half a jig, half a jig,
> Half a jig, onward,
> All in the valley of death
> Rode the Six Hundred."

I forget what came next. It was Blenheim I think. At any rate all of our pieces were about death and battles. Miss Wilkinson smiled in a vacant way and preened herself busily. Her hands fluttered about, as she smoothed her flowing velvet skirt of rich purple, and adjusted her veil, and poked at the bird in her hat, and felt of a leaf on our rubber tree.

Everybody brightened up a little when Harold's turn came. He was last, he was chubby, and, as Mother explained, he was too small yet to say a whole poem. Mother smiled lovingly at him as he knitted his brows and began:

> "Forever float zat standard sheet
> Where bweezy fo-bit—"

" 'Where breathes the foe but falls,' darling," Mother said softly.

Harold reddened with embarrassment at being called "darling" in public, and set his fat little jaws with an obstinate look. "Where bweezy," he repeated:

> "Where bweezy fo-bit falls afore us,
> Wif fweedom's soil beneath our feet,
> An' fweedom's banner stweaming o'er us."

He bowed with a jerk. The performance was over. "Such good boys," Mother said to Miss Wilkinson proudly, as we started out. We tried not to run as we left, but we went through the door in a second, and in the hall there was such a rush for the stairs that Harold fell down with a bang, and was kicked in the head.

Whenever Harold got hurt, which was perhaps rather often, the important thing to do was to choke him. If we had tried to comfort him first, his wails would have brought Mother up on the run. We also had found by experience that it was a great mistake to choke him in silence, because that silence itself would make Mother suspect that something dreadful had happened. Consequently, while choking our indignant little brother, we had to make joyful sounds. This must often have given us the appearance of peculiarly hard-hearted fiends.

On this occasion, Harold was instantly jerked to his feet with our hands over his mouth. The other two boys began whistling and cheering, in a loud nervous manner, and while Harold was struggling for breath I shook my fist at him fiercely.

"But you knocked me down," he managed to whisper.

"All right," I said, "I'll let you hit me back. I'll let you knock me down, honest, no fooling. You can do it the minute we get to the top of the stairs."

"But I'm hurt in two places," Harold sobbed, rubbing his head, with the tears running down his round cheeks.

"Well, if you'll shut up about it," I said, "you can knock George down too."

"What *are* you doing, boys?" Mother called from the parlor in horror. "You aren't knocking each other down, are you!" We heard her start for the door.

"We were just fooling, Mama," George explained reassuringly, as she came through the curtains. Harold was on his way upstairs by that time. He was in a hurry to get to the landing where he was to have his revenge.

Mother stood there a moment, but there didn't seem to be anything wrong. She said that we mustn't disappoint her like

this and make a bad impression on everybody by being so noisy
and rough when we were leaving the parlor.

"No'm," we said. "We didn't mean to."

"And if any boy hits one of his brothers," she said, "I'll have
to have Papa spank him."

Dead silence.

She went back in to those tiresome callers. It was all their
fault, really, we felt. The second she disappeared through the
curtains, we dashed up the stairs.

At the landing we stopped. Harold was waiting for us, eagerly
shouting, "You promised, you promised!" I let him knock me
down, as agreed. His eyes shone as he punched away at me
with his soft little fists.

"Now it's your turn, George," I ordered.

George wasn't at all in the mood to be knocked down however. He said that the last time he had allowed Harold to do it,
Harold had given him a kick on the shins. We were wrangling
about this, when Mother again came to the door.

"Why, boys," she said to us reproachfully.

We rushed off to the nursery.

As we slammed the door shut, we forgot all about the callers
and Mother and everything else, Harold even forgot about hitting George, in our haste to get back to our battle. There was
Admiral Harry, in his jack-boots, bobbing around in the waves,
and Captain Sinkem's ships were more than ready to go on with
their fire. Harold sprang up on the bed and sounded a bugle call,
George shouted "Surrender!" and the cannonade began again at
the exact point where it had left off.

Our battles with toy soldiers and paper ships were realer to
us and much more exciting than the warlike poems we recited.
Those didn't seem gory or horrible to us. They seemed almost
tame by contrast. Besides the former were ancient history while
the latter were of Today.

NOBLE BOYS

Like most children I was taught to admire high ideals in my boyhood. These teachings were well-meant of course, and I took them all in good part. I didn't really admire some of the ideals much, and I made no attempt to live up to them, but at least I regarded such things with a wary respect. Though they sounded to me like standards meant for much better boys than myself, I saw that I too would have to adopt them if I ever became really good, and consequently it interested me to hear about them and filled me with awe—much the same kind of awe I felt at ghost stories, only more far-off and solemn. Meantime they brought home to me the acute disadvantage of goodness, and kept me content with not having any very great moral ambitions.

These doses of high ideals came in various ways, each one unexpected. Sometimes they were administered to me in the form of little talks by my teachers. Sometimes they appeared in a book. On my seventh birthday, for instance, old Mrs. Caister gave me *The Christmas Child* by Mrs. Molesworth. This child's name was Ted, and his history was given at great length from his babyhood to the day he was twelve. I read it all the way through, because a book was a book, but although this one had bright red covers and pictures it was kind of depressing.

It began with a lot of Ted's cunning baby talk. I had to skip some of that. I went on as fast as I could till Ted was seven, like me. But at this point I ran into a long account of his unselfish acts, and about how he joined in "the merry games" of the sons of his father's employees, all of whom respectfully addressed him as "Master Ted" in their play; and then about his going away to school and becoming "a first-rate croquet-player."

According to Mrs. Molesworth, Ted was always "a boy of

nice feelings. Not rough and knockabout in his ways like many
school-boys," she added, in what I felt was a reproving tone,
directed at me. He did have a fight with another boy named Rex
in one chapter, but he felt it was "so horrid" to hit Rex that he
ended by kissing him.

Ted worried about this kissing business afterward and went
to his mother. "Was that unmanly, Mother?" he asked.

"His mother drew him toward her and looked lovingly into his
anxious face. 'Unmanly, my boy? No, indeed,' she said. 'Kindness
and goodness can never be unmanly.' And Ted went off to bed."

I was disturbed by this incident. It made goodness seem more
unnatural to me than ever. But it deeply moved Mrs. Molesworth. She admired Ted so much that she kept saying so, in little
asides to her readers. "I think he had a sweet and brave spirit,
don't you, children?" she said in this chapter; and she went on
to describe how considerate and patient he was, and how "he
was *never* guilty of any rudeness." It was plain that Ted had all
the virtues.

Ted died at the end of the book, just before his twelfth birthday. Very good children often did die on the last page, I had
noticed. They never had anything violent or awful the matter
with them, they just took sick and expired very gently of some
vague and unnamed disease.

"I would have liked to tell how Ted grew up into such a man
as his boyhood promised," Mrs. Molesworth explained. "But,
dears, I *cannot* tell you this, for it was not to be so."

I didn't like books with unhappy endings, but I didn't mind
this one. It seemed sad, in a way, and yet suitable. I regarded
it with much the same feelings that I later regarded Greek trage-
dies. The Olympian deities in their hate stacked the cards against
Œdipus and Jehovah and Mrs. Molesworth did the same thing
to Ted, out of love. It was a comfort to feel that Heaven neither
loved nor hated me yet, and I earnestly hoped that it never would.
I felt pretty sure that I could get along all right by myself, if
Heaven would ignore my existence and let me alone.

There were very few books of this pious sort on our nursery

shelves. Piety of an extreme type was becoming old-fashioned. It was all right but it really didn't seem modern. People talked more about true nobility and noble deeds in the eighties. The atmosphere that my generation grew up in was thick with nobility. Not the atmosphere of our homes or the streets of course, but that of our books.

When I was eight or nine I was given a book called *Noble Boys*. It was by the editor of Peter Parley's Annual, a gentleman named William Martin. Mr. Martin, looking around him in the eighties at the Victorian era, felt a distressing lack of something in the air. He was too up to date to go back to piety, but he had so much heart that even that era seemed sometimes to give him a chill. "It is too much the custom in this cool, matter-of-fact age," he said, "to ignore the sympathies and affections." He felt that most books for boys were not elevated enough, and his purpose in compiling his volume was to remedy this.

He started off well, I thought. The first noble boy whose history he brought forward for my emulation was Cyrus of Persia, the great warrior, son of Cambyses. Among the others were Alexander of Macedon, the Chevalier Bayard, Sir Philip Sidney, the Iron Duke of Wellington, and Garibaldi. All Mr. Martin's selections, he said, were chosen as examples of "the spirit of bold and hazardous enterprise." He was very English about it, however. He detested some of the Scots. I sat down to read his book right after breakfast on Christmas, and by New Year's I had finished Garibaldi and reached the last of his bold heroes, the late respected Prince Consort.

"It is a bright summer's morning," Mr. Martin's story of Albert began, "and the sunlight gilds the rich foliage of the stately trees which encircle the residence of the Duke of Saxe-Coburg. . . . Since the castle clock has struck three there have been anxious watchers within the Schloss, and grooms with horses ready saddled stand in the court-yard. Voices speak in a whisper, but all is hopeful. . . . The clock strikes six, and the firing of guns announces the birth of a Prince."

After thus recording Prince Albert's impressive arrival on earth,

Mr. Martin went on to say that "ere he had reached his second year, his grandmother wrote to her daughter, the mother of our beloved Queen: 'Little Alberinchen, with his large blue eyes and dimpled cheeks, is bewitching, forward, and quick as a weasel.' " On and on through this noble youth's infancy I plowed step by step. Mr. Martin remarked that the Prince was in some ways very like Sir Philip Sidney. Sidney was a poet, and Prince Albert, he said, was quite fond of music.

Up to this point, although the Prince had done well in his studies, he hadn't performed any heroic deed like the other boys in this book. But now that came too. Early one morning in the young Prince's apartment at Coburg he was awakened by an unpleasant smell. There was smoke in the room. He got out of bed and discovered that one of his rooms was on fire. There was no plumbing of course, and he had nothing to put out the fire with except "two pitchers of water and a jug of camomile tea," but he and his brother and their valet threw these on the fire and then summoned help. The sentry rang the fire-bell, help arrived from all sides, and the smoldering flames were extinguished.

In order to make sure that his readers had not missed the point, or failed in some way to appreciate this as a companion piece to Wellington's Waterloo, Mr. Martin told the story all over again, ending by saying that it was thus that the Prince saved "the noble edifice from destruction, with but two pitchers of water from the washstands and a jug of camomile tea." I don't know just why, but I felt that he did right to repeat it. On the next page the Prince married Victoria, and at the bottom of that page he died.

The effect of Mr. Martin and Mrs. Molesworth was to create in the back of my mind a Valhalla, peopled by lofty but shadowy figures, Wellington, Prince Albert and Sidney, Garibaldi and Ted. I never dreamed of taking a critical attitude toward these figures. The only thing was that no matter how much I read about them I felt empty inside. They were as resplendent and as striking as the wax-works in the Eden Musée, and I looked at their effigies one by one, with solemn respect, but they had been dead a long time. I never thought of Gulliver or Robinson Crusoe as dead.

I had heard a good deal about a writer named Horatio Alger who wrote books for boys. One day a cousin of mine, Parmly Clapp, offered to lend me a few. They were easy to read and they came into my life at just the right moment. I had become convinced that splendor and holiness were out of my line. Alger opened my eyes to a brand-new attraction—the ways in which boys could earn money.

I was fascinated by that idea. If I could only earn steady wages I could buy lots of new things. I already had all the food that I wanted—except chocolate caramels—and as to better clothes I was indifferent, but I needed more lead soldiers and some rare stamps and a printing-press badly.

"A long train was running at moderate speed over a Wisconsin railroad. Among the passengers was a stout, gentlemanly-looking boy, who looked much more than sixteen, although he had not yet reached that age. On the seat beside him was a large carpet bag." That is the way that *Strive and Succeed* by Horatio Alger began, and the stout, gentlemanly, fifteen-year-old boy had already done some work as a book-agent and a clerk in a store. According to the preface this book was "reprinted from the pages of *Young Israel,* a New York juvenile magazine." It wasn't only the young Israelites who liked Alger however, it was young Yankees too. I suppose that a youth with a soul above business wouldn't have cared much for a story like *Cash Boy* with its honest and hard-working hero, but my soul wasn't that kind. I also read *Bound to Rise, Slow and Sure,* and *Paul the Peddler.* The boys Alger introduced me to were level-headed youngsters, not dreamers, and they seemed to be right on my level, or not too much above it. They were manly, but in a sensible way; they were brave but they also were practical; and they didn't make me uncomfortable by devoting themselves to honor and glory. I didn't re-read them as I did Gulliver, their interests were a little too narrow, but they were more my own kind than Alexander of Macedon. They were business-like heroes.

MOTHER GIVES FATHER A SURPRISE

I must have been a chronically suspicious small boy, for I remember thinking to myself that Father needed a great deal of watching. When he was in an expansive and jolly mood, a boy could trust him, but not when he felt thoughtful. At such times the danger was that he would think of some brand-new ambition. Not for himself, but for me.

One such ambition, which I blindly felt was harsh and unnatural, was that in addition to French I should learn German. He seemed to have all sorts of hopeful pictures in his mind of my future, and one of these was of my traveling widely in Europe, conversing in an affable and condescending way with all nations. When I earnestly protested that I didn't want to converse with them, he laughed at my spluttering and told me that I would, later on. He added: "I decline to have any son of mine grow up to be a damn blockhead, and blunder around the Continent in a helpless and ridiculous manner." He said that was no way to travel. All self-respecting young men should learn enough languages to feel at ease while in Europe.

This made even the very thought of Europe objectionable to me. If a boy had to go through all that, just to travel, I felt I'd rather stay home. I was having quite enough trouble with French without studying German. But I couldn't get Father to sympathize with this point of view. His own travels abroad as a young bachelor and later as a young bridegroom had left him with such pleasant memories that he had become, from my point of view, kind of romantic. I was impatient with this. I felt like a young but clear-headed critic arguing with some hopeless dreamer.

I felt more exasperated than ever when, on questioning Father,

I learned that he hadn't traveled in Germany or had to learn German. He had picked up a smattering of it somehow, but the only tongue he knew well was French. When I said resentfully that it was not fair to make me learn something he hadn't, he said that that was the very reason he wanted me to, so that I wouldn't miss it, as he had. All his life, he said, he had regretted not knowing that language. I told him I'd bet I'd never miss it, but he assured me I would.

At odd moments he tried to teach me the rudiments of German himself. For some reason he began with the word Ich, which I could never pronounce. I could not or would not lend myself to saying such a word right. I was willing to call it either Ick or Itch, but that was as far as I'd go. We had I don't know how many heated and long-drawn-out sessions before he resigned me to what he called my "barbarous fate."

One winter some friends of Mother's, the Garrisons, introduced her to an elderly German lady who was in want. Her name was Fräulein von Pilch, and she was a majestically heavy and slow-speaking person. She had a meditative expression, voluminous skirts, and calm eyes. When the Garrisons brought her to the house and introduced her, she clasped and held Mother's hand, and said to her affectionately, "But you are eggsackly der teep." Mrs. Garrison explained this meant that Mother was just the type to learn German, and that Fräulein von Pilch would be only too happy to teach her.

Mother was always sorry for anyone who was old and hard up. She didn't really want to learn German, but she suddenly saw that, if she did, she would be giving a wonderful surprise to Father the next time they went abroad. As this idea enchanted her, and as this really seemed to be the right moment, and as Fräulein was in such very sad circumstances, Mother agreed to take lessons. Then Fräulein explained that the price of each lesson to Mother would be very much less if she signed a little written agreement to take a full course of them; and Mother, who besides having a soft heart had a sense of thrift too, simply couldn't resist taking advantage of such a bargain, and signed.

The German language and Mother then began to make each other's acquaintance. The beginning was pleasant enough, but yet somehow not promising. Fräulein shook her head several times thoughtfully at certain developments. Mother's head was so full of other things that Fräulein didn't seem to feel sure there was going to be room enough in it for a language like German. Also, Mother seemed to expect the German language to behave like a gentleman and not be too hard on a busy woman who had several small boys to take care of, and who was studying it out of pure kindness, merely to help poor old Fräulein. This feeling of Mother's was concealed out of politeness at first, but it was burstingly strong; and when neither the German language nor Fräulein seemed to feel grateful, and when on the contrary they became too demanding and difficult, they were vehemently told that they really would have to change for the better.

Fräulein went off to think this over until the next lesson. She loved the German language just as it was; and even if she hadn't she didn't see how she could change it. That had never been done. She had no wish to change herself either. She was a good German. On the other hand, she wasn't a mere teacher, she was more like a missionary. When she came across unfortunate foreigners, who were living in darkness, and held up the light of German before them, she wished them to bow reverently before it and take it into their hearts.

She came back determined to get it into Mother's heart somehow, even if she had to go very slow and pretend to yield here and there. She yielded on some irregular verbs and the prepositions before the dative for instance. The one thing she wouldn't give way on was the general structure of sentences, with the ingredients properly arranged in an orderly row, and the verb where it belonged, at the end. That was the essence of German. That however was the very thing about German that antagonized Mother. She said it was impossible for her to talk that way. She couldn't keep the verb back. She had a quick, darting mind and her way of thinking and talking was lively, and every time Fräulein with her stately tread entered the house Mother pounced on

her and tried to make her and the German language become
lively too.

A worried look gradually appeared on Fräulein's once-peaceful
brow, and her slow, quiet eyes grew distressed. She could be
patient, she could be affectionate and steadfast, but she could
not become lively. She was probably secretly troubled by the con-
cessions she had already made—they had not been exactly disloyal to the Fatherland but they were on the borderline—and
she neither knew how to nor dared to keep on making more. She
at last put her foot down. Mother was brought face to face with
all the undisguised rigors of German, and Fräulein flatly informed her that she would have to accept them.

Mother was appalled to have a worm turn in this way and
threaten her—an ungrateful worm whom she had befriended.
She tried to break off the agreement. This stirred up still deeper
depths of "Germanness," as Mother called it, in Fräulein. She
stubbornly held to her rights and insisted on going ahead.

When she left the house at the end of that lesson she was in a
hard mood, and Mother was in a depressed one. She had me
come down to her room and we had a long talk about it. I was
too young to be any real help to her but Mother felt desperate.
We read over the agreement together. "The mean old thing,"
Mother wailed. She burst into tears of vexation. It couldn't be
broken. The idea of paying Fräulein the money for nothing was
not even considered. We neither of us knew what to do.

The next time Fräulein came to the house Mother again summoned me, and I found to my horror that she was now turning
to me in earnest. The only way out that she could see, she said,
was for me to learn German.

I was very much agitated. My devotion to Mother was pulling
me one way and my loathing of German the other. Fortunately
Fräulein, upon being consulted, looked at me with disfavor. I
couldn't even pronounce her name right, she said, and she had
never taught children.

I said to Mother that the one who seemed fondest of German
was Father.

That night after dinner Mother explained to Father about the surprise for him that she had planned but told him that she didn't feel well enough just then to do very much studying, and that as she thought she was going to have a baby she would have to take a short rest. She said that Father had better take her lessons for her until she felt better.

It took quite a little explaining to make this plan at all clear to Father. When he had at last got it straight and had looked at the contract, he said that of course he had no time for German, it was out of the question, but he felt that a few lessons from Fräulein wouldn't hurt me a bit. He looked at me and laughed as he added that he wished the old woman luck.

Mother then had to make him understand that Fräulein never taught children. She said also that she didn't know what was the matter with me but I couldn't even say Ich, and the money would really be wasted if Fräulein and I spent the winter on it. Father got out of his chair and walked up and down when he had to admit this. He said that Mother was everlastingly throwing herself into hasty and ill-advised projects and then turning to him to be extricated, and that he was tired of it. He said that he was overburdened with heavy responsibilities and problems and cares, and that although he wished very much he had learned German when young he now had no leisure to study it. After all of which he said that since there was no other way out of the mess, he would take a lesson or two, while Mother rested, but that then she must take her own medicine.

This step proved to be fatal. Although Father felt indignant and put upon, he made good progress in German. After two or three lessons, which he had to take at night, when he had finished his dinner, he insisted that Mother must stop shirking and go back to work, but although she seemed to be always about to do this, somehow she never did. He could never quite pin her down. He grumbled, he protested, but every time Fräulein arrived, either the hairdresser was there, or the dressmaker, or maybe Aunt Emma, or else some sudden household emergency kept Mother from taking the lesson. Or if she did try to, after the first fifteen minutes Mother felt very faint, and Fräulein would come downstairs, beaming, to give Father the rest of the hour. She was delighted with Father because he was thorough. No matter how cross he got at her she smiled tenderly at him, while he faithfully though unwillingly filled her copy books with a fine German script.

FATHER BUYS US A BOAT

We boys wanted a boat. Spending our summers at the Pequot, a colony of cottages near New London, where the Thames flows into the Sound, we wanted to be out on the water. Charlie Ogden had a rowboat, but that wasn't enough to go round. There were nearly a dozen boys from New York at the Pequot in the eighties. There were four of us Day boys alone. And though Charlie was hospitable, he insisted on having at least as much use of his own boat as we did. He also had a sister who liked to use it, and take out other girls with her. A boat full of girls seemed to us a ridiculous sight, but they brazened it out, rowing up and down near the shore, in their starched white frocks and stiff little petticoats, while we boys commented loudly and mockingly on their performance.

One summer after we had all learned to swim, we four brothers at last got Father to promise that he would buy a boat for the family. Mother said he was to make very sure that he selected a safe one. Although she went in bathing and splashed around, close to the shore, she regarded swimming as an unnatural and mysterious feat, and she deeply distrusted the water.

In the circumstances, a sailboat was out of the question. Sailboats were always tipping over, Mother said, or else being blown out to sea, or striking holes in themselves by dashing against rocks, and then sinking straight out of sight. A canoe, or even a light skiff or rowboat, seemed almost as dangerous. She didn't want to keep her boys from enjoying themselves on the water, but couldn't Father get something solid for us to go out in?

Father at last found an immensely broad rowboat, long enough for three sets of oars, with a great, roomy, square-cut stern and a tiller, and a rather fat bow. She was so stalwart and solid that we could leap in or out of her without disturbing her balance, and it took a great deal of muscular effort to compel her to rock. Other rowboats could be upset by main force if we wanted to do it, as we now and then did when in swimming, but not this boat of ours. In dignity, weight, and durability she resembled a barge.

This boat seemed especially designed to promote family life. If one of us went out by himself in her, he seldom went far. He came back breathing hard and exhausted, and tried to find reinforcements. George and I, who were the oldest, could get along by spelling each other, but if our younger brothers wanted to come we liked to have them, and Cousin Julie besides. When Julie came, she usually began by sitting in the stern like a lady and trying to steer so as to satisfy the various oarsmen, each of whom had different ideas; but we often got caught in such a strong tide that we had hard work getting home, and Julie would then find that in mere self-preservation she would have to turn to and row.

As Julie was beginning to go to teas and other young-ladyish parties, she didn't have a great deal of appetite for boating, at least of this kind, so when Harold, my youngest brother, was six, he was promoted to be coxswain instead. We then began having races with Charlie's boat. This was a stern business. It was particularly hard on our knuckles and the backs of our heads. Each boy rowed with a pair of oars instead of one, to better our speed, and when he crossed the handle ends over, in his excitement, he knocked all the skin off his knuckles. And in rough water anybody who missed a stroke fell over backward and banged his head good and hard. After going through all this it was kind of exasperating never to beat Charlie's boat.

When a yacht or a man-of-war visited the Pequot, what we boys most admired about it was the crew of its gig. There were no gasoline launches in those days. A gig with six sailors and a coxswain would put off from some splendid yacht and bound swiftly over the water. Four fascinated red-headed Day boys would stand staring in awe at the perfect rhythm and timing of the oarsmen, with their short, snappy strokes. Best of all, as they rounded the dock, at a word from the coxswain the oars would spring out of the rowlocks and stiffly point to the sky, while the boat glided easily in and laid itself alongside the float.

Having a boat ourselves now, and a fairly large family to man it, we of course tried to imitate this performance and make a smart landing ourselves, especially if there was anyone watching. One day when we had the tide with us, George and I for once got a magnificent momentum on our sleepy old craft. On that particular day, too, Harold, our coxswain, had been hungry for hours and was in a hurry to land. In order to be sure to avoid any delay, he held back his order to up oars till the very last moment, and then steered too full at the float besides, so as to be sure not to miss it. Our boat flew through the water. It rammed the float, head on, with such violence that George and I and our four shaky oars were instantly spilled off our thwarts, and as we clattered to the bottom of the boat the bow man and his boat hook fell over backward on top of us. Mother, who was waiting on the dock, started screaming for help. This, naturally, drew everybody's attention to us, to our great annoyance. And while we were scrambling to our feet, Harold leapt out and fled.

Below the Pequot House, sticking out into the river, stood the dock, broad and spacious. Once or twice a day the little river steamer passed by. If signaled, she stopped and made fast to the easterly end to take on a passenger, tooting her whistle in triumph. Or sometimes the dinghy of a visiting yacht would wait at the float, while its owner sat in a rocking-chair drinking lemonade on a cottage piazza. At other times the dock was deserted by grown people, except Cap'n Finch.

Cap'n Finch was a lean, sharp-eyed man of possibly thirty or forty, who owned a beautiful white sloop, the *Hattie,* which was to let, by the hour. As an investment, the *Hattie* paid slow and irregular dividends. She lay, spick and span, at her moorings, day in and day out, and Cap'n Finch sat under a shed on the dock, watching her and chewing tobacco. He looked discontented. He had a restless way of shifting about, and a tart and abrupt way of speaking.

Once in a while, though, his bronze face would relax a little and he would become less forbidding. This was when visitors at the hotel would stroll down to the dock, and after protracted negotiations go for a sail on the Sound.

It seemed to me, as a boy, that the most glorious thing on earth was a sloop. I often ran down to the dock to look at the *Hattie,* rocking gently in the waves at her moorings. And on the rare occasions when Cap'n Finch avariciously took a party on board, made sail, and winged his way down the river, I felt enthralled by the sight. Because, I suppose, of the sum that such an outing required, I never got a chance to sail in the *Hattie.* Mother didn't like sailing, and Father didn't like Cap'n Finch. The situation was hopeless.

Meanwhile we kept tugging away at the oars of our rowboat. Sometimes we rowed up the river toward the town of New London, to visit an old whaling man we called Amos, and read a valuable book of his about how and where to catch whales. One day Amos, looking over our rowboat, suggested that he could step a mast in her, for'ard, with a leg-of-mutton sail, all complete. With a centerboard, I could then sail her anywhere. This excited me greatly. As neither Amos nor I had any money, however, we did nothing for some weeks but talk. Then Amos found a spar, a rather little one, that would do for a mast, and enough old canvas to patch up a sail out of, and although we couldn't afford blocks or halyards, he and I went to work.

Owing to the high cost of lead, we had to give up the idea of a centerboard. Amos shook his head over this. He said a sail would be no use without one. I didn't agree. Though I knew little or nothing about sailing, I knew a whole lot about rowing, and I was tired of pulling my arms out of their sockets, tugging away at those oars.

Amos yielded at last. He kept making predictions of difficulties, but, as I pointed out, perhaps those very difficulties would open Father's eyes to our needs.

The New York Yacht Club fleet anchored off the Pequot during its cruise every summer. One dark morning the yachts fought their way in against a wet northern wind, while George and I were pulling up the river to get the new sail from Amos. He had all the gear ready. He showed us how to step the mast and how to unship it again when we were through, he screwed in a cleat or two for the sheet, and after a while we were off. We didn't ask Amos any questions about how to handle a sail. We supposed that we knew. So did Amos. He had never met boys who didn't.

The wind was gusty and strong, and it was blowing almost directly downstream. The tide was running out, and the current of the river was swift. We sped along at a rate that was intoxicating to a pair of weary ex-oarsmen. Sprawled insolently at our ease in the stern, we hardly noticed the rain. All went well till we bore down on the crowd of yachts that now lay at anchor.

It was necessary to do some careful steering. George had the sheet, I the tiller. I not only felt thoroughly competent, I felt happy and proud. It seemed to me that even the great yachts ahead of us would admire our boat, and that their crews would perhaps man the sides and give us a cheer as we passed.

To my consternation, I then found that our boat wouldn't do what I wanted. It obediently pointed its nose in any direction I wished, but this had very little effect on the course it took through the water. I could sail it downstream bow on if I steered due south, straight ahead, or by pulling the tiller I could present one of its fat sides to the wind, but whatever I did we still went due south, with the wind, tide, and current. I began to understand better why Amos had wanted a centerboard.

We didn't hit any of the first yachts that we passed, I hardly know why. Both they and I fully expected it. We had some narrow escapes. As the yachts became thicker, however, naturally some had to suffer. Many more of their crews manned their sides than I had let myself dream, but they didn't stand and cheer us, they cursed. At first they were incredulous, they couldn't believe we'd dare to harm them, but as they saw our boat ram and rebound from some neighboring craft, they suddenly realized, crew by crew, that they all were in danger.

The yachts were of various sizes. There must have been a hundred, all told. Some had crews of only one or two men, some had dozens. Large or small, all the crews seemed to think it would help to save them from being damaged if they threatened us fiercely enough as we bore down on them. It didn't. Nearly all these yachts were freshly painted, and this was the first leg of their cruise, and one or two red-faced owners whose yachts we bumped into, or scraped, ran along their decks shaking their fists at us and roaring like madmen.

George was groggy by this time. He had nearly fallen overboard at our second or third bad collision, and as for me, I was half-stunned with fright. Then, just a little way down the stream, I saw the *Hattie*. I realize now that she was probably only a rotten old tub, but that was not how I saw her in those days. She was a far more sacred craft in my eyes than any yacht in the harbor, and on top of that I was scared of Cap'n Finch and of what he might do. I came to my senses, abandoned the tiller, and we lowered the sail. As the sail was nailed fast to the mast, this involved lowering everything.

Disguised now as an innocent rowboat, George and I rowed ashore, and unobtrusively made our way home in the rain. On the dock we had to pass Cap'n Finch. He had probably seen at least a part of our disgraceful adventure, but as we went by he averted his eyes and grimly gazed out to sea.

The next day some of the yachtsmen gave parties on board their yachts, and one very youthful yacht-owner, who was attentive to Julie, invited all the Day family. George and I consulted privately together about what we'd better do, and when the hour came for us to start we were not to be found.

MOTHER ON HORSEBACK

Father liked company. He was a sociable man and he liked to have his family do things with him. And particularly he liked to have Mother do things with him. So, after he had been riding horseback awhile he began to urge Mother to take it up too.

Mother however had a deep distrust of horses. Her father, to be sure, had had a stock farm in Ohio where he raised horses, but that had been way out of town, and she hadn't taken to horses. Or they to her.

In the city she seldom even rode in carriages, until she was fifty or over. Before that she trusted her legs. She preferred to. Of course, she used street-cars and buses, which had horses to draw them, and once in a long while she sent to a livery stable and hired a cab. But the horses that drew cabs and street-cars seemed of some milder breed than those which she saw led out in the ring of the Riding Club where Father wanted her to learn to ride.

However Father continued to urge her. He assured her confidently that it would take her no time at all to learn. "As to managing a horse," he said, "there's nothing to it. Just make up your mind what you want to do and see to it the horse does it."

This did not make it any clearer to Mother just how she was ever going to manage such a beast; but she went to a great deal of trouble to have a riding habit made and one fine day she went to the Riding Club for the first lesson.

When I saw Mother on horseback I felt a solemn horror. She who had once been so slender and young was now plump. Her tight riding habit accentuated her figure and, to my troubled eyes, she looked all wrong, even before she mounted.

And to make matters worse, she approached any horse with

misgivings; she got aboard without any liking for or confidence in the animal. He never got any clear idea of what she wished him to do, and even if he did he wouldn't have felt any particular desire to comply with her wishes. She wanted a horse to understand everything without being told, or at least to interpret correctly her ejaculations and jerks. He, in his turn, only became more bewildered. Both of them were soon in despair. At brief moments one of them would hope a little for better things, they would start on a trot with some courage perhaps, but no use— hope would die as my mother bounced tightly along on his back and both she and the horse grew more wretched and at odds with each other.

Father, however, was cheery. He was blind to the horse's misery and firmly disregarded hers. Bent on giving her encouragement he followed her around the ring telling her what to do. He could always tell though he couldn't teach. He fully believed that if she kept on she'd learn. He was completely surprised and baffled when, after a few lessons, Mother said:

"That's enough, Clare, I am too busy to go there just now."

He did not give up, however, but said that New London, next summer, was just the place to learn. He said that riding in a ring didn't have much purpose to it anyway and that the country was the place. Besides, out there we had not only Father's horse, but also the family stand-by, a horse named Dick. All of us boys had jogged up and down on old Dick's back while learning, and there seemed to Father no reason why Mother should not do so too.

Mother agreed readily enough. She wanted to end the talk, and next summer seemed a long way off. For the time being the whole thing was over and done with.

No sooner had we arrived in New London, though, than Father began to make plans for taking Mother out with old Dick. Mother, however, said firmly that she was much too busy getting settled. The truth was that the ring had been bad enough but at least it was enclosed. She shuddered to think of herself on the back of a horse in the open country. With nothing to stop the creature there was no telling where he would run to. She secretly made up her mind that nothing on earth was going to get her on the back of any horse way out here in the country.

While she was thinking of an excuse strong enough to silence Father, old Dick settled the matter for her. Dick was a middle-aged, slow-witted, good-looking horse. He was black all over except two white fetlocks and a star on his forehead. We boys thought he was handsome. So did other people who didn't know horses. His coat was kept so glossy that although the hairs were coarse they looked fine. His eyes were large, liquid and friendly, and they seemed to glow with intelligence, or even with fire, although as a matter of fact Dick had neither.

When he stood outside our front door and held his head high and pricked up his ears, hoping for sugar, only a mean person would have noticed that those ears were the longest a horse ever had. His disposition was agreeable and his general appearance somehow was gentlemanly.

Father never rode Dick himself if he could possibly help it. He had bought him because he was a safe horse for us little boys. We felt that it was only when he went into action that he didn't live up to his looks. He had a solid heavy-footed gallop that jolted us hard at each bounce, his legs were thick and he had never learned to raise them at all; he always hung his bony head low as he pounded laboriously on, and he stopped short in the middle of a gallop whenever he wanted to rest. He stopped very often, to indicate that he was done for, and he had to be yelled at and kicked to persuade him to start again.

Having a far more gentlemanly nature than I had, Dick took those kicks in good part. It seemed boisterous to him, I suppose, but he took it for granted I meant well. As soon as he got over his surprise at the exasperation I'd shown, he would cheerfully bestir himself and plunge ahead again, just to be pleasant. And a moment or two later he would once more suddenly come to a halt.

No matter how rudely I shouted at Dick, his behavior toward me was invariably urbane and considerate. Every time I fell off, he immediately stopped and began eating grass. While I was picking myself up and climbing on again he continued to eat. After I had got on his back and hauled his head up and begun thumping his side with my heels, he would look around in a friendly way at me, until it became finally clear to him that I wanted to go on with our ride.

A horse of this temperament, conservative, slow and respectable, was the last horse that we ever thought would run away with us some day. Yet one afternoon that's what happened.

George and I had driven Dick in the dog-cart along the shore road all the way from our summer cottage at the Pequot up to the town of New London. We had started early and Dick had taken his time about it. At the place where the road turned off from the shore and passed under the railroad tracks, which ran overhead on a low, stumpy, ironwork bridge, we faithfully stopped, according to promise, to make sure that no train was coming, and then drove on into New London and through its narrow winding streets to meet Father.

We sat waiting a long time near the station in the hot afternoon sunshine. The train was way behind schedule that Saturday. That was bad luck for Father. He could get away only for weekends. On Sunday night he would have to take the night boat to return to New York. Every hour of his week-ends was precious to him.

Dick hung his long head down, crooked a knee or two, dozed in the shafts.

The very second the train rolled into the station we saw Father spring out. He walked swiftly over to us and got into the dogcart. George was sitting in the front seat beside him. I sat behind, facing backward. Father took the reins, touched Dick up with the whip and away we drove toward the Pequot. There still was a chance of our getting there in time for a swim.

Dick was still half-asleep. When he found that he was expected to hurry, he got rather flustered. He snorted, he threw his legs around, and shook his head. George and I laughed. Before Father drove under the low railroad bridge we stopped for a moment, but it was only a moment, and none of us heard the fast train. As we started through, it came with a roar, less than ten feet over our heads. Dick's brain was never very clear and it now ceased to work. The noise was so great and so alarming that he leapt wildly forward, and the next I knew he was speeding away with us down the shore road. I was rather pleased about this at first. The sooner we got home the better. But as the heavy dog-cart lurched and I saw Father sawing away at Dick's leathery mouth, I realized that the big animal was out of control. I held on tight to the side-rails. At one place where there was a thank-you-ma'am in the road, I was bounced so high up in the air, holding on to the side-rails, that the cushioned seat rose from its frame underneath me and pitched out of the dog-cart. I came down on the frame with a bang, and stared back at my seat as it sailed through the air and fell plop on the road far behind us.

I was astonished at Dick. He had always trusted the family before. But he'd been more than frightened, he'd been shocked by the noise under the bridge. He behaved as though we had tried to lead him into a loud and terrible death. No matter how hard Father pulled, Dick galloped ahead. He wasn't going to trust anybody but himself from now on. He had to get away from that bridge and he had to keep going.

Dick ran in all for nearly two miles. He was puffing and coughing most of the time and making a great deal of noise. So was Father. Father was calling upon Dick to stop, and calling on us to hold tight, and on the world in general to look out and keep out of the way. After a little, George tried to help Father pull on the reins, but Dick had the bit in his teeth and he was still in a panic.

The one good thing about the situation was that our speed was not great. Dick was going much faster than usual, but that was not very fast. It was a kind of slow-motion runaway.

The worst of it was when we got to the Pequot. We roared helplessly by in full view of the cottage piazzas and the crowded hotel, at an unseemly yet ponderous gallop, and swung on toward the hill.

Even on the hill Dick didn't stop, which astonished George and me greatly. He went up and over the crest and plunged on past the Haven place and down the road toward the lighthouse. It wasn't until the road got so sandy that the going was bad that Dick solemnly slowed down and made up his mind he was safe.

Father got out when he stopped. He said that the damned horse had pulled his arms out of their sockets, and demanded to know where the cushion was and why I had lost it. When I told him, he said it was very peculiar and he'd have to send the coachman to get the cushion. Then he looked at his watch and brightened up and said he'd have time for a swim. He turned Dick around and we drove sedately back to our cottage.

After Father had his swim he came out on the porch, refreshed and at peace with the world. The runaway was comfortably a thing of the past. Mother however had no intention of letting this opportunity slip by her. She began right away to say firmly that she had always known horses were dangerous, and she could not see why he had ever urged her to ride.

"An accident can happen to anyone," Father said easily.

"That's just why I shall never ride, Clare," Mother returned.

"But this did not mean anything, I tell you," said Father. "That damn train just rushed out of nowhere and that crazy horse took the bit in his teeth."

"Well, I should think that you would have looked first," Mother said as she gathered up her sewing before going in to make ready for dinner.

"I tell you I did look but the—" Father started to explain again.

"If you looked I don't see why you went under the bridge with the train right there," said Mother severely as she went through the door.

Father, who had been so genial, was now red-faced and angry. He puffed violently at his cigar for a moment, then strode up the road to the cottage where his friend Mr. Ogden lived.

As we came along to the Pequot House for dinner a few moments later, we saw Father quietly exhaling his cigar, and his voice, always full-bodied, came to us distinct on the early evening air.

"And where that train came from I'm damned if I know."

MOTHER AND BESSIE
SKINNER'S RING

The women whom Moher knew in the eighties didn't discuss women's rights. When Mrs. Belva Lockwood ran for President, they knew it was ridiculous. When votes for women were advocated, later on, they disapproved of that program. They sometimes are pictured, accordingly, as meek, supine creatures. This is a mistake. In their marital relations they were particularly firm and demanding.

Their underlying feeling was that a woman had certain "prerogatives," which God and Nature had given her. They often talked to each other about these and the best ways to get them. When Mother was in her thirties she listened to such talks intently. She had no very clear idea as to what a woman's prerogatives were, but whatever they were she thought she might need them, and her feelings about them were vigorous.

This attitude was partly an outgrowth of the way Father talked. He didn't seem to think that a woman had any prerogatives. He never put it that way exactly, but whenever one was claimed it surprised him. He professed never to have heard of the most ordinary feminine privileges.

One grievance of Mother's, which had seemed a small matter at first but which grew bigger each year, was that Father had never given a ring to her when they got engaged. She had been a little surprised, even at the time, when she didn't get one. She had supposed every girl got an engagement ring as soon as she promised to marry. Father had once had an unpleasant experience, however, which had left a dislike of engagement rings fixed in his mind. He told Mother not to be young and foolish. Engagement rings were all nonsense. He said they were going to get

married so very soon anyway that she didn't need one. She was
in no mood to quarrel with him. He was twenty-eight, she was
twenty, and his ideas prevailed.

As time went on, and as Mother talked over things with other
young married women, she felt more and more injured. Not only
that, but she began to fear she had made a dreadful mistake.
Her young women friends explained to her the awful conse-
quences of letting a man evade his plain duty. Any man who
had successfully evaded one duty, they said, would naturally
suppose he could keep right on evading for life.

The next thing Father knew, he found himself being heatedly
urged to buy an engagement ring for his wife, several years after
they had married and settled down and begun to have children.
Not having the slightest idea as to why Mother wanted it, he
was immensely surprised. He was still more surprised to see her
cry when he refused her request. He patiently explained to her,
as though she were a petulant child, the senselessness of his presenting an engagement ring to the woman he was married to,
damn it.

This encounter was only the first of many that they had on the
subject. As the combats continued, Father became more and
more convinced that women were completely unreasonable, and
also that Mother had a mysterious mania for rings; and Mother,
whose jewel box didn't have very much in it, felt more and more
sure that the women she had talked with were right, and that
unless she could get that ring out of Father, she'd never get any
of her just dues again.

Meanwhile, having got it into his head that Mother had a
strange love of rings, Father bought her a handsome ring every
time she bore him a son. Once in a long while he even brought
home a new ring on her birthday, if he had been sufficiently reminded in advance that her birthday was coming. Mother was
delighted each time she got one. She had a great love of jewels.
But from her point of view none of these gifts could make up
to a woman for the lack of ever having had an engagement ring,
and she kept right on wanting one.

One afternoon, down at Grandpa Day's, while I was playing on the floor with a wooden engine that Grandpa had made for me, and while Mother was talking with Grandma and old Mrs. Caister, something was said about Bessie Skinner.

Mother sniffed.

"That was the one that Clare got engaged to first, Vinnie," said Grandma.

Mother said, "Yes, I know, but what really happened? What broke it off?"

Grandma shook her head and said evenly that she never knew.

Mrs. Caister laughed to herself. "They were cousins," she said. "They were both of 'em Days, Vinnie; that's why. Whenever they had any difference, neither one of 'em would give in to the other. So finally Bessie up and returned the ring that Clare—"

"*What!*" Mother shrieked. I looked up from my engine. "He gave that woman a *ring?* What became of it?"

Mrs. Caister said that she supposed Father had it. She remembered distinctly that he had given Bessie a ring and a watch, and that she had never sent the watch back to him, but she certainly had sent the ring.

The next thing I knew Mother was hurrying with me through East Twenty-fifth Street over to Fourth Avenue and we were getting on an uptown horse-car. I looked out at the thin, dirty white horses. It was cold and my legs were not quite long enough to reach to the floor of the car, where the straw would have kept them a little warmer. I squirmed around and knelt on the seat to look out of the window. There wasn't much to see but long rows of red-brick houses, two or three stories high, with shops on the street floors and furniture or baskets of vegetables out on the broad sidewalks. Every two or three blocks a big wooden Indian with a bunch of wooden cigars in his hand stood offering them to passers-by, at the door of some cigar shop. Presently the conductor struck a match to light the tiny kerosene lamps, one at each end of the car, and we went in the tunnel. When we came out again, in Forty-second Street, the buildings were all twice as tall, and the streets twice as crowded with horses and wagons and hacks, cutting in and out every which way, with the drivers yelling like mad at each other.

It was nearly six o'clock when we got home. Father was dressing for dinner. He was at his washstand in the passageway, in his trousers and undershirt, with his suspenders hanging down, sponging his face and head and snorting with pleasure.

"Clare!" Mother cried, as she ran in his bedroom. "Why did you never give me that ring?"

Father looked up from the wash-bowl, dripping with water. "What are you talking about?" he said. "Go away."

"Where did you put it, Clare?" Mother said urgently. "Don't pretend you don't know!"

Father rubbed his head and hair with his big Turkish towel and stared angrily at her. "Go away, Vinnie!" he roared. "I gave you a ring only last year. I don't know what on earth is the matter with you. I never saw such a woman!"

"I want that ring you gave Bessie Skinner, Clare!"

Father got red. He laughed. "Where did you hear about that?" he asked.

"Never mind where I heard about it," Mother said. "I want it. Is it in this bureau drawer?"

"Shut that drawer!" Father shouted. "No, it's not. Leave my things alone, Vinnie!"

I ran on upstairs to get ready for dinner myself.

A few days later, after Father had taken down from an upper shelf an old box of mementoes, he found the ring he had once given to his cousin and handed it over to Mother. It was a very little ring. Not nearly so handsome as those Mother had. Father had been young and unable to afford a better one when he had bought it. It was only a thin band of gold with two tiny white diamonds, but Mother clutched it victoriously.

"I don't see what you want that poor old thing for," Father said.

Mother didn't exactly know, either. She only knew that she felt much better, now that she had it. She looked at the two tiny diamonds, wondering what could be done with them. She looked speculatively at Father. Her eye fell on his shirt front.

"What do you wear those pearl studs all the time for?" she asked him.

"I don't," he said. "I haven't worn them for weeks. I just screwed them in tonight for a change."

"Your plain gold ones are handsomer, really," said Mother.

Father went back to his newspaper. Shirt studs didn't interest him. Or at least so he thought. He didn't know that he was wearing his full-dress pearls for the last time.

A few nights later a small box from Tiffany's arrived at the door—a box that Mother had been waiting for eagerly. It contained a new ring—a pretty little ring with three fine pearls in it and two tiny diamonds. Much handsomer than Bessie Skinner's.

"See my new ring, Clare!" she cried.

Father examined it but without recognizing the jewels. "More extravagance," he said, with a frown.

"But isn't it pretty?" said Mother.

"I don't say it's not pretty, Vinnie, but how much did it cost? I've given you enough rings by this time."

Mother gave him a kiss.

"It didn't cost anything, darling, except for the setting. And now that I've got this you needn't give me rings any more."

Father looked at her incredulously.

"What I'd really like now," Mother said, "would be a nice diamond necklace."

FATHER BRIGHTENS THE SICKROOM

Throughout Mother's illness, Father hadn't been very much troubled. But now that she was beginning to get well again, he felt quite alarmed, for he realized at last, as he watched her, how feeble she had become. He kept patting her hand and saying "Dear Vinnie," and telling her he couldn't stand it.

Mother was pleased by his being attentive. When she saw other women being fussed over by their husbands, she often wished she got more of such attentions. But she was not really the kind of woman to linger much over endearments. She liked things of that sort to be electric, and to come in quick flashes, and pass. She hadn't time or patience to give herself up to long interchanges.

So after Father, who wasn't very inventive, had patted her hand twenty times, she snatched it away in annoyance and said: "Stop it, Clare! That's enough!

"Get your hat and stick, dear," she added. "It's time you were starting."

Mrs. Nichols was giving a tea which Mother wished to hear all about, and she had coerced Father, much against his will, into saying he'd go. What had made him consent was his desire to do something for her. She said that if he told her about the tea it might brighten her up, and he felt that she probably needed a little amusement.

He looked spruce and handsome in his formal cutaway coat. Mother smiled at him. She felt she was being generous to Mrs. Nichols, and executive, too, to send Father there in her stead—such a distinguished-looking, ruddy, agreeable man would be a help at any tea. It would be pleasant for Father, besides. She only wished she could go, instead of sitting in bed with nothing more interesting to look forward to than chicken broth. Things tasted so good at a tea.

"Anything I can do for you while I'm out?" Father asked her.

"Yes, Clare," she said suddenly, "there *is* something I'd like. Do bring me some of those little sandwiches Mrs. Nichols has— they'd be nice with the broth."

"Sandwiches and *broth?*" Father said in dismay.

"No! Just sandwiches," Mother said. "Those little thin sandwiches. Bring some in your pocket."

"Oh, some sandwiches, eh?" Father put on his high hat, took his stick and gloves from the table, and left.

He enjoyed himself more than he expected to at the tea. Met some men he knew, and was spoken to by a great many ladies whom he knew more or less. It made him feel expansive and jovial to be kept busy responding to all of them.

He was on guard, however. There were some women present whom he knew of old and took care to avoid: women who talked every minute, or who had masculine airs, or who dressed like old frumps. But he picked out a good corner to sit in where there were none of these persons, and where he could be gallant in his jolly way to others of a much nicer kind. And their daughters. He had a cup of tea, too, and a plate of sandwiches that one of the attendants had given him.

As he munched them appreciatively, he remembered that he was to get some for Mother.

He looked around to see where the sandwiches had come from and observed a long table at the other side of the room piled high with delicacies. But how could he possibly march up to that table publicly, and amaze everyone by juggling the sticky things into his coat-tail pocket?

One of the young girls was asking him a question. He turned to her to respond. As their conversation went on, his mind went back again, once or twice, to the sandwiches, but he didn't see how he could go over there and put a supply in his pocket. It

would be an odd thing to do. He had never done such a thing
in his life. It had never even occurred to him to do a thing of that
kind. He was sure that Mother would understand how impossible
it was when he told her.

He had too good a time to leave early, and he stopped at the
club for a moment before walking leisurely home.

Mother's broth had been brought up to her and she was lying
there, waiting. She heard him let himself in the front door and
put away his hat and things in the coat closet. He seemed to take
forever to do it. She heard the closet door shut. She tasted her
broth. It was flat. But Father's step was coming along the hall
to her room now, at last.

He beamed cheerfully at her as he entered and started to sit
down in a chair.

"Don't sit on my sandwiches," she warned him.

He half put his hand to his coat-tails, then remembered, and
frowned.

"Oh, Clare!" Mother cried disappointedly. "Didn't you bring
them? It's been so tiresome sitting here waiting. Didn't you even
bring one?"

"Now wait," Father said, "wait a moment and let me explain."

"Weren't there any there?"

"Yes, but—"

"You *forgot* them!"

"No! I didn't forget them!" Father said crossly.

"Why didn't you bring me some, then?"

"Will—you—let—me—ex—plain?"

"Never mind. I'm tired," said Mother, "and I knew you
wouldn't anyway."

"I insist on your listening to me," Father shouted. "I intend
to be heard."

Mother lay back on her pillows, looking deeply hurt and
closing her eyes.

"The table was at one side of the room," Father began. "Over
here, say. There were the sandwiches, there. I remembered you

wanted some, and I noted where they were, several times. But—
they—it was impracticable, Vinnie. In short, there was no way
to do it."

"What did you do all the time, then?" Mother sighed. "Who
did you see?"

"I saw everybody," Father said. "I had a very nice talk with
—er—Mrs. Fisher. No, Folsom? Wait a moment. What is that
woman's name? She's a cousin of Mrs.—well, I can't remember,
but I know the name perfectly. Finley. No, not Finley. Anyway,
she lives on Park Avenue."

"Oh dear," Mother said. "And who else?"

"Well, let me see. Mrs. Palmer, of course."

"Mrs. Palmer! Why, she's in the South."

"Oh. Well, maybe it was Mrs.—er—what's-her-name, then.
The woman whose uncle owns that ugly house on Quaker Ridge."

"I don't know who you're talking about."

"Why, yes you do. You've seen him fifty times, damn it. The
man who drives that lopsided pair of flea-bitten grays."

"And you talked to *him?*"

"No! The confounded blatherskite. He wasn't there. I talked
with his aunt, I tell you. His niece, I mean. The one who looks
like an Eskimo."

"Can't you tell me about *anybody* who was there? Anybody at
all?"

"I can't remember all their names. No."

"Well, Clare!" Mother said. "I hope you spoke to Mrs.
Nichols."

"Yes, I did. We had quite a talk."

"What did she have on?"

"Let me think, now. Something fuzzy, I remember. With
chains."

"What color was it?"

"I think it was some shade of green."

"That's funny. She wore that green dress when she received
with her sister, last month."

"Maybe it wasn't green. Perhaps it was purple."

"Oh, Clare!"

"Good God!" Father roared. "Don't be so unreasonable. I can't give you an account of all the little details of every stitch she had on. I'm not a damned couturier, Vinnie."

"But you aren't telling me a thing about anybody," Mother wailed. "I did hope you'd bring home a little news for me, even if you didn't remember my sandwiches." She looked at him sharply. "Did you eat any yourself?"

"Yes," Father said, recollecting the taste with pleasure. "I had several. They were very nice."

"Oh, Clare!"

"Don't begin on that again," Father said. "I *wanted* to bring you some, Vinnie." He searched his mind perplexedly for a way to explain. But he didn't quite understand, himself, why he hadn't brought those sandwiches home. He looked helplessly at her.

"You never will do anything that you think isn't 'suitable,' " Mother said irritatedly.

"Why, of course I won't," he said, frowning. "Why should I?"

"Not even for me?"

"Oh, damn! Oh, damnation!" said Father.

MOTHER GETS AN ALLOWANCE

Mother came back from a trip to Egypt with a few hundred dollars left in her letter of credit, which, much against Father's will, she kept for her own. This Egyptian hoard lasted for years though only a few hundred dollars; but as it dwindled Mother grew worried and restless. It shouldn't have dwindled. It should have grown. She said that she should have something coming in every month. What she—and still less Father—didn't clearly realize was that she was half unconsciously groping toward a life of her own, in a random, haphazard, inactive way.

Some of the younger women whom Mother knew had been putting ideas into her head. They had told her that it was childish and undignified for her to have to keep asking Father for money to pay the household expenses; and worse still to have to struggle with him over each dollar. The right way to fix it was to have an allowance. But although she listened with interest to this tempting idea Mother had reservations. She had heard two kinds of stories about allowances and one friend had given her some solemn warnings against them.

However the younger women told Mother, "Just estimate how much you need for the house and yourself, and have Mr. Day hand you a monthly check with no talk about it."

Mother told them that they didn't know Mr. Day. She really liked the plan they suggested. The only thing was that she couldn't figure how much to ask for. If she asked for too little she'd be in a trap, and she didn't want to get in any trap— especially one of her own making. On the other hand, she knew it would be no use at all to ask Father for any very large sum because he wouldn't give it. Yet she knew very well that any allowance that wasn't large might sometimes be too little. What would she do then? She didn't want to be always trying to live at some fixed monthly rate, there were too many unexpected emergencies. She felt that the plan wasn't safe.

She talked it over with Father, however, just to see what he'd say. Father said a great deal. He said that of all the damned nonsense he had ever heard this was the damnedest. He told Mother that she was a lovely woman and he was very fond of her, but that neither she nor any of her family knew the first thing about money.

Mother immediately told him she knew as much about money as he did. But she secretly realized that she was not good at figures. She wouldn't have put it that way, even in her own thoughts—she would have merely said that she didn't like figures or that figures were tiresome. The idea of having some money of her own every month was attractive, but the prospect of having to make careful estimates wasn't.

She played with the notion for years without really pushing it. She liked to poke Father up on the subject. When he made a row about some bill, and when she had no good defense, she counter-attacked him by declaring that it was all his own fault, and that he wouldn't have any such troubles if he gave her a proper allowance. He replied that he would have nothing but trouble if he did anything as crazy as that. And in the excitement of denouncing allowances he would lose sight of the bill.

Father's opinion of the financial ability of women was small, also the custom of the times and of his generation made Mother's talk of an allowance seem preposterous to him.

Even as recently as thirty or forty years ago, in New York, a lady was not supposed to have any occasion for cash. Two or three dollars to keep in her purse for car-fares and candy was plenty. There were very few cabs in the streets, and it wasn't customary for a woman to hail one. A lady usually had an escort anyway, and he, of course, paid all expenses. If she had any shopping to do she made her purchases at places where she had charge accounts. If she lunched out without an escort it wasn't at a restaurant but at the home of some friend.

Ladies were elaborately dressed beings in long, trailing skirts, and whenever they walked in the street, they had to hold up these skirts with one hand. They had to do this gracefully, of course, and at just the right height, so as not to reveal too much of their ankles and yet keep the hem free from dirt. With the other hand they carried an umbrella or parasol, or on cold days a muff.

In the side seam of their skirts was a pocket which held a tiny purse, a handkerchief, and a silver-topped vial of smelling-salts to use if they felt faint. But this pocket was not easy to get at, and it was embarrassing to feel around for it, so when women got on a street-car they tucked a nickel inside their buttoned gloves. All conductors were supposed to lend a hand to help them get on and off.

When I was a little boy Mother wore bonnets, tied under her chin with gay ribbons. Later on, when bonnets went out, she had a hard time with stiff hats. Ladies' hats were perched up on top of their hair, and although they were pinned on with long jeweled pins they were insecure in a wind, and their hair was skewered with quantities of hair-pins, which kept falling out. No matter how thoroughly ladies were buttoned up, they were always coming apart. Their escorts protected them however, swelling with whiskers and grandeur.

Men knew the world. Women didn't. Women were not fitted to deal with the world. A wife's fortune, if she had one, was usually controlled by her husband. And men's manner in supplying women with money was supposed to be tender but firm. This attitude was so general, and so few of Mother's friends were exempt from it, that in spite of her self-reliant nature she accepted it as inevitable. The idea of her ever becoming independent, even in a small way, in money matters, and having a life of her own seemed a dream.

Nevertheless Father felt they should be business-like and one of the great objections, he said, to giving Mother an allowance was that she would give it all to those parsons. He said the

minute he died she'd give all of his money to them too. Or she'd
lend it to one of those incompetent friends of hers.

He had plenty of reasons to think this, for once in a while the
Rev. Dr. Garden, the rector of our church, would drop in to see
Mother. He usually left a loving message of some kind for Father
—at any rate Father always heard that he'd been there. And he
didn't like it. If he himself was at home at the time, it was all
right, because in that case the rector got nothing more than a
cup of tea from his visit and he departed as poor as when he
came. But when any clergyman succeeded in seeing Mother
alone, he always got something out of her, and not only that but
it was invariably something of Father's.

Mother explained again and again that Dr. Garden had to
visit all his parishioners, and that he didn't ask them for anything,
at least not very often, he merely talked about the needs of the
parish and the opportunities. However, Father remained down
on all the clergy. He also remained down on all charities except
the Charity Organization Society and its woodyard. This was
another trouble, for when appeals came to help a hospital, or a
fresh-air fund, or a home for orphans, Mother couldn't bear not
to give something. But Father would never give her money for
any such purpose. He said charity began at home and if he was
going to give money outside he must investigate first. He asked
questions. He said he had never heard of whatever hospital had
sent the last circular. He looked at the signature to the appeal for
colored orphans suspiciously, and wanted to know "who the
devil is this Father O'Brien?"

Mother loathed these inquisitions. So she would tuck a five-
dollar bill in the envelope and mail it quickly, and not dare to
tell Father.

As years went on however, and as he gradually lost all hope of
molding Mother into his pattern he began to admit that the
allowance plan might not be so bad—if it worked. And the more
Mother heard how many other women there were who now had
them, the more confident she began to feel that she could do it if
they could.

What finally brought the thing to a point was a milliner's bill from Mlle. Mimi. Father came to Mother's room holding it out between his thumb and one finger as though it were almost too repulsive to touch.

"I will not send this person a check," he said.

Mother flamed up at him. "Why, Clare! It's the only hat I've bought since November, and it was reduced from forty dollars."

"I do not object to your buying a hat if you need one," he answered, "though it is beyond my comprehension why you require so many, but the person from whom you bought it isn't fit to be in the hat business, or in any other kind either."

"Poor Mimi!" Mother interrupted. "She does sell her things very cheap."

"Her bill gives no evidence of any such habit," said Father. "But that is not what I'm talking about."

"Well, really," Mother cried, "why don't you *say* what you're talking about then? You just stand there going on and on talking about this wretched bill."

"If you will be so kind," Father elaborately and sternly rejoined, "as to cease interrupting me for a moment and allow me to speak, I will tell you. I have made out thousands of checks in my life, payable to this or that firm or person, but I never have and I never will write a check that says 'pay to the order of Mimi.' "

"I never went there before," Mother said, "but it's a very nice place and I don't see why you object to it."

"I object to it because this confounded person doesn't put her name on her bills," Father shouted. "What the devil is her name anyhow?"

"Why you saw it yourself, Clare. It's Mimi!"

"Mimi what? Mimi O'Brien? Mimi Jones? Mimi Weinstein?"

"How do I know! It's just Mimi."

"It isn't just Mimi. She must have some other name, damn it. And you can tell her to print it on her bill if she wants to be paid. I will not make out a check payable to Tom, or to Dick, or to Mimi. It's impertinent of her to expect it."

The final outcome of the conversation was that Father agreed to give Mother an allowance although he was still in doubt just what it would cover.

"I hope to God it will work," he said pessimistically.

What happened was that Mother, despite her charitable leaks, began hoarding. She had a nest egg and was determined to add to it. The household expenses she still considered Father's duty. She had got too accustomed to his paying the regular bills for her to change easily and pay for them herself. As this began to dawn on Father his surprise and grief were acute.

"It doesn't cover a single thing," he said to me one evening.

However, the matter was settled in Mother's mind. And Father was never allowed to pass up a single month. It was not an easy allowance to get, it didn't just come. But it was something due her, and before the month was ended she would receive it, exhausted but triumphant.

Father, when at last he had brought it home, would be extra glum. On these nights he sat in his room, or on the piazza, if we were in the country, talking to himself a long time. It was impossible to catch the words at first, but gradually as his feelings reached a climax he got up and addressed the universe reproachfully, and always in the same words.

"Just an added expense," he groaned. "Oh damn."

FATHER AND OLD MOTHER EARTH

Father said he was "getting damn tired of being cooped up in the city all summer," while Mother and we boys were enjoying ourselves at New London. He could spend only his week-ends with us there. He wanted some place nearer town. His former partner, Mr. John A. Gwynne, had bought a pleasant country place in Rye, only twenty-odd miles from New York. Not far away, in Harrison, old Mr. Macy had laid out a large private park and had built several cottages in it to rent. Father rented one.

George and I came home from boarding-school to that large private park. We disliked it. Mr. Macy's men were always working at it to make it look trim and neat. It was the kind of park that boys were not allowed to muss up. There was nowhere we could play games of any kind except on one tennis-court.

We not only played tennis on that court, we held a track meet there every day. Each of us four brothers became an athletic club, all by himself, and he entered a complete team of athletes consisting solely of himself in every event of each meet. Harold, the youngest, called himself The Pastime Athletic Club, and, although he was a roly-poly, fat little boy, he often won the standing high jump by means of his handicap, and even the hundred-yard dash.

What with all our jumps and shot-puttings and dashes and heel-and-toe walks, that tennis-court had a hard time, and Mr. Macy's men had about all they could do to repair it. Meanwhile Mr. Macy himself began to have a hard time with Father. Father had taken a deep interest in the park—deeper than we felt it deserved, and much deeper than Mr. Macy seemed to find quite convenient. Mr. Macy liked his tenants to appreciate and admire his park, but he turned out to be unreceptive to advice about changing it.

He had fenced in all the roads he had built, with fences of neat iron posts, strung with wires. Father said these were ugly. Those roads, he said, should be lined with hedges. Mr. Macy said he didn't want hedges. Father looked up the best kinds and recommended privet as most suitable for Mr. Macy.

The roads were surfaced with coarse bits of blue-stone which had sharp, cutting edges. This blue-stone was supposed to get ground down gradually till it made a hard road-bed. As it didn't get ground down as evenly as it should, Mr. Macy was always renewing it, and dumping loads of fresh stone on the bad places —stone with fresh cutting edges. This was hard on shoes, bicycles, horses' feet and the thin rubber tires we had on one of our carriages. Father looked up the best kinds of surfacing and recommended trap-rock.

Many years later Mr. Macy became a convert to privet, and planted the borders of all his roads with fresh green hedges— which really was an improvement. But he stuck to his blue-stone, and Father and he were still arguing away about trap-rock, pro and con, when the automobile era overtook them and put them both out of date.

Meanwhile, even that very first summer, Father said he liked Harrison, and he found that he liked it better and better the longer he stayed. He began to talk about buying a place there, to settle down in for good. He considered making Mr. Macy an offer for one of his cottages. He liked Mr. Macy, and, in spite of all the advice that Father tendered, Mr. Macy liked him. But somehow there didn't seem to be room for them both in the same park.

Adjoining the park was an old run-down forty-acre farm belonging to a farmer named Smith. Mr. Macy regarded this farm as an eye-sore and he greatly desired to buy it. The difficulty was that he found Mr. Smith hard to deal with. Mr. Smith was one of the oldest inhabitants of that section, and he didn't like it

when he heard down at the postoffice that his farm had been
called an eye-sore. Year in and year out he had refused even to
listen to offers. His farm was not for sale. For some reason or
other however he turned out to be willing to talk the matter
over with Father.

Father wanted to buy that piece of land. He climbed over the
old stone wall night after night to have a chat with Mr. Smith,
and see whether they could come to terms. He always came back
from these visits fervently declaring that he didn't like farms. He
said that farming might be all right enough if it was carried on
properly but the trouble was that it usually wasn't. He talked
disparagingly about the ragged overalls that most farmers wore,
and their slouchy way of walking and talking. On our horseback
rides in the back country, when we passed by a farm, Father
would point out its neglected, unpainted sheds and say, "Pah!
What a damned low-class way of living!"

I didn't agree with him. Boys were always kept dressed up in
those days, and some of them didn't mind it, but I could never
master the secret of feeling at ease in fine clothes. I even had
secret leanings toward overalls, and the more ragged the better.
I liked to see a long dripping watering trough in the farmyard,
and horses pushing their noses into the water, with their traces
knotted up at their sides. I liked to watch cows lounging along
as they filed into a barn, and hay bursting out of a hay-mow,
and noisy chickens crowding around a back door to be fed.

There was one farm I especially liked where we sometimes
bought cider. I knew old Eben Sedley who ran it, and when I
was out on a ride by myself I used to stop there and listen to him.
I was a city boy, I knew nothing whatever about how a plow
handle felt, and Mr. Sedley's remarks about his corn or his
potatoes were meaningless to me, but as he talked on I somehow
understood that he was engaged in a long and strange struggle,
and that the force he was struggling with, Nature, was too big
to control. He reminded me of Amos, the whaler, with whom
I had talked in New London. I respected men like farmers and
sailors who worked with the soil or at sea. They seemed to me to

have a look of long-suffering endurance about them, as though
they had learned not to be much surprised by calamities.

Of course I said nothing to Father about any of this. Father
seemed to regard all calamities as things that must be controlled.
They were manifestations of a rebellious and unruly spirit in
nature. They were a species of intentional perverseness which
mankind ought to discipline. He often said that old Eben Sedley
was shiftless and slack, and that Mr. Smith wasn't much better,
and that if he, Father, ever succeeded in buying Mr. Smith's
farm, it wouldn't be long before that piece of land wouldn't
know itself.

In spite of Father's objections to farms, he said he was fond
of the country. He liked fresh country air. He liked to gallop on
horseback along shady lanes and dirt roads. The roads had to
smell right, however. They could smell of hay, for example, or
flowers, but they must by no means smell of pigs. The trouble
was that every once in so often they did smell of pigs. Father
would then declare that this was intolerable, and demand to be
informed why such a nuisance was allowed to exist.

I never felt sure myself whether Father liked the country or
not. When it was on its good behavior he did, but whenever it
wasn't he was rather severe with the country. His attitude toward
it wasn't quietly stoical, like Mr. Sedley's; Father was a far more
hearty lord of the soil, and a great deal more hectoring.

He especially disapproved of the country wherever it was
wild and uncultivated. It ought at least to have trees growing
on it or animals grazing. He was not interested in wasteland, he
said. He had no objection at all to allowing the sea to be wild.
The sea, like the air, was an element, and wildness was suitable
to it. Father would not have felt at home with tame elements or
enjoyed living among them. Good, roaring, wet, tempestuous
winds and rough seas gave him pleasure. But the land was another matter entirely. The land was more female. Its duty was to
bring forth its fruits in abundance for Father, not forgetting addi-
tional supplies of hay and oats for our horses. Land should do all
this readily too, and give men well-flavored products. If it didn't,

Father despised either the fields or the spineless fellows who tilled them for not being firm with those fields and making them do what they should.

Father's feeling toward old Mother Earth in short was not sentimental. He was prepared to be very fond of her, but only if she did her part.

When he and I got back from our ride together, early one morning, Mr. Smith was waiting to see him. I dismounted and went on indoors to breakfast. In a few minutes Father came in too and said to Mother, "It's settled. I've bought it." The Smiths, I learned a day later, would move away the next month; and after that, even if Nature continued to misbehave elsewhere, it looked as though she'd have to mind her p's and q's on Father's new farm.

FATHER INVESTS IN A LIVERY

Father's first coachman, Morgan, had never been a coachman before. He had worked in the Riding Club's stables and it was there that we got to know him. He seemed to be just the right man for us but the one objection was that he had no livery. Father blamed him for this. In fact he came near not taking him. The idea seemed to be that a man who had no livery wasn't a genuine coachman. All genuine coachmen had liveries, just as all good dogs had collars. Morgan said, "Where would I be getting a livery, sir? A man like meself hasn't the money, and I never heard tell of any coachman that bought his own anyhow." Mother said that then he should have brought a livery from his previous place. Morgan touched his forelock and respectfully explained to us that this wasn't done, and that anyway the livery hadn't belonged to him but to the Riding Club.

None of Father's New England ancestors had ever had a coachman in livery. Father felt it was a great expense. He said he didn't like it. But as it was considered impossible for a coachman to drive our dog-cart, or even sit on the back seat, without wearing a high hat and a white ascot tie and either a bright green or blue suit, with nickel-plated buttons, Father sent Morgan to a medium-priced shop to get his outfit. He saw to it, too, that Morgan's suit was of good strong material, so that he never would have to buy him another livery for a great many years.

Morgan was an alert, hopeful man, and we liked him, but he had done better as a stable-man at the Riding Club than he did as a coachman. So long as we had only two horses and a dog-cart he got along pretty well, but when in the course of time we got a third horse the strain made him nervous. He had always been fond of his liquor, it appeared. Now he got so he depended on it. As a result, coming to New York on the night boat from the country one autumn, feeling weighed down with the duties and responsibilities we had placed on his shoulders by entrusting him with three costly horses and Topsy the cat, he sat up all night trying to keep his eyes open and dismally drowning his worries. When he arrived in New York in the morning and came to report on his journey, he stood in the hall, pale and speechless, staring vacantly at us, then collapsed on the hatrack, in tears, and confessed that Topsy was lost.

He was immediately discharged, and he stayed discharged for over a week, all of which time he spent—or declared to us that he spent—on the boat, making inquiries and running down clews, but in vain, for Topsy never was found.

One night he surreptitiously came back to our house with a basket. He was let in the basement door without our knowing it. He left the basket and fled. Margaret, the cook, then came upstairs, with her lips tightly pursed and yet with a pleading look on her face, and asked Father and Mother if they would please kindly step down to the kitchen. We all trooped down at once. There, on the floor, in Topsy's old basket, was a new-born lamb.

"What's this miserable thing?" Father demanded.

We boys poked at the strange object, curiously. It shut its eyes and said, "Ba-a."

Margaret said Morgan had told her that he had got this lamb at the butcher's. He had apparently intended it to be a peace offering. It wasn't taken as such. If Morgan had been present, he would have been discharged all over again and for good, for daring to incommode Father with this attempt at atonement.

The Day family didn't know what on earth to do with that lamb. They couldn't bring themselves to connive at its murder and send it back to the butcher. Yet to bring up a lamb on Madison Avenue seemed quite a problem. We boys were all in favor of keeping it, hoping that it soon would grow up and become a great big ram with curved horns. We planned to chase it up and down stairs, and sic it at other boys, and hide it underneath the piano. At the moment however it was so weak and wobbly that it could hardly stand up. It just lay in its basket beside the kitchen range and plaintively bleated for milk.

Margaret petted it and warmed up saucers of milk for it, and offered to let us feed it too. We boys didn't see any fun in feeding warm milk to a lamb. We wanted to put its basket upside down on top of it, as we'd done with Topsy, and then poke it up and make it drag the basket around on the floor. When Margaret stood her ground and shooed us off, we had to drop that idea, but we felt that she was depriving the lamb of having any good times at all.

It ended in the lamb's being sent out to Audubon Park, a tract of wooded land between the Hudson River and what is now upper Broadway, where Aunty Jane's country home was. Tall apartment houses and the Hispanic Museum are standing today where that lamb used to nibble the grass, alongside my cousins' pet rabbits.

Morgan was taken back as our coachman after a suitable period, during which he was supposed to be sitting in purgatory and cleansing himself of his sins, but still he was never quite forgiven for losing old Topsy. He worried about it; he knew he was under a cloud. Furthermore we had discharged him so often that it had dampened his spirits. Iron discipline, which strengthens some natures, had completely floored Morgan's. He grew worse and worse. Father had kept him years longer than he wanted to, because of that livery. He now at last hardened his heart and told Morgan to go.

In choosing a new man Father and Mother tried to be guided by their experience. They decided that there were two fixed requirements that they must now keep in mind, aside from honesty, industry, steadiness and knowing how to take care of horses. One was that the man must be a total abstainer who hated strong drink, and the other was that in order to wear that livery he must be the same size as Morgan.

A series of men, all of wrong sizes, came to our house, one by one, and put on Morgan's livery in the basement before coming upstairs to be interviewed. They one and all insisted that it was a good fit. Tall men whose bare wrists hung down, red and hairy, below Morgan's coat-cuffs, came boldly upstairs like scarecrows, trying in vain to look natty. Little men appeared with only the tips of their fingers showing and the coat flapping around them. All had their fists full of good references that smelled of horses and harness dressing, and if these references were to be believed, not a man of them ever got drunk.

They were all sent away. Whether it was that the marks of drink showed on them, in spite of their references, or whether they made too disreputable an appearance in poor Morgan's livery, none of them quite suited Father. They didn't look right, he said. The only one of them who seemed really eligible was a severe and respectable man who came up from the basement carrying Morgan's coat on his arm. It would fit him, he said, but he would prefer not to wear it. He wanted a new one. He was sent packing instantly for having high and lofty ideas.

Another man with excellent references came the very next evening. He was a round jolly man with an honest eye. Father said after questioning him that he could see he knew horses. His name was O'Dowd, and in addition to his references he had brought a certificate with him, signed by two parish priests, saying that the bearer had a wonderful character and never touched liquor. The only objection to him was that he was fatter than Morgan. He had managed to squeeze himself into Morgan's coat somehow, however, and although some of the buttons wouldn't button he said "it could be easy let out," and furthermore it would take him no time at all to train down. He chuckled and said all he needed was plenty of work.

As he seemed to have the right attitude about this, O'Dowd was engaged, on the distinct understanding however that his weight must come down at once. He immediately went into training. He drew in his stomach every time Mother looked at him, and he rubbed his hands with delight when Father bought a new pair of horses, which made five in all, a stanhope and a victoria to add to our dog-cart, and a new set of harness. O'Dowd busily trotted around the stable attending to these, and said that with all that to do surely any man would peel like an onion.

Mother kept declaring that she couldn't see that he got any thinner. She complained that he "bulged." Sitting behind him every day in the victoria while he drove her about, she noticed this much more than Father, who used the stanhope and drove his horses himself. She also said that O'Dowd had the largest ears a man ever had. This was probably true. At any rate, as they stuck out straight, they looked it. They were red, thick and hairy, and on some afternoons they got redder, when Mother, sitting below looking up at them, couldn't get her mind off them, and made some remark about their unfortunate size to a friend.

Another objection to O'Dowd was that he had too many children. He had three when he came, and although he was warned to stop they kept coming until he had seven. There were more little O'Dowds on the Day place than there were little Day boys.

O'Dowd was instructed to keep them close to the stable, and on no account to let them be seen near the garden or lawn. This left them practically no place to play but the manure pit and paddock. One or another of them was always venturing out to trespass on those forbidden acres when no one was watching, and scampering wildly back through the bushes when his crime was discovered.

The eldest boy, Morris, was held to blame, by both O'Dowd and ourselves, for every bit of disgraceful behavior on the part of his little brothers. He was a thin, lanky boy, with sad eyes and a querulous voice. As O'Dowd had all he could do, grooming the horses, cleaning the harness, and driving, the responsibilities of fatherhood fell more and more upon Morris. "The melancholy Morris," as Mother sympathetically called him. When the district school opened in the fall, we would sometimes come upon a procession of small O'Dowds on the road, led by their pale eldest brother, walking to or from the dingy, wooden schoolhouse. By that time all youngness had gone out of Morris, and he walked with a round-shouldered stoop.

The district school was not far from our place. It was rickety-looking and old. One summer evening a citizens' meeting was

held in it, to vote on building a new little schoolhouse with
modern improvements. Father heard of this at the last moment,
just in time to walk to the school after dinner and enter a protest.
He had paid enough taxes as it was, he told Mother, and he
didn't propose to pay any more.

He found that the meeting was in full swing as he went in the
door. A man with a loud bellowing voice was haranguing those
present, urging them to vote for this splendid and much-needed
improvement. He had seven fine children to send to it himself,
he declaimed, and if God was good to him maybe he'd have seven
more.

The room was so thick with pipe and cigar smoke that it was
hard to make faces out, and Father could scarcely believe at first
that it was O'Dowd who was bellowing. None of us had ever
heard his voice raised above a respectful low key. But it was he,
no mistake. "O'Dowd!" Father called sharply. "What are you
doing here? Stop that damned noise at once."

It was the voice of authority, and this was the nineties.
O'Dowd wilted, touched his forelock, said "Yes, sir," and looked
for his hat.

"Go outside and wait," Father said.

"That man isn't a citizen of Harrison," Father said to the
meeting. "He doesn't pay taxes. I do. What is all this nonsense
about? The property owners of this neighborhood don't want a
new school."

"Mr. O'Dowd said he wanted it," somebody got up and said.

Father stared at him, and motioned him with his cane to sit
down. "O'Dowd is my coachman," he said. "He doesn't know
what he wants. There's no one else in my part of the township
who has any children to send. And if a new school is put up in
my neighborhood and I move away, there will be no O'Dowds to
go to it either. I move that this plan be quashed."

A citizen who wanted a new school over on his side of the
township, instead of on ours, quickly seconded the motion. There
was no more debate. It was carried.

Father walked home angrily and in silence, with O'Dowd in

the rear. At our gate Father halted. He had put up, in spite of Mother's objections, with O'Dowd's staying fat, he had permitted this ungrateful man to bulge, year after year, on the box, he had striven to overlook his criminal carelessness in having too many children, and now if it hadn't been for Father's promptness, O'Dowd would have raised Father's taxes. "What have you to say for yourself?" Father asked him.

O'Dowd had been thinking things over. "I niver thought of the taxes, sir," he explained. "It won't happen again."

It didn't look at that time as though the O'Dowds would ever pay taxes themselves. The blackest part of their family outlook was the stupidity of poor Morris. O'Dowd shook his head over Morris. "He's not taking to the horses," he said.

Neither Morris nor any of the rest of us knew in those days that the era of coachmen was ending, and the era of automobiles was about to begin. When it came, the melancholy Morris, who had never liked horses, woke up. He had apparently been born with an instinctive love for gasoline engines. If they hadn't been invented, he'd have gone through life as a second-rate coachman or maybe a failure. As it was, he became one of the best of the very first crop of chauffeurs. He not only made better wages than any old coachman, he was regularly taken to Europe, where he drove his employer through countries that no other O'Dowd of his line had seen. One of his brothers went along as a helper, on the third of these trips—Patrick Gorman O'Dowd, who had been the most impish and wild of the lot, as a boy, but who later became a two-hundred-pound plumber, with a big gold watch and chain. Patrick didn't care much for scenery, and he had a poor opinion of Europe. He inspected it thoroughly, but only from one point of view. "The plumbing in some of them castles there," he told me, years afterwards, "would make any decent American ashamed to be using it." He looked around to make sure that no lady was near who might hear him, cupped his hand to my ear, and wheezed in a shocked, portly whisper, "Just a hole in the wall."

MOTHER AND OUR WICKED MARE

Mother never thought of the horse as the friend and companion of man. She looked at all horses suspiciously. Perhaps they were not wild animals, in the sense in which lions and zebras were wild, but still there was something strange about them. They weren't really tame, like our dogs. She loved dogs. She liked ponies too, they were more our own size, but horses were too large to be trusted, and they had ironshod feet.

Once in a while she grew fond of some special horse after she had watched it for years, but even then she never undertook to drive it herself. Driving was a man's job. That didn't mean that she thought men in general were good drivers, however. Mother hadn't any more confidence in men in general than she had in horses. Men were always assuring her that they knew how to do this or that, when they didn't at all. If it had been safe to do so, she would have liked to trust herself in their hands, it would have been so convenient, for as she was a woman she felt that she had to have certain things done for her. But men, although stronger, were childish. They greatly over-estimated their ability as drivers, for instance. All of them firmly believed that they understood horses, whereas Mother knew better. When she saw a horse and a man having trouble, she privately bet on the horse.

In the nineties everybody used horses—if in no other way at least in horse-cars and buses. Our family needed several every summer when we lived in the country. One was reserved solely as a saddle-horse for Father to ride. Father rode early every morning before breakfast and then took a train to the city. The other horses were used for all sorts of things. What with catching trains, mornings, and meeting them again, afternoons, and going for the mail, or taking some of us down to the beach, or trotting along the dusty country roads with Mother when she paid an afternoon call on some friend three or four miles away, or when she went to the village to shop, our horses were kept pretty busy, and when one of them had to be turned out to rest, it was hard on the others.

Mother at last went to Father about it. She said that things had come to a point where we had to have one more horse.

Father said, "The trouble with you, Vinnie, is that you don't use enough forethought. You don't plan these things out. With a little careful management you can get along with what we have now."

Mother replied that there wasn't a woman on earth who could plan every minute, and she'd like to see forethought pull the station-wagon when Brownie went lame, but if we used Father's saddle-horse in the dog-cart perhaps that would do.

From Father's point of view this was blasphemous. "Any time that I can't have even one horse in condition to ride," he told Mother, "I'll sell the whole lot of them, hide and hair, and the family can walk. Do 'em good."

He got thinking things over after this conversation however, and made up his mind that he'd better do something about it and look around for some decent animal that could be got cheap. He heard of one soon at the club, a dark brown, muscular mare.

The member of the club who owned her had gone abroad and couldn't be reached. He had posted the mare for sale with the cryptic phrase, "Warranted sound." The usual guarantee, when there was any, was "Warranted sound, kind and willing," but we thought that perhaps the omission was inadvertent. The price was low. Father bought her.

This mare's name was Uarda, a strange name, but somehow it fitted her. We heard later that an Egyptian princess named Uarda, of evil repute, had lived a bad life in some dynasty centuries back. Whether Uarda the mare had come from Egypt too, nobody knew. She looked it, however. She looked like the horse of some genie in the *Arabian Nights*. She was slithery, bony and lean, and her coat had a glitter, and her eyes were unnaturally greenish and wild and unfathomable.

There was plenty of work in her. She never went lame or got tired. She seemed made of steel. Sudden sights or sounds that made other horses shy, Uarda ignored. She was wholly without fear, and there wasn't an ounce of love in her either. She was oblivious of the Day family, and not interested in her surroundings.

O'Dowd the coachman was frankly afraid of her. "She's always brooding, sir," he whispered to Father, as though she could understand what he said and revenge herself on him. She certainly had a remote and contemptuous look.

Uarda's contempt could be seen in her eye. Her hatred she expressed with her tail. All carriage horses were docked in those days, many of them too much, but Uarda from O'Dowd's point of view hadn't been docked enough. She had an extra long bone in her tail, he explained, and it had only been shortened a trifle. And the muscle in her tail, which was strong as steel, hadn't been nicked. The purpose of nicking the under muscle was to weaken it, so that a horse's little bobbed tail would stand cocked up and look stylish, and aside from looks there was a practical advantage to this, because it prevented a horse from catching a rein under his tail and clamping it down. When that happened, he couldn't be reined in or guided, and now and then that led to a runaway or some bad collision.

Humanitarians were always denouncing men who docked horses' tails. A horse with a docked tail was helpless in fly-time, they argued, and when it was chopped off it hurt. Father pished at these arguments. He said that it wasn't his fault if there were flies in the world, and that nobody wept over him when his teeth were chopped by the dentist.

He wouldn't have a horse docked himself though. He simply bought them that way. When O'Dowd wanted Uarda's tail shortened, Father wouldn't allow it. O'Dowd shook his head over this. He said we'd live to regret it.

We came to see what he meant. As Uarda sullenly trotted along, thinking of sin, or black magic, she would flail her tail round and round powerfully, like a propeller. Sooner or later, no matter how careful O'Dowd was, she'd catch a rein under it, and hold that rein tight as a vise. With some horses you could watch till the muscle relaxed for a moment and then vigorously yank the rein out, but no one could do this with Uarda. The only thing to do was to reach over the dashboard and yank at her tail, and yank hard with all your strength too, and yank over and over, hoping that she wouldn't lash out and kick you before you got the rein loose. This was an undignified performance to go through, and O'Dowd felt it shamed him in public.

What mortified him still more was the way Mother behaved at such moments. At the very first sign of trouble Mother's one idea was to get out of the carriage just as quick as she could. She couldn't jump, her skirts were too long and voluminous and there were too many petticoats under them, but she could and did shout to O'Dowd to stop, at the top of her voice, and then gather up her dress in one hand and clutch at the arm of the seat and feel around with her foot for the inadequate little round metal steps, which always seemed so high from the ground when she hadn't any horse-block to step out onto, and then while the springy surrey was shaking, and giving a bit on one side, she would precariously descend in a hurry, getting dust or mud on her skirts from the wheel, and more on her high buttoned shoes in the old-fashioned dirt road.

Standing there in safety she would stare at O'Dowd while he yanked. She would also make comments. When this happened way off on some deserted road it wasn't so bad, but sometimes it happened on Purchase Street in Rye, where other coachmen were watching, or outside old Mr. Raser's store opposite the station in Harrison. "Mercy on us, what takes you so *long*, O'Dowd?" Mother would cry. "If you can't drive any better than that, why don't you say so?"

O'Dowd was a good-natured soul, but he knew he could drive as well as most coachmen, and he used to get silently exasperated on these occasions. It was useless for him, though, to attempt to lay the blame upon Uarda, or to say he had never seen such a horse in all his born days. "Never mind about all your born days,

O'Dowd," Mother would tell him impatiently. "That horse knows more than you do, this minute, and I should think that you'd be ashamed to sit there and admit it."

As O'Dowd had never even dreamt of admitting it, this kind of attack used to stagger him. "I know as much as any horse in the stable, Mum," he would begin, in confusion.

"But you ought to know *more* than an animal!" Mother would interrupt swiftly. "That's what we pay you your wages for, O'Dowd. You're a *man,* not a horse. If you don't know any more than our horses you ought not to be driving them. It really isn't safe for me to go out with you."

"Not an accident have I ever had on my soul, Mrs. Day, in all the twenty years that—"

"You'll have one this very minute if you can't get that rein out," Mother would interrupt sharply.

As O'Dowd knew that this was highly probable he would concentrate upon Uarda, and when he had got her under control again Mother would climb back into the carriage, still talking, and off they would go.

Somehow O'Dowd never seemed to feel any resentment toward Mother, after a scene of this sort. He understood Mother. His hostility was all toward that mare. On Uarda's bad days he got into such a bitter state, as he drove her about, that he used to carry on a one-sided conversation with her, in a low growling mutter. "Oho! That's the way of it, is it? Trying it on me again! Ye black-hearted Eye-gyptian! Bad scran to ye, ye limb of the Divil, ye!"

After a while he invented an arrangement of buckles and straps, which moored Uarda's tail to the shafts. This contraption left her tail just leeway enough for her to arch it but kept her from flailing it around or getting it over the reins. She was in a cold fury about it. O'Dowd wore a broad grin.

These moorings were so elaborate that they were unsightly, however. They looked very odd. Mother complained that everyone stared at them, which was perfectly true. People even asked questions. Mr. Read, who was a judge at the horseshow, and who had supposed himself to be familiar with every kind of harness there was, couldn't get his eyes off them when Mother went to call on his wife and when he came forward to help her get out at his door. "Ah," he said, staring fixedly at the bright silver buckle in the middle of Uarda's slick tail, and the leather shrouds and stays that led down from it to either shaft, "Ah! May I ask what this—er—? Why this—?"

"Oh, don't pay any attention to that, Mr. Read," Mother answered. "Our coachman seems to feel he can't drive without it. It's just some idea of O'Dowd's." And she hurried up the piazza steps, leaving O'Dowd red and speechless, and taking Mr. Read with her, so mystified by what he had seen and so baffled for the moment by Mother that he became speechless too.

As for Father, he said it was a disgusting arrangement, the first time he saw it, and he ordered O'Dowd to "remove that infernal rigging at once." But the fact remained that when we used them those straps were effective, and every time we went out without them, we got into trouble. Uarda never actually ran away when she got a rein under her tail, but she never would quite admit that she wasn't going to bolt, and she had such a wicked look about her that we knew things were dangerous. We all gradually came to tolerate letting O'Dowd strap her up, even Father. There was really only one safe alternative, when he left O'Dowd home and drove us around in the low surrey himself, and that was to hold the reins up very high, at the level almost of his nose. Father couldn't and wouldn't do that.

One day Father and Mother and George and I were out in the surrey. Father was driving of course, and I was sitting beside him on the front seat. Uarda was in a vile mood. Her tail strained at O'Dowd's straps and buckles. It writhed like a snake. Two or three miles from home she triumphantly tore it loose. "Oh, oh!" Mother wailed.

"Be quiet, confound it," said Father. "Clarence, can you strap it down again?"

I got out and tried but I couldn't strap it securely enough. Only O'Dowd knew the secret. No matter how I adjusted the buckles and hauled on the straps, Uarda contemptuously flicked her tail out. "Take it off altogether," Father ordered. "We'll never get home at this rate."

"I want to get out then," said Mother. "I'd much rather walk."

Father gritted his teeth. "Sit still," he said sharply. "I've driven horses since I was a boy."

Back-seat driving was invented long before motors, and when Mother was nervous she had a really deadly gift for this art. She tried to control herself that afternoon, at Father's repeated requests, but she couldn't. Uarda's tail was too much for her.

"I only bought this horse to please your mother," Father said in a loud, oratorical tone, as though he were making a speech, addressing his sons and the landscape in general as Uarda trotted along, "and if I ever saw any animal that came straight from hell—"

"She's swishing it, Clare," Mother called to him.

"She can swish and be hanged," Father said, feeling that he had his hands full, fore and aft, with these two unmanageable females who were spoiling his drive.

"Look out! Look out, Clare dear!"

"Vinnie, will you keep still!"

"I'm trying to, darling," screamed Mother, "but that awful horse—Oh! Oh! Look *out!*"

Father cut at Uarda's flanks with the whip.

"Clare! *Do* please be careful!"

"I *am* being careful. Be quiet."

"There she goes again! Oh Clare, let me out!"

"See here," Father said to her sternly, turning half-around in his seat, "if you cannot control yourself—"

Swish! Uarda's tail caught the rein.

Father swore and leaned forward and pulled on it. Uarda came to a stop. We were on our way up a long hill at the moment, and Father had just begun walking her. Luckily for us, she now decided it was a good place to rest.

Father jerked at the rein twice more—once cautiously, and

once with more force. Uarda held it clamped tight to her rump. Her ears went back. She snorted.

"Oh mercy! Let me get out of this!" Mother shrieked, and climbed down onto the road. "Come on, Georgie!"

George jumped out beside her. It was a narrow road with a ditch on each side. She scrambled across the ditch to safety, and stood on the steep, grassy bank.

Father felt deeply insulted at this lack of confidence in him. His blood surged to his face, his eyes popped with passion. He stood up, facing a little sidewise, took the rein in both hands, set his jaws, and gave one mighty yank. At that very instant Uarda, with the skill of a demon, let go. Father fell over backward out of the surrey and crashed into the ditch.

Mother screamed.

I leaned over the dashboard and got the reins. George ran to help Father. Uarda tossed her head and stood still.

Father rose from the ditch, muddy yet somehow majestic, and said to us, "It was your mother."

"Why, *Clare!*" Mother shouted indignantly from the opposite bank.

FATHER'S TROUBLESOME
NEIGHBOR

The house next to ours on the north, No. 422 Madison Avenue, belonged to the Robinsons. No. 418 on our other side was occupied by the Higginses. These three little houses were squeezed so tightly together that they had a combined frontage of only about sixty feet. The three families in them, not having been introduced, never spoke. They could have, of course, if they had wanted to, but none of them did. Instead, they merely bowed to each other, in a blank, distant way, and neither the Higginses nor the Robinsons ever entered our doors during the twenty-five years that we lived there, nor did we enter theirs. The Robinsons looked down on us; and we looked down on the Higginses.

Mr. Douglas Robinson wasn't an ordinary Robinson. He had an estate in West Virginia which he had inherited from the Monroes, and he also had a large house called The Mansion, in the Mohawk Valley, near Herkimer. He was in the real-estate business, and when he formed a partnership with his friend, Mr. Brown, later on, he couldn't bring himself to let the firm be called Robinson, Brown & Co., so their names were printed in full, "Douglas Robinson, Charles S. Brown & Co.," on every one of their signs. They were such an active firm and they had so many signs that this name became famous. It was this Mr. Brown, by the way, who afterward founded Brown, Wheelock & Co.

Mr. Robinson's wife was a dignified but lively young lady who had been Miss Corinne Roosevelt. She knew how to write poetry, turn cartwheels and stand on her head. Not that we ever saw her do any of these, though I longed to. She was the sister of a youth named Theodore Roosevelt who was getting to be active in politics, and who talked too much, Father said. Later, he became President. Distinguished visitors often went up and down the steps of 422.

There was nothing distinguished about Mr. Higgins, who lived in 418. He was an undersized, depressed-looking man with lanky side-whiskers who was in the insurance business. His house had a mortgage on it, and Father said that he looked it.

Father said that all solid, substantial men owned their own homes. "There must be something the matter with Higgins," he said. "I don't wish to have anything whatever to do with the fellow."

Nevertheless we had a good deal to do with him, although he never knew it. Our house and his, instead of each having a wall of its own, had only one thin wall between them. After we moved into 420 Father began saying that the Higginses made too much noise. What the Higginses thought of all our noises I never knew. They had no piano, no children, no quarrels, and it seemed to me they kept very quiet, except that now and then we heard a faint sound resembling a sneeze.

Father disliked this intensely. He had always lived in solider houses, and he wasn't used to hearing sounds of any sort come through a wall. It interfered with the feeling of privacy that a house ought to have. No matter how meekly and politely Mr. Higgins might sneeze, Father said that it was simply intolerable, and that it must be the dust in his whiskers.

Some nights Mr. Higgins was out. On others, perhaps he succeeded in controlling himself. But every time a sudden, subdued "A-choo" floated into our dining-room, Father would set down his claret glass, turn around in his chair, glare fixedly at the wall, and indignantly say to us: "There he goes! Sneezing again!"

The only two places where we ever heard Mr. Higgins were the dining-room and the front hall. Our hall had a solemnly dramatic atmosphere about it to all of us boys, because that was where the black hatrack stood, at the foot of our stairs, and it was usually there that we got spanked.

As this hatrack was the first thing that visitors saw when they entered, it had to be, and was, most impressive. It consisted of a long, black-walnut chest, low enough to sit down on, hidden away in which were all the family's galoshes and rubbers and two or three baseballs. Mounted on this chest was a mirror, seven feet high and five wide, in a fluted black-walnut frame, and this frame had a spreading carved canopy overhanging on top. At each side were some gleaming brass pegs, long and straight, on which hung Father's hats; and under these were two umbrella racks with deep brass pans underneath.

In the dining-room there was a black-walnut sideboard, much broader and fatter than the hatrack, and with an even loftier top. At the other end of the room, facing this sideboard, was a combination mantel and mirror. The mirror ran up nearly all the way to the high ceiling, and when I climbed up on a chair I could see the black sideboard in it. On each end of the mantel was a heavily ornamented bronze urn, about two feet high, to match Uncle Hal's immense bronze clock which stood in between them. And in the center of the dining-room, between the mantel and the sideboard, was a great round black-walnut table.

Dark red curtains hung in the windows. There was a thick red rug on the floor. The lower three or four feet of the walls was painted a deep chocolate color. Above that they were a dull bronze, with a Grecian pattern made of flat strips of felt molded on them in relief. Two gory battle scenes and a crayon portrait hung on these walls. The cheeriest thing in the room was the fireplace. It was a rather small one however, with a little brass grate in it, and the overhang of the mantelpiece dwarfed it.

Every evening from six to seven o'clock, while Father and Mother were having their dinner, this dining-room became as sacred a scene, in my eyes, as a high court or shrine—although owing to the imperfections of the service and Father's temper it was considerably noisier. I sometimes leaned over the banisters in the narrow hall outside, looking down in through the doorway.

After seven, when the table had been cleared away and covered with a Turkish cloth of soft reds and gold, we boys went trooping in. The dining-room became a sitting-room then. It was the one room in the house where we all met. It wasn't nearly as commodious as the parlor but nobody ever went into the parlor, except of course to play the piano, or when visitors made formal calls.

One November night when I had had a birthday and was seven years old, Father said that I was now old enough to join him and Mother at dinner, and sit at the dining-room table. I strutted around in the nursery beforehand, with my hands thrust into my pants pockets, saying goodbye to my brothers, who, as I condescendingly explained to them, were still little boys. George would have to wait two solid years before *he* was promoted, I told him, and the others of course even longer. I then went down to dinner.

In our dining-room, I found almost at once that the honor I had won was a hollow one. It was also oppressive. The free and easy interchange which I had been used to at my meals with my brothers, down in the basement, was gone. I had been cock of the roost in the basement but now I had to keep still, and respectfully say Yes sir and No sir, and submit to being taught what seemed to me many superfluous manners. I had to use plain china too instead of the interesting kind we had in the basement, where one of my brothers had a saucer with a picture of a cottonfield on it, and the other had one depicting a train on the Central Pacific, making its way through herds of buffalo to some remote place called "the Coast." My own saucer had been better still. It had no picture on it at all, which of course was unfortunate, but to console me for its barrenness in this respect, it had a flavor of glory. It bore the arms and insignia of the Seventh Regiment, done in dull red and gold; and Margaret, our cook, had told me (quite erroneously) that it had "gone through the War."

On one of my first stately but saucerless nights in the dining-room, we had turnips for dinner. Father noticed that I didn't take any. "Have some turnip," he said.

I was happily stowing away several flaky boiled potatoes with bits of green parsley on them, and a chunk of hot juicy steak. "No, thank you, Father," I said, and foolishly added, "I never eat turnip."

He laid down his fork and stared at me in amusement. "You will begin now, then," he told me.

"I don't like it, Father."

"I'll tell you what you like and what you don't like," he said. "You're not old enough to know about such things," he added, and although his tone was peremptory his look wasn't unkind. "You've no business not to like turnip. It's good."

I said that I hated it.

"That's enough," he said. "We won't discuss it." He took the dish and deposited on my plate two generous tablespoonfuls of mashed turnip.

I looked longingly at my steak and potatoes. They seemed more delicious than ever. I put a little turnip on my fork and raised it to my mouth, but as the smell got nearer my nose I felt so repelled that I put the fork down again.

Father was watching me. He said: "Eat that turnip. At once."

The sadness of an exile on some foreign shore flooded my heart. I thought of how gay it had been in the basement. "I don't *want* to eat it!" I wailed. "I'd rather go without dinner, Father!" I pushed back my chair and stood up, suddenly ablaze with rebellion.

Father roared at me, "Sit down, sir!" I wouldn't. He was now ablaze too. Mother gave a frightened cry and begged us to stop. She couldn't ever bear to have Father and me clash with each other. But Father didn't much care whether she could bear it or not, when his temper was hot, and the next instant he was leading me off by the ear down the hall toward the hatrack.

When we got there he sat himself down on it, laid me across his knees, lifted my jacket, and gave me a spanking. After he had finished we rose and returned to the dining-room.

I then began eating my turnip.

Mother looked sympathetic but said nothing. The table was still. Father sat back, puffing a little from his recent exertions. I was boiling with rage. This occasion was a turning point, I fear, in my relations with Father. I could see no sense in being made to eat turnip, and Father didn't explain. He never explained anything, I discovered. It didn't seem to him necessary. I on the other hand, although open to reasoning, no matter how specious, always felt full of combativeness and obstinacy when an order seemed arbitrary. The fact that Father loved me and cherished me and worked and planned for my welfare meant nothing to me, as a boy, when he ordered me around. If I had received only cold justice from him I'd have wanted affection. As it was I undervalued his affection because I thought him unjust. The taste of that turnip choked me; it was sickening. I sobbed as I tried to swallow it.

Then a faint sound came through the wall. Compared to the noise I had made on the hatrack it was only a far-away whisper, but it came from 418, it was an intrusion, and Father promptly resented it.

"Damn that Higgins!" he said.

He turned half around in his chair and sternly frowned at the wall.

I had been waiting for just such a chance and had my handkerchief ready. I quickly slid the rest of my turnip off into my lap.

MOTHER MAKES A
MUSTARD PLASTER

Mother was a curious anomaly in her generation. For one thing, she never learned to cook. Just to go into a kitchen put her in a helpless confusion. It seemed simpler to her to go hungry than to try to do anything with all those hopeless-looking ingredients that sit around on kitchen shelves. Now if it were a matter of sewing on buttons or darning socks, Mother could do that, but she never sewed for the fun of it, or made fine lace covers like Grandma Stockwell, or knitted.

When we children were sick she used to take care of us. But when Father had a cold and wanted to be taken care of, Mother said, "That's enough, Clare. It seems to me you are making a fuss about that cold." Of course Father wanted a great deal of care, and if he was not getting it every moment he lay on his bed and groaned. After he had groaned long enough, Mother would go in, rather upset and touched, and lean over him for a moment. "There, there, Clare," she would say. "What can I do for you?"

"*Do!*" Father roared. "No one does anything. What I want is something to cure this cold."

Now and again Mother would rub his back, and Father loved it. It was attention, and sometimes it was soothing, even though her method was to make rather quick, short dashes up and down the spine. However, just as Father began to relax and close his eyes, Mother's own back would commence to ache, bending over him, and she would then feel that she had been rubbing a good long time. As she straightened up briskly, giving one last rub, she destroyed whatever small rhythm she had achieved before.

"Oh, damn," Father would say.

"Clare!" Mother would cry. "Just after I have been rubbing your back for you."

"But you had only just begun," Father would say.

"Heavens, Clare! Nobody has their back rubbed all day long," Mother would reply as she tucked in the sheet.

It wasn't that Mother took Father's or anyone else's sickness lightly. It was only that she had a quick nature and hated to be handled herself. If she were ill, all she asked was for people to keep out of her room. But if one of her loved ones felt bad, she was instantly worried and concerned.

One afternoon in the late summer, when we were still in the country at Harrison, she was troubled because Father would not go to bed although he was obviously miserable with a cold.

"Clare, do go and take a hot bath. I'll have Matilda make you some hot lemonade."

Father answered stiffly that he was all right if she would only leave him alone.

"But you are not all right," Mother said. "Your eyes are watering, and your nose is red, and you are all stopped up."

"I tell you it's passing," Father said hotly. "Let's play a game of bezique." His voice was thick and hoarse.

Mother hesitated. She really ought to send him to bed, but she did love to play bezique. She ended by acquiescing.

He and Mother sat down near me in front of the fire. They had opened the game box and were about to play when the waitress appeared, begging our pardon for disturbing us.

"It's the mare, sir. She's got loose again and all the men have gone and it's Neville's day off."

"Can't you see that Mr. Day has a cold, Annie," Mother said, "and can't go out after horses? Why don't they keep the mare in her stall like the other horses?"

Mother knew as well as any of us did that the mare, Uarda, had a bad way of slipping her halter and stealing out into the rocky pasture across the road, where she would eat grass quietly enough until someone came within a foot of her, when she would slither off and commence eating again about ten feet away. She was apparently unaware of anyone around, but there was a malicious glint in her eye. She would keep up this teasing for a while, then suddenly permit herself to be caught and be led quietly back to the stable. Although catching her was a nuisance, and needed more than one person, the proceeding was in no way dangerous.

Father and I got up to go out and Mother said she might as well come too. She tried to make Father put on his coat, but he shook his head impatiently, saying that it only took a moment to catch the horse.

To our right lay the cornfield. Father had liked the corn he had in the garden so much that he had tried a whole field of it. It had not been successful; for one thing, the Italians across the tracks stole a lot, and then it had not grown the way it should. As we came along now the earth looked thin and cold, the corn weary. "You see that corn?" Father said.

"Oh, don't get started about that corn now, Clare," Mother cried. "Let's get that mare out of here first."

Father insisted on crossing the field at right angles to the way it was plowed, stepping over each furrow. He and I could do it easily, of course, but Mother disliked it, and it was hard on fat Fritz, the dachshund; his legs were so short at each end and his body so low-slung in the middle. Looking back, I could see him heaving over the furrows, like a ship out at sea, and leap as he would, each furrow scraped his poor, plump little paunch as he plunged up and over.

It took a little longer to catch the mare than Father had thought, but soon we were on the way back with her.

"Corn," Father said on the way back, as we again came through the cornfield, "should be green. Green is, I believe, the customary color for its leaves and its stalks. Why should all the corn that is planted in my fields be yellow from birth? I know what my corn ought to look like. But it doesn't seem to. Every time that I talk about corn to the farmer, *he* talks about bugs. He has the utmost difficulty in finding me a good healthy stalk, with good healthy ears of corn on it that my family can eat, but it's no trouble at all to him to find the stalks on which he grows bugs. 'I engaged you,' I tell him, 'as a farmer, and I expect you to farm. When I want an entomologist I'll send for one. What I want now is something to eat!' "

"That's enough, Clare," said Mother. "You're getting hoarse."

Father tightened his lips, looking hurt. "Nobody on this whole place cares a hang about things except me," he said, scowling around at his fields. His eye lit on Fritz. His scowl disappeared. "That's taking a pound or two off him, I'll wager," he chuckled.

The next day Father's cold was so much worse that Mother sent for Dr. Markoe. Dr. Markoe was a famous and very busy surgeon, but Father had been one of his early patients when he was just starting his career and still in general practice. Although Dr. Markoe had announced that he was giving up medicine, Father had seen no need for changing doctors just because his doctor had added what Father called a side line. So, most unwillingly, and often with a real feeling that a general medical man would be more fitting for the particular case, Dr. Markoe continued to treat not only Father but the rest of us for our measles, typhoid fever, or ordinary colds. When Dr. Markoe died we were left stranded, and for years had no regular doctor at all.

That morning Dr. Markoe had an important operation, and as Father's symptoms were not bad enough for him to leave his surgical patient and come out to the country, he gave Mother a list of instructions, among them that she was to make Father a mustard plaster.

If Mother had had a recipe for making a mustard plaster all would have been well. But she had none, and although nowadays anyone can walk into a drugstore and ask for a mustard plaster which will come all prepared and dried on a piece of paper or cloth, in those days plasters were mixed at home by women who usually grew up knowing that the recipe called for at least as much flour as mustard in the mixture. Mother, however, had never made one. It seemed simple enough to her, so she sent for a spoon, a bowl, some mustard and some water, and mixed a thick paste.

Father, in the meanwhile, was watching the proceedings with interest. As she spread a linen cloth on his chest and began to cover it with her thick paste of pure mustard he was already envisaging prompt relief from the congestion in his chest. In a few seconds the mixture began to soak through. Father's roars were loud and immediate. Mother paid no attention, but continued to spread her mixture, making sure that it was plentiful and even.

"Damn! Vinnie! I say—oh, God! Vinnie, stop!"

"Clare, do be still. You know I have to do this."

"But Vinnie. Take that stuff off—you're burning me up, I say. Stop it!"

But Mother knew what she was meant to do, so despite Father's alarming shrieks she kept right on. A mustard plaster always burns, and Father always roared at any slight discomfort.

Father's anguish was real this time, but he always made so much noise anyway, no one believed him.

Dr. Markoe had told Mother just how many minutes to leave the plaster on Father's chest, and no amount of swearing or roaring stirred Mother into taking it off one minute sooner. At the end of that time, when the plaster was removed, to her horror Father's skin came with it, and Dr. Markoe had to come out after all.

MOTHER AND PUG DOGS
AND RUBBER TREES

There were two special things that it was considered chic to have, in good New York homes, in the eighties. One of these was a fat pug dog with a ribbon around his neck, tied in a bow. The other was a rubber tree.

Father's instinct was to do the right thing, and to live in the right way, according to the ideas of his times, but he drew the line at pug dogs. He said he had owned dogs himself as a boy, and he wasn't fussy about their breeds either, but "I must positively decline," he told Mother, "to begin domesticating monstrosities." He said he doubted whether pugs were dogs anyhow. They looked too Chinese. He said that quite possibly in China they filled a niche of their own, though he couldn't guess what, but no pop-eyed pug dog would ever be permitted to waddle around Father's home.

As to rubber trees, he was still more emphatic. He said he liked to be cheerful himself and to live in cheerful surroundings, and of all the disconsolate plants in the world a rubber tree was the most dismal. A rubber tree wasn't a tree, it was nothing but a stick with three leaves on it, and why or how such an unsightly plant had ever become a craze was a mystery.

The trouble was that Mother felt a longing for these two things, she didn't know why. She saw pug dogs and rubber trees everywhere but in her own home, and gradually her home came to seem bare. When visitors looked around the parlor it embarrassed her. They were too polite to say, "Where's your rubber tree?" but she was sure they were thinking it.

On Christmas morning Father found one of his socks fastened with a bent pin to his mantelpiece. It had a small china dish in it.

His one hope and prayer was not to be given anything whatever on Christmas, but he recognized this thing. "Why, this is my soap-dish," he said. "What's it doing here, damn it?"

Mother's eyes were sparkling with mischief. "I thought you might need it, Clare dear," she said sweetly, "when you were feeding your nice new pug dog."

She pointed to what looked like a hat box, done up in red ribbons. Father opened it and took out the tissue paper. A life-sized pug dog, made of china, was sitting inside.

"Hah!" Father said in relief. This objet d'art wasn't beautiful by any means, it was in the way and it was awkwardly large, but it wasn't alive. He could stand it.

Mother adored that pug dog. And as it was such a handsome piece of china, she said, and had cost her so much, she had to think carefully where would be the best place to put it. After trying several sites she decided on a place in the parlor, facing the door as you came in For years and years there it sat on the floor, where it deceived and amazed Mother's visitors. They exclaimed in delight at its lifelike appearance and its big bulging eyes. Mother added to the effect by tying a broad red satin bow round its neck.

A rubber tree followed. A real one. It was hidden in the narrow hall bedroom next to Mother's, at first, and spoken of as "the new plant," and by the time that Father became suspicious enough to investigate, it was practically a member of the family, the way Mother felt, and she couldn't be parted from it. After a battle or two, Father made up his mind that he needn't bother because the lanky thing would soon die, and until then he might as well ignore it, as he did the imitation pug dog.

That rubber tree seemed to me a most lugubrious object to look at. It had had five dark green leaves when it came, but three of these soon turned a horrible mottled yellow and dried up and died. After that nothing happened to it for weeks. It just stood there, with its thin, twisty stem tied for support to the bookcase, sullenly drinking up all the water Mother poured into its pot, and looking more utterly forlorn and sick of this world every day.

Mother however had plenty of determination and spirit, whether her tree had or not, and her will at last prevailed. The rubber tree still looked to me quite as doleful as ever, but it took up the burden of existence once more and put out a new leaf. A more tedious and deliberate unfolding of a bud I'd never seen. Mother didn't mind how slow it was. It was responding to her, and that made her happy. As soon as the new leaf had uncurled itself and spread itself out, the rubber tree was borne downstairs in state to the parlor, to stand on an Empire table by the china pug dog.

After dinner, Mother took Father's arm, coaxingly, and led him in there to look at it. He stood, smoking his cigar, and watching her as she cooed over it and patted its little new leaf. "Don't smoke too near it, Clare dear," she said, over her shoulder. Father stroked his mustache, said "Humph," and walked thoughtfully back to the dining-room. He winked at me presently and said, "Your mother has a very warm heart."

A year or two later, when the rubber tree began to get tall, it was replanted in a much larger flower pot, and put in a tray on the floor; and as time passed by and as it kept growing, it was given a green wooden tub. It went with us to the country every summer and came back in the fall. It was as much trouble and worry, almost, as a baby.

The only possible way to transport it on these two annual trips was to entrust it to Morgan, the coachman, to take in the dog-cart. Morgan hated that rubber tree. It had a good many leaves on it now, but if even one fell off Mother missed it. Morgan explained that neither he nor all the angels could keep a dog-cart from joggling, but Mother said she knew that very well, and that was why she had reminded him specially that he must walk the horse, and three large leaves were missing from the bottom this time and two from the top.

I was sorry for Mother because I knew how she watched over that tree and loved every leaf, but I also felt sorry for Morgan. I had heard other coachmen make fun of him. On these trips he had to drive one horse in the dog-cart and lead two others behind. He had to stow quite a sizable cargo on and under the seats. His livery, his high hat, his bedding, light and heavy blankets for each of the horses, curry-combs, cloths and brushes, buckets, hoof-picks, two saddles, several bridles, a bag full of bits of old harness, and Topsy, the cat. Morgan used to arrive at our front door in town with everything on board except the rubber tree and old Topsy, find room for these too, and unhappily drive off down Madison Avenue, feeling very conspicuous. Topsy, who didn't like Morgan, yowled and wailed in her basket, and the rubber tree, sitting beside him, was now eight feet high.

His destination, and ours, every summer was New London, a hundred and twenty-five miles away. We went on the train of course. Morgan and the horses and Topsy went on the night boat. I never knew, nor could I manage to picture to myself, what kind of a time Morgan had. A veil was drawn over those dark experiences. All I knew was that Morgan and his caravan arrived a day after we did, the animals dejected and dingy, and Morgan dejected and drunk.

If it hadn't been for the rubber tree, which according to Mother's orders he had to deliver at once, Morgan wouldn't have had to exhibit himself to us in this state. He could have gone direct to the large boarding stables and slept himself sober. As it was, he was faced with a problem that he could never quite solve, the problem of how a man in his cups could get a rubber tree out of a dog-cart and carry it up a tar path and into a cottage, without self-betrayal.

He tried being jaunty about it. He tried being hearty and jolly. But as he was in reality profoundly depressed, by what he had gone through on the boat, his attempts to be pleasant rang hollow. They sounded slightly insane. When he tried being grave and judicial instead, he alarmed Mother dreadfully by his sweeping gestures and his important-looking nods of the head. "For Heaven's sake, Morgan," she would cry, "do get out of this cottage. Don't stand there by my poor rubber tree wagging your head at me that way."

The next day Morgan always had to go through a long, trying

session. It began with his being discharged, and it ended with his taking the pledge. This consisted of his solemn assurance that he would never again touch a drop. He freely invoked on himself the most picturesque dooms if he did. "May the Mother of God tear the gullet out of me, bless her sweet heart, the very next drop I take, Mrs. Day, and I won't take it neither." He would continue in a loud, rising scale with his eyes fixed upon Mother's, until he reached a crescendo of fervor that convinced her, and that I think convinced him.

"Morgan," she said, at the end of one such interview.

Morgan respectfully touched his hat. "Yes, mum?"

"You don't deserve it, but I'll try to believe you once more."

"Yes, mum, thank you, Mrs. Day," Morgan replied, looking brighter.

"But if you should ever *dare*," Mother vehemently added, "to take another drink of that wicked stuff I hope it will *choke* you!"

Morgan paled. "I hope not, mum," he hastily muttered, again touching his hat.

After we got a place of our own in the country where the tree had more room to grow than ever, it grew far too much. It stood on the piazza, in the one place that wasn't roofed over, and it became so tall that its upper branches reached to the second-floor window. This window unfortunately was Father's. He began to complain. He said that damned tree was too noisy. He said he had built himself a home in the country, at great expense, so as to have some peace and quiet, instead of which here was an outlandish rubber tree tapping on his window all night.

Mother got prouder and prouder of it, the taller it grew. She began busily cutting slips from it and planting numbers of these in new pots, all the way around the piazza. These slips were tall but weedy and weak. Every one of them had to be tied to one of the piazza's square wooden pillars.

The old original tree was now far too big to go into our city home any more. It had to be left in a greenhouse belonging to Mr. Fremd in the winters, and it lived with us only in summer. It would have been out of place in town anyhow. The rubber

tree craze had ended long since, and all the pug dogs of New
York were gone, too. Those once popular animals had completely disappeared from the city, even our china one, which one
of us boys had broken. New fads had sprung up. One was for
"favrile glass" which Louis Tiffany made lamps of, and another
was for old-fashioned warming-pans. Mother of course had one
of each. Her favrile lamp was in the shape of a swollen and
adipose lily, glittering with curious hues, far more hues and more
glitter than Solomon had in all his glory. Her warming-pan,
which she had bought somewhere in New England, had been
fixed up to match. Its honest old oaken handle had been stained
to look like polished mahogany, and a broad red satin ribbon
was tied in a bowknot around it, like that which the pug dog
had worn.

Mother was not one to be fickle however, and she was faithful
to her rubber tree still. It was on her mind all the time. When
we moved up to the country each spring, that tree was the first
thing she greeted.

It was becoming quite a job for her to water it sufficiently, on
account of its size, and this was particularly difficult when there
was a drought. What made it so hard at such times, at least in
Mother's eyes, was Father's bath. Drought or no drought, he
said, he had to have his cold bath every morning. Mother said
that her tree would die and he wouldn't, and what was his
answer to that? His answer was that he had always taken a bath
every day of his life.

For years he had tried to get Mother to take an icy plunge too.
As he grew older he said less about it, but he took a tubbing
himself just the same. Mother said that if he insisted on a daily
bath, even in droughts, he must leave the water standing in his
tub so that it could be used for her rubber tree.

Father let her use it but he didn't like it. He said Mother was
messy. She tracked water all over his floor, he said, when she
walked back and forth, filling her pitcher from his tub and then
pouring it out of his bedroom window to splash it on top of that
tree. Mother said she didn't splash the water, and had not tracked

up his floor, and when Father pointed indignantly to the pools and wet spots by his sofa, she said that those were just a few drops from the outside of the pitcher.

One cold, dark autumn morning, Father was longer than usual taking his bath. The water was icy, and things hadn't been going well with him, and altogether he wasn't feeling as vigorous as usual that morning. When Mother dipped her pitcher into his bathtub she found that it wasn't cold. He had secretly warmed it a little to take off some of its chill.

"Why, Clare!" she laughed. "I thought you were such a stickler for taking cold baths!"

"Damnation!" said Father. "Get out of my bathroom. Leave my bathtub alone! I swear to God no man ever had so much to bear from a rubber tree."

Mr. Fremd, although he was a professional nursery-man, felt the same way. He was getting tired of the rubber tree too. One winter, without telling Mother, he cut off its top. In May, when his wagon climbed our hill again, bringing back his maimed victim, and when Mother expressed the grief and fury she felt at his conduct, Mr. Fremd was defiant. He had simply had to do it, he said. The roof of his greenhouse wasn't high enough for that tree any more. Mother quarreled with him about this. She warned him that he must never again behave like that to her plants, and that summer she helped the old tree to regain its full height. Mr. Fremd retaliated, the following winter, by keeping it lying flat on its side for the seven or eight months that he had it. He said, what else could he do. That was the only way he could get it indoors. From that time on the tree spent over half of each year lying down, never standing up except in the summers, and it gradually became rather towzled.

When this strange pet of Mother's had finally completely outgrown her, and when she had vainly appealed for help to all of her friends, she happened one evening to hear my brother George speak of the Marsh Botanical Garden at Yale. The next I knew she had presented the Botanical Garden with her rubber tree. They tried to explain to her that they didn't have any rubber trees, but this did them no good, it only made Mother the prouder to bestow hers upon them. Her one stipulation was that as the coachman couldn't very well drive it all the way up to New Haven, the Marsh Botanical Garden must come down to Harrison and get it themselves. To my private astonishment they apparently did so. Although years later George told me that he had hired a truck for the purpose, letting Mother believe that the University had done so, as he knew that Mother would never have been willing to let George do it—or to do it herself. And George was unwilling to have the University pay. The last I saw of our tree was its top sticking way out of the rear of a Forestry truck, rounding a turn down the road.

MOTHER PLAYS HER ROLE

Mother had a strong and instinctive desire to play her role to the full. If she had been the queen of a court, she'd have started right in being regal and gracious, stirring up the lord chamberlain, and making sure the king toed the mark. Anything that it was customary for an energetic queen to attend to, Mother would have at once had a go at. So just as soon as Father had laid out the grounds of his new home in the country, and Mother could see that there was something more to it than a lot of mess and workmen, she christened the place Upland Farm and determined to fill a useful role there.

She was handicapped because she really didn't know anything about farms or farming. As to the proper method of growing crops in a field, that was a mystery to her, and anyhow it was a man's job. Even our vegetable garden was too large a problem for her to tackle. What she liked to do was to grow flowers in little pots on the piazza. This got to be a department in itself, she had so many pots, and they all had to be watered. On hot summer nights after the gardener had finished his other work, we would hear his unwilling footsteps around the corner of the house as he came to fill the big watering can at the faucet near the steps. However, if there was a drought, the gardener said these plants were not important. Mother would then bestir herself to preserve their lives by taking water out to them herself.

Though this was interesting enough as an occupation, it did not give her a role. Of course there was the moving back and forth —and Mother felt no one understood the magnitude of this task —but it was an exceptional thing that only overtook one twice a year. And most of the impending catastrophes were avoided anyway. When Father discovered that the jar of preserved strawberries had been packed with the tea and his cheese in a wash boiler with many other articles, and remonstrated, Mother knew of so many more dangerous packages than the strawberries that she brushed him aside with the remark that as nothing had happened to anything, why was he making all this talk.

However, almost any situation has a role in it for a wide-awake woman, and Mother finally found hers through prodding up Father and the farmer to make Upland Farm more and more farmlike, so that the name would seem right and fitting to others. Of course the very first year there had been a kitchen garden, but it wasn't enough for her to serve vegetables from our garden at dinner, and tell her guests triumphantly that the peas had come right out of our own pea patch, and promise to march them down after dessert and show them the beans, too, and the place where the melons were to have been if they hadn't all dried up in infancy. This sort of thing didn't content her, because we didn't have enough guests.

We boys benefited at first from her extension of the production of vegetables because we used to take all that we could lay our hands on and drive off in the farm cart and sell them. This opportunity to earn money so easily made up in part to us for our former summers at New London; but it was not destined to last, for we found before long that there did not seem to be so many vegetables that wouldn't be missed. We also discovered that our market was being spoiled, for we soon noticed that Mother would go out in the victoria, dressed in her fresh, ruffled dresses, and holding her lace parasol so as to shade her face, and make calls on her friends in the afternoon. With her she would carry a basket of vegetables to those who had no garden of their own, or, to the more fortunate, something not to be found in their garden. The next morning when four red-headed and freckled boys drove up to sell their vegetables, all the houses would be mysteriously stocked.

But it was the cows who gave Mother her first real responsibility in her role of chatelaine. At first there had been only one cow, but there had come a time when she went dry. In order to avoid any such stoppage of our milk supply, the next year a second cow had been added; as the years went on, more cows were about the place. Father bought a fancy one to improve the stock, or kept a heifer, until finally there were always five.

When we first settled there, Harrison was out in the country, but little by little it became a suburb. The farms, old and new, disappeared. Even the parklike estates were split up into smaller holdings or turned into clubs. Almost none of our neighbors had barns or kept cows any more. It was easier to buy milk and butter. Mother didn't like to depend on bottled milk, though, and as she also was proud of our butter, she clung to all our cows.

Father and Mother had no use for five cows, especially when the time came that they were alone on the place; but by that time, each of the cows had become a member of the family, even the two cranky ones and the stupid old white one which none of us liked.

For a while it was a problem to get the milk down daily to the city for the family use during the winter. Express companies, while willing to take on the order, did not feel they had to be at our house at any appointed hour to deliver a can of milk. Mother, who had to deal with the cook, felt strongly they should be. Certainly the time for milk to come to any house was early in the morning—everybody knew that.

However, right near the Grand Central station was a grocery store the family had used for years, a comfortable, established firm. There they mixed Father's coffee just to his taste, and saw to it that his cigars were right. As the station checking system for parcels was not as well arranged then as now, old customers left their bundles behind the grocery-store counters to be called for later in the day. I can't remember how or why, but we once left a grandfather's clock there for over a year. The name of this long-suffering grocer was Charles.

Since the store was so near the station, Mother felt that it would be no trouble at all to them to have a man run over and get our can of milk off the train from Harrison and send it up to the house with the first delivery. Perhaps it was because the family had traded for a long time with them, or perhaps because they had been accustomed for an equally long time to Mother's and Father's difficult requests; at any rate, they consented to do this. The arrangement worked very well for us, but if Charles' was so unfortunate as to be only half an hour late in delivering the can, they were called right up and scolded roundly. If the farmer did not put the can on the usual train, or if it was delayed, Charles' found themselves not only apologizing but anxiously meeting each train from Harrison until the milk arrived. They would then send a man straight up to our house on a special trip with the can.

Meanwhile the cows gave milk—more milk than the family knew what to do with. The farmer and the coachman and their children and wives were chock-full of it. So were the chickens and the pigs. Moreover, Mother did not play her part—she lived it, and she insisted that all the milk be set for cream. This meant that in summer the cream became pretty sour by the time the farmer got around to churning a large part of it into butter. We none of us thought of complaining about the taste of the butter, except one of my brothers, who always loathed it.

When the family got smaller, we not only had too much butter, but the house was drowned in cream. Great bowls and pitcherfuls would come on the table. Mother, knowing about all the cream down in the dairy waiting to be churned, would wearily order any cream that was left after luncheon to be brought out on the porch. There she would sit on a broiling hot day whipping it into butter. Sometimes the butter was obstinate and Mother would have to leave it while she went and changed her dress so as to be ready for callers in the afternoon. On those days, when visitors drove up they would find Mother sitting there in her chair still beating away.

There were two things about our butter that prevented it from being really good. One was that Father had started out with the best of pedigreed Jersey stock. This strain of cow gives delicious, rich milk and cream, but the butter has a strong taste.

The second was that our farmer never washed the butter suffi-ciently to take all of the buttermilk out of it. The color, however, was always beautiful and both Mother and the farmer took great pride in never having to use any artificial coloring matter to give it that rich, golden look.

By the time the family had been reduced to just Mother and Father and they had grown old and had fewer and fewer guests, Mother found that the butter was not only a responsibility but a real problem. Some of it she gave away to friends who were sick or poor. There were one or two families, however, who were rich and who, Mother felt, could well afford to buy themselves nice fresh country butter. I don't know whether they really intended to do so, but at any rate they did buy our butter. And Mother was very particular that these orders should never fail to be de-livered. When she returned to town from her weekly trips to the country, one of the most precious articles she carried with her was a large stone crock which was placed in the car last, because on the way home the chauffeur would have to stop at Mrs. Dickerman's and walk up to the door, bearing in his arms, pa-tiently or disdainfully according to the nature of the chauffeur, this large earthenware crock full of round pats of butter. If these friends did not like the butter, they never said so; therefore Mother continued to be serene about bestowing it as a special privilege.

Once, some especially bankerish and well-tailored people came to dine. They were English friends of my brother who had never liked the butter. They innocently asked if there was anything they could take back to England, where he was now living, in the country. Mother was equal to any emergency of that variety and instantly took them up on this offer.

The day they sailed home Mother stopped in to see me at my apartment in town and spoke of how kind they were.

"What did you send?" I asked.

"Why," said Mother, "I sent him some of the farm butter."

I had seen these people; tall, slim, elegant. They had no

wrinkles in their clothes and their manners were studied and quiet. I had a quick vision of their carrying something rather bulkily wrapped in brown paper, for Mother, although she dearly loved to do up parcels, had never the patience to make them come out just right. I hoped that they would be able to get it from the ship's refrigerator to my brother quickly, so that no tell-tale grease spots would greet my brother's eye as he put out his hand to receive this gift.

"Don't you think you might have sent something else?" I asked. "They rather specialize in fresh butter over there."

"But not our butter from Harrison," Mother proudly answered.

FATHER'S HOME DISAPPEARS

Father wanted to buy a home that would be permanent. He had been married five years, and he felt that it was high time to settle down once and for all. The little house at 251 Madison Avenue, which had been all right for a young bride and groom, was getting too small, now that there were boys in the family.

Grandpa Day smiled and told Mother that there was no such thing in New York as permanence, and that he had been forced out of four comfortable homes in his day. Father agreed that this had been so in the old days, and he also admitted that of course the town was bound to keep growing, but he thought that a man who picked the right district could now settle down.

Every respectable citizen in the seventies owned his own house. A decent three- or four-story house, unencumbered by mortgages, and situated within one or possibly two blocks of Fifth Avenue—and it oughtn't to be above Fifty-ninth Street or below Washington Square. Those were the usual requirements.

Father looked around carefully, he got the most expert advice that he could, and then he used his best judgment. As a result, he selected and bought 420 Madison Avenue. This was a sunny house, just below Forty-ninth Street, it was fairly near Central Park, and it was in a new and eligible district for good private residences. Brokers said that "the permanent residential quality of that whole section" was guaranteed by the fine public edifices which had been built in the neighborhood. St. Luke's Hospital stood on Fifth Avenue, from Fifty-fourth Street to Fifty-fifth, surrounded by big, shady trees and a broad grassy lawn. St. Patrick's Cathedral, at Fiftieth Street, had been recently dedicated. And Columbia College and its campus occupied a whole city block from Forty-ninth Street to Fiftieth, and from Madison

Avenue over to what is Park Avenue now, but what was then a broad open cut full of locomotives and trains.

In the seventies, there were almost no apartments, and people didn't move nearly so frequently as they do today. The old saying was that three moves were as bad as a fire. This move of ours from 251 to 420 bulked as large in my mind as the flight of the Israelites from Egypt, all except the Red Sea, and they didn't have to carry such heavy furniture as a Victorian family.

Mother used to tell us little stories about it for years. As I remember, the hardest thing to handle was Uncle Hal's clock— the wedding-present that he and Aunt Addie had given to Mother. At the top of this magnificent structure—which would have been more in place, really, if it had been erected in Central Park—was seated a robed and amply-built woman; below her was the clock face, and on each side, lower down, was a man, one of whom had a hammer, and both of whom looked kind of cross. I suppose it was an allegory of some sort, but I don't know what about. The woman seemed to be in favor of harmony, but the two men were not. To save this massive bronze statuary from injury Mother actually carried it up in a cab, in her lap, bouncing about on the cobblestones, and then went back for her five-months-old baby.

Our new home was a four-story brownstone-front house with a stoop, and it had all the modern conveniences of 1879. It had gas-lights in every room, even the cook's. We used kerosene lamps in the parlor, but that was only because the gas chandelier was too high to light without climbing up on a step-ladder. There was a convenient little gas-jet even in the cellar, which didn't burn very well to be sure, as it had only a small bluish flame, but which saved us from bothering with candles, which struggled to light up the ghostly pillars and dark silent shadows. Another convenience was that the big kitchen range had a grating in front that slid open, and a mechanical shaker to let the cook stir the coal fire. There was a round little Dutch oven for basting besides. In the long white-washed cellar there was a coal-bin, a wood-bin, a wine-closet, and barrels and barrels of potatoes and

cider and apples. And there was a fine hot-air furnace that roared
and rattled and misbehaved itself wildly, which had to be
wrestled with by Margaret, the cook, and probed into by Father.
Most of the rooms had fireplaces too, which burned cannel coal
or small logs, and gave out a fragrant glow on chilly evenings.
The waitress was always lugging a coal scuttle or an armful of
logs up the stairs, and until after we boys were older she had
no one to help her.

On every floor except the fourth of the new house we had
running water, and there were two shining tin bathtubs—one for
Father and Mother and one for the rest of the family (three boys,
Cousin Julia, an occasional visitor, and later a nurse and new
baby). The cook and waitress didn't have a bathtub, but there
was a white china water-pitcher and bowl in their bedroom, the
same as in mine, and off at one end of the cellar they had a cold
little water-closet.

All the plumbing was completely boxed in, of course, except in
the cellar. When we opened the great, stately door of Father's
bathroom and looked in there, in awe, all we saw was a long
dark mahogany case in which his tin bathtub shone, and a forbidding mahogany structure beside it, three feet square and
three high, with a solid closed cover on top. All the woodwork
and trim of this room was somberly polished, not painted. A pure
white Victorian bathrobe on a hook was the one touch of light.
The walls were dark and the one little window was up in the
high ceiling, where it opened into a narrow interior airshaft. The
whole place had a dim, brooding tone, like a crypt in a church.

There wasn't any washstand in the bathroom—that wasn't
the custom—but there was one in a box at each end of the
passageway between the two bedrooms.

In nearly every room there was a bell-pull which jerked at one
of the eight dangling bells that hung in a row in the kitchen. In
each of the three upper hallways was a speaking tube too, and as
these also connected with the kitchen, Margaret, our cook, had
her hands full. The way to use a tube was to blow into it vigorously, ignoring the dust that flew out, until one of these blowings

succeeded in working the whistle which was affixed to the mouth-piece below. On hearing this whistle Margaret was supposed to spring to the appropriate tube and shout loudly up it. But Margaret was so short that she had to climb up on a chair before she could do this, and then, if it was the wrong tube, get down again, move the chair, haul up all her petticoats once more to make another climb, and when she had done all this howl up the next tube instead. By that time Father or Mother had lost patience and begun pulling a bell, and Margaret would clump upstairs to answer it, muttering to herself, "Such a house!"

On the first floor, a little above the street level, were the dining-room, pantry and parlor. On the second were Father's and Mother's rooms. The furniture in Father's room and in the dining-room was dark and severe. In Mother's room and the parlor it was dark but ornamental or rich. In all four of these rooms it was massive.

Our quarters up on the third and fourth floors were more simple. Little beds, light walls, plain hard carpets, and three shelves full of toys. Soldiers, building blocks, marbles, a Punch and Judy show, and five red iron cars. As we were all boys there were no dolls of course, and we had no books by women authors.

Our toys were made for hard wear and tear, and they got plenty of it. It was only at Christmas that any additions were made to our stock. We knew every battered lead soldier, individually, we knew almost every nicked block, we could tell at a glance just which boy every marble belonged to, except those made of clay which we called migs. And each brother had his own sacred place where his own toys were kept, except when the waitress cleaned the room and mixed everything up.

Our books were few but we read and re-read them, *Robinson Crusoe* the most. *Gulliver's Travels, Tanglewood Tales, King Solomon's Mine,* and *Pilgrim's Progress* came next. Christian's adventures were more exciting and real to me than anything in other story-books, and I was especially taken with Apollyon and poor old Giant Despair.

Down below our nursery windows, on the sidewalk, was a little gas lamp-post. A German band of three or four pieces used to come of an evening and stand under its flickering light, reading their music, and tooting away on their horns. We were thirsty for music, there were no phonographs or radios then, and we huddled in the window, squirming ecstatically, and listening to their stirring marches. Sometimes Father would stick his head out of the front door and tell them to go away and be damned, but as soon as we heard him shut it again we'd toss down our pennies, wrapped in twisted bits of paper, so that they could see them, and they'd play one more tune.

Down the murderously dark and steep flight of stairs from the dining-room was the front basement. We boys had our supper there, and sometimes we played games on the floor under Father's big billiard table.

The daylight filtered in through an iron-barred window, which looked out into our "area." Sitting on the broad window seat, we could see the legs and feet of passers-by walking along on the sidewalk above. On days when the postman was in a hurry or when nobody answered the bell, he reached in his hand through the bars, pushed this window up, and tossed in the letters.

On the mantel was a clock of black marble, shaped like a tomb from the Nile. On one wall was an engraving of Rosa Bonheur's rearing horses being led to a fair. Each of us boys had his favorite horse in that cavalcade—in fact I had three. On the opposite wall was an engraving of Landseer's "Stag at Bay." We stood and stared at him in awe. Our other heroes, Crusoe and Christian, and still more of course Gulliver, in spite of all the adventures they had, were somehow at heart pretty humdrum. That stag was quite different. He was tragic and male and magnificent.

On the other side of the room from the stag was Father's brown walnut desk, where he made entries in his ledger of investments, or his household accounts. His mood while he did this was cheerful, if he and the country were prosperous. In bad times he flung up his head in defiance, and looked at bay, like the stag.

The top of the billiard table was kept covered with a grey rubber cloth. On nights when Father went down there after dinner and lit the four hooded gas-lights and took off and folded up that cover, the whole room seemed transformed. The engravings on the walls were in darkness, but the broad top and the gleaming rims of the table were flooded with light. A scarlet ivory ball and two white ones rolled on this rich green expanse, and Father stood studying them in his snowy-white shirt-sleeves, with his polished cue, inlaid with mother-of-pearl, in his hand.

Years later when I read about how artistically the Japanese could arrange single flowers, and how it made mandarins happy to stare at Ming yellow, I thought of this scene in our basement. It was my introduction to beauty.

For the first ten or fifteen years that we lived in 420, the neighborhood got better and better. Father's judgment as to its permanence seemed fully justified. It had become thickly planted with residences in many of which friends of our family were making their homes. We had grown fond of 420 by that time. Birth and death and endless household events had taken place inside its walls, and it had become a part of ourselves.

Then business began invading upper Fifth Avenue and spreading to Madison. A butcher bought a house near us and turned it into a market. We felt he was an impudent person and bought nothing from him for months, until in an emergency Mother sent in there for a rack of lamb chops. We then discovered that this butcher was not only an upstart, he was extremely expensive, and he was catering to the fashionable Fifth Avenue families and didn't care a rap about ours.

More and more of the old houses around us were made into stores. After 1900 some of the best people left, and soon that whole district began steadily sliding downhill.

All these changes didn't at first seem as though they would last. Many owners resisted them, hoping against hope year by year. But the Indians had to give way when the white men arrived, and when a group of gigantic white buildings sprang up into the air at and around Forty-second Street, most of the old brownstone houses in our neighborhood finally disappeared too.

Father held on to his as long as he could. What drove him away at last was the noise of the new street-cars all night. The old horse-cars had had something human about them—they wouldn't have been much out of place even in ancient Rome. In size and appearance they fitted into the old human scale. The new cars were monsters, and the strident and unnatural din they made wrecked Father's sleep. After tossing actively around in his bed for what seemed to him hours, swearing resentfully at the misery they had brought into his life, he sometimes threw off his blankets and strode to the open window, in his bare feet and nightshirt, and shook his fist at them and yelled until he woke Mother up.

She slept in the back. She offered to take his front room instead. He would not give it up. She begged him at least then to stuff his ears full of cotton at night. He said he would not go through such indignities. He seemed to feel that adopting her remedies would be giving in to those street-cars. He said he'd rather move and defy them.

It was years after we left, as it happened, before I went back there. Then one day I had an appointment to keep in an office on the twelfth or thirteenth floor of the sky-scraper which had been put up on that site. We still owned the land and I knew there was now a sky-scraper there, but I hadn't seen it, I'd been living out West for some time, and after getting back I'd been ill. On my way down my mind was preoccupied by other things, and it wasn't until I stepped out of my taxi that I took a look at the street.

My nerves or my brain cells must have been unconsciously full of old memories, for apparently what I expected to find were two rows of short houses, set well back from the sidewalks, with the cheerful rattle of a wagon or two, or a cab, going by. Instead of that, there were what seemed to me immensely high ramparts that I couldn't—from the street—see the tops of. They rose up into the air directly from the inner edge of the sidewalk.

I felt them crowding against me. In the street between these ramparts there was a rushing bedlam of sound—hoots, roars, grindings, clashing. And on those once quiet sidewalks where we had spun our tops and slid down the railings, I found myself jostled by masses of hurrying people.

On the corner where the three pretty Lyons girls used to live, in a fat little house full of windows, there was a gigantic and grimy white tower heaving up to the sky. The sunny, irregular, red brick buildings which Columbia College once occupied, the lamp-post where the band used to play, even the flagstones were gone.

I went into the new and modern 420 and got into an elevator. Up we shot, past the floor where Father's four-poster and bureau had been, past the level of the nursery and my bedroom, on and on, up and up; and there, suspended almost in the clouds, high above our old life, was the office where I had an appointment. I don't know why I felt dizzy. I had been up in hundreds of sky-scrapers higher than this. I tried not to keep thinking of my childhood home, way down below. I pushed the button and in a moment the man inside opened the door, as casually as though everything were perfectly natural and he were living on solid earth.

MOTHER TRAVELS ALONE

When Mother was a girl she lived in a small town and journeys were Great Events. They were not to be undertaken lightly. Although later in life she traveled often she couldn't get over her early feelings. Nevertheless when she was nearly seventy she decided to go and see her grandchildren in Europe. Father was not well enough to take the trip, so after getting him settled in Harrison she started off by herself.

The house in town was all boarded up and watched over by the Holmes patrol. There was a large red seal on the door, and if anyone tried to get in, a bell rang in the main office. Of course if you let them know beforehand the exact time you wanted to get in, a man would come and open the house up; but the thought of all that red tape and arranging made Mother tired even to think of it. So she always said to everyone: "After the last things that go to the country are taken down the steps, I walk out, and behind me comes the Holmes man; and after that," here her voice sank to a whisper and her eyes opened wide, "no one can get in until fall, not even I."

Since she felt the house in town was impossible, she had to spend the night before sailing in an hotel. Although she rather enjoyed going to hotels in other cities she felt that going to an hotel in New York was forlorn; as though she had no home or family. However a friend of hers said that she could have her apartment at 270 Park Avenue, which would be much more homelike.

Wherever Mother went she had to have a personal contact. When she went to a store, for instance, she did not say she was going to Wanamaker's, Altman's or Lord and Taylor's, she was going to "Miss Smith's, at Lord and Taylor's you know." Lord and Taylor did not always care so much about this because Mother's favorite saleslady had to sell her everything, gloves, dresses, coats or material by the yard—whatever she had a mind to get in the store. If it took rather long to find the article Mother just put it down to the general slowness of stores and waited with what patience she could muster. It was the same at 270 Park Avenue.

George had arranged to meet Mother at my apartment and from there take her to 270 Park Avenue. When they arrived although Mother had been there only long enough to leave her bags, and was to spend but one night, he found everyone smiling and jumping around, acting much more human than most New York apartment-house employees.

Mother was in high good humor as she introduced him to the doorman, the bell boys, the clerk and the elevator man. They could now see that she wasn't alone; although she was to be alone there for the night. George said that they had evidently all been told about "My son, Mr. George Day."

As she shepherded him in to see the apartment and have "a bit of a talk," she was just like a child with a new toy. She had to show George both baths, the beds and chairs, the view and all the closets—everything.

It was something to see and enjoy however, not really to use, for a little later she moved a chair to sit down and telephone me. She talked happily for a few minutes but as she got up she found she had forgotten where the chair had come from. "Oh my soul!" she wailed, "it would never do to disarrange things!"

George left about eleven with the understanding that Philip, Mother's chauffeur, would call for him at the Yale Club at quarter to nine the next morning. George, knowing Mother, however, was at the door at eight-thirty, where sure enough he found Philip waiting. They hurried around to 270 Park Avenue where they were just in time for Mother as she appeared at the front door with all her luggage.

The drive down to the pier was comfortable. As the boat did

not sail until noon even Mother felt that there was enough time to get there if the traffic did not stop too much.

But at the dock a public porter took all the precious luggage, paying no attention to Mother's cries that Philip would attend to that. Worse still, this rough-looking man did not keep it with him but stolidly dumped it on an escalator which shot it up and out of sight. With no knowledge of whether or not she would ever see her beloved things again, Mother was told to go with George, up an elevator. What wore Mother out most was that she felt the public porter did not hurry but slowly marched up the stairs taking no pains at all to be at the top of the escalator by the time her bags were there. Anybody might walk off with them, leaving her an odd assortment of unfamiliar things she did not want in the least.

Mother looked as though she were undecided whether to go on the escalator herself with the bags, which she had planned to have constantly in sight, or to run up the stairs after the public porter. George saved the situation by having the presence of mind to seize hold of Mother's famous old black Gladstone bag and take this into the passenger elevator. The bag acted as a magnet to draw Mother in after him.

When they arrived on the main floor the public porter was standing there waiting for them with the other five bags, and was at once taken into high favor. All became peaceful as they marched down to the gangway, but there new alarms arose. For the public porter was by now a private family retainer as it were, highly trusted and indispensable. But under regulations he had to leave the five bags to be carried on board by stewards of the ship, who, while said to be numerous, were not visible. Furthermore, Mother as a passenger had to go up one gangway, while George, as a visitor, had to go up another.

George pointed out that they both came out close together on the deck above, so after she had a conference with the ticket inspectors and other officials which ended in their all laughing together, she proceeded up her gangplank and George up his. He commandeered two stewards for the luggage, so that Mother and all the bags and the stewards and George met at once in her stateroom and promptly overflowed in the hallway.

Mother at once wailed that she was never going to be able to get in the stateroom and what should she do, and counted the bags and patted each one. However in a few minutes the bags were in and the stewards out and Mother exclaiming over how nice her stateroom was—not a bit stuffy and *very* comfortable.

Just then the stewardess came in. She was a pretty, fresh-faced woman to whom Mother immediately took a great fancy. When George left they were joking together and the stewardess telling Mother she must be Irish or at least have kissed the Blarney Stone.

Beside this to take a train from Harrison to come to town on a summer's afternoon might seem less trying. Not to Mother. Trains were great implacable, roaring monsters. They had a frightful ascendancy over her.

She used to take one down each week from Harrison to see me. She took an afternoon train arriving at 125th Street at 3 and went back on the 5:27.

She always came dressed carefully in traveling clothes with the ancient black leather Gladstone bag clutched in her hand. In it she brought me eggs and butter—such rich golden butter—and spinach. We had good talks and laughs. We got all smoothed out and happy from seeing each other. But then came the ordeal of catching the 5:27.

I used to drive over to the station with her, and we always had plenty of time for if we left my apartment at quarter to five we got to the 125th Street station at five minutes past five at the latest. Nevertheless as we drew near, a sensation of urgency seized her. "Here's the station," she cried. It was like being possessed. Her eyes changed; she no longer saw me. She said, "Goodbye, dear love," automatically; hurried out of the carriage, gripped that much-enduring black bag tight, and ran up the stairs. That long flight to the platform! It used to shake her all up to run, with fear clutching her: but this was a STATION.

She said to me afterwards when she was describing it all, that she used to feel only very callous people dared pretend to be calm in a station, abnormal creatures, who were certain to come to bad ends. "Lord help and save us," she said, "they probably missed their trains and killed themselves."

As she got to the top of the platform a train appeared, instantly. She tried to think of the fact that it was twenty minutes early, and going in the wrong direction, but it made such a noise she couldn't think. She just felt that if it once got away from her it was gone—it would never come back.

She called to the announcer: "Here, man! Man!" He wouldn't listen. Perhaps it would be safest to get aboard, to take no chances. There were the car-steps where all those people were.

So she and the black bag, which I really think shared her excitement, pushed madly to the steps of a car and attempted to climb up. But because it was so crowded, she had time to ask the brakeman, earnestly, if he were sure it was her train. And it gradually developed that this was *not* her train, but some huge impostor, some really impossible train that would not do at all. Several persons confirmed this. Officials. It was probably true. "You are *sure*, porter? Well. . . .

"I am going to Harrison. . . .

"What! I am on the *wrong platform!* My soul!"

She didn't quite cry, but the frightened little tears were right there, only she had no time to do anything but run back down those awful stairs. Other people were using them. She remembered that afterwards. But at the time she didn't see them. Her eyes were fixed, her legs blindly felt their way as though they were at a fire—if they would never be good for another step, no matter, they must simply race now.

Down those stairs and then up the other flight. Oh they were so long. *And all this time she could hear trains on the platform above!* Trains coming and going. They're *cruel*—when she was hurrying so. Oh please wait!

From then on she said she didn't know what she was doing. She got on the right platform, with about sixteen minutes to spare, but she couldn't collect herself. She was so shaken up.

Every cell in her body and brain was focused on one pressing need —that of catching that train—and convinced of the imminent danger of its getting away. In those sixteen minutes four or five trains came in, before hers, and in spite of all that anyone could say to her she tried to climb on each one. The announcer himself took pity on her, after her third excited attempt, and led her away, promising to point out her train when it came. But when the next wrong train appeared, she began trembling again, and felt she couldn't stand there, so as soon as his back was turned she made for it. And again was thrust back. She felt so ashamed! But not ashamed enough to stop trying.

The next though was hers.

Once on board, she soon relaxed, and recovered quite promptly. The blessed relief of having come safely through so many perils, and the sense of having triumphed over a large, loud, deceiving old train, were soothing enough to make up for her exertions. She had already turned her mind on the problem of telling Dennis, the gardener, just how much spinach she wanted to bring down to me the next week. Her agony she forgot, just as when a hypnotized person comes out of a trance in which he has suffered, he leaves all pain behind in a moment. It was sponged off the slate.

MOTHER AND THE
SERVANT PROBLEM

When old Margaret cooked for us, although there was not a great variety, what she cooked was just right. But Mother was not so successful with her waitresses. There is something about good service, at table, that adds to the pleasure of eating. Even the best of food, with bad service, isn't fun at all. That was only too often what happened at our house. Mother knew that Father valued good service, but because he yelled at her so much to economize, she did not know that he would probably have been willing to pay for it. Although she felt guilty when he criticized the way she ran the house, she was sure she did the best she could under the circumstances.

Most of the time she felt it was Father's fault that things didn't run smoothly. He made such a fuss, she said. But the fact was that she couldn't make a house run smoothly. It was not that she neglected it. She worked very hard at it and got all tired out. But what she loved to do was to make a house look pretty and home-like. She created a pleasant atmosphere by the way she arranged flowers and furniture, and she was always busy moving things around and planning new effects. She also worked hard planning the meals, or training green waitresses so that Father's dinner would be properly served. But training waitresses and planning meals was not her forte. So in a room with flowers and a pleasant look to it, we'd have dreadful scenes with Father red-faced and angry because his dinner never seemed just right.

One night we had a new waitress, of whom Mother had great hopes. But while serving Father she held a dish so high that he could not help himself. When he roared at her to put it down lower she began to tremble. After Father got hold of the spoon he held it in mid-air while he addressed himself to Mother.

"How many times," he said, "have I asked you not to engage a girl who doesn't even know how to hold a dish properly?"

"Clare," said Mother, "hush! Can't you see she is new and doing her best?"

"What I want," said Father, "is service."

He then felt better and helped himself calmly from the offending dish, immediately forgetting the waitress. He tried the food, found it good and started to enjoy it. Meanwhile the trembling girl walked toward Mother. Halfway there she broke down and ran out of the room sobbing.

Father turned in surprise. "What now?" he said, as she disappeared through the swinging door.

"Oh Clare," Mother wailed, "see what you've done."

The next day when a friend of hers came to call, Mother told her about this scene, and bemoaned the departure of the waitress. Her friend was a large commanding woman, who ruled her husband carefully but firmly. She nodded her head several times but said nothing until Mother sank back exhausted from her tale. "What you need," she told Mother impressively in her deep controlled voice, "is a housekeeper."

Mother said that a housekeeper was out of the question. She knew Mr. Day would never consider such a thing. Nevertheless her friend described in detail the peace that reigned in the homes that had housekeepers. And what was more astonishing, she knew the exact person to make Mother's home perfect.

By the time the afternoon was over, Mother could hardly wait for Father to come home so she could tell him all about the treasure she had engaged.

"Clare," she called, before he closed the front door, "come right up here. I want to talk to you."

Father was astonished. This was the time when she was generally so busy with the last minute details about the house or dressing that she was in no mood for talk. He stuck his cane in the tall pinkish-brown jar, carefully placed so that the large roses painted down one side showed to good effect. He then put

his hat on the closet shelf and his coat on its hanger. After he
shut the door carefully on them, he ran up the stairs, two at a
time.

"What is it, Vinnie? Is anything wrong?"

"Wrong, Clare? Why should anything be wrong?"

"You said you wanted to talk to me."

"Of course, I want to talk to you. Aren't you glad Mrs. Abbott
is coming to be our housekeeper and make everything pleasant
for you?"

"Mrs. Abbott! Who is Mrs. Abbott? And what, may I ask, is
she to make pleasant for me?"

"Why, the *house,* Clare. Don't shout so."

Father and Mother saw the house through different eyes. They
each felt strongly that it was their own home, but the idea that
it might be a common one had never entered their minds. Right
now Father began loudly: "This is my home and I won't have—"

"Of course, it's your home, Clare. I don't understand what
you are talking about."

"I'm saying I wish my home run with some regard for my
wishes."

"That's just what I was telling you, Clare," said Mother. "I
have just taken a lot of trouble so that all your wishes can be
taken care of perfectly."

"Since when has it been my wish to have a stranger thrust into
my home?"

"A housekeeper isn't a stranger, Clare," said Mother. And
quickly reminded him that if he did not hurry and change he
would be late for dinner.

After the first enthusiasm was over, Mother began to wonder
how it was going to feel to have her home reduced to perfect
order by some determined woman. She looked forward to Mrs.
Abbott's arrival so uneasily that when she came, Mother was
astonished to find her gentle and rather vague. Although there
was nothing really wrong with her clothing, somehow she gave an
effect of things being just askew. Also, her pale eyes never seemed
fixed in the direction in which they were looking. None of this

bothered Mother. She was so relieved that she was not to be ordered about in her home like the husband of her commanding friend. But on the other hand, she knew the situation was difficult and wondered if it might not really be better if Mrs. Abbott looked more like a general.

Father's reaction from the first—when he spoke to her at all —was to address her in a loud tone, as though she were across the street. If her replies were not satisfactory, as they generally weren't, he then spoke about her, as though she were not present. Mother could never quite make up her mind whether she wanted her to have more spunk or not. She felt that if Mrs. Abbott did talk back to Father there was no telling what he might do to her. Deep down inside her, Mother almost believed that it might even endanger Mrs. Abbott's life if she were to do anything so daring. However, as she didn't, Father declared again and again that she had no backbone; and that she was a pudding-head.

Mother dreaded the evenings when Father decided to go into the pantry to open a bottle of wine, because it seemed as though every time he did so Mrs. Abbott was sitting there at her table waiting for her meal to be brought to her. Father never waited until he got all the way back into the dining-room but, while the door was still open, demanded of Mother the reason why that woman was sitting around out there.

"For your comfort," Mother said.

"She's not doing anything for me," Father said, "she's not doing anything at all."

Mother felt that somehow this was all very annoying of Mrs. Abbott.

To make matters worse, Mrs. Abbott always saw the gloomy side of everything, which especially upset Mother when she was ill. For although naturally a buoyant person, she was highly susceptible, and needed bright, cheery people and gay flowers around her. Mrs. Abbott was anything but cheering.

As Mother began to feel better, she would send for Mrs. Abbott to see how the household affairs were going. Mother did so one June morning, when she had been ill with a cold, but was feeling stronger. Mrs. Abbott took quite a long time to come upstairs and Mother began to wish she had never sent for her. Just then Mrs. Abbott sidled vaguely into the room, her eyes fixed on the far corner. She made a little rush at Mother's bed as though to stand right by her head.

"Good heavens, Mrs. Abbott, don't stand where I can't see you. Go to the foot of the bed."

For a few moments they talked of household matters. But Mrs. Abbott kept stopping. Her eyes wandered to Mother and rested intently on her face. From time to time she shook her head. Once, right in the middle of a sentence she became silent, then leaned forward staring at Mother.

Mother became alarmed. "Mrs. Abbott," she said, "what is it?"

Mrs. Abbott looked at Mother and said in her simple way: "I think you look *sicker* than yesterday."

Mother jumped up in the bed. "Oh! My Lord, Mrs. Abbott, you must not talk that way." Feeling that maybe something dreadful really was the matter with her, Mother fell back on the pillows.

Mrs. Abbott continued to look at Mother without saying anything.

"What a way to tell anyone sick in bed that they look *sicker!*" Mother wailed.

Mrs. Abbott was frightened at Mother's vehemence, but she replied in a faint but defiant voice, "Well, I *do* think so."

Mother by this time was unable to lift her head. She turned and feebly closed her eyes. It did seem as though she felt worse.

"Go," she said in a voice almost as weak as Mrs. Abbott's. "Go back down in the kitchen. I am not well enough to talk any longer."

The main difficulty in dealing with Mrs. Abbott was that her mind wasn't steady or fixed. It had formed the habit of blowing around like the wind wherever it happened to list. She had no proper control over it. In fact, her mind controlled her. One morning, when Mother was saying urgently, "Now, Mrs. Abbott, you won't forget about that soap, will you?" I saw a vague look

float into Mrs. Abbott's wandering eye, and her mind snatched
her up, as it were, and deposited her at a distance. She stared at
the fireplace dreamily and said, "This isn't the right beach for
soap."

"What!" Mother demanded.

Mrs. Abbott came back with a start.

"What on earth are you talking about, Mrs. Abbott?"

Mrs. Abbott looked injured. "I didn't forget about the soap,
Mrs. Day, but it wasn't there."

"It is too!" Mother shrieked. "Park and Tilford's are *never*
out of Pears' soap! You haven't even got your hat on to go and
get it yet. What's the matter with you, Mrs. Abbott?"

Mrs. Abbott sighed and looked forgivingly, though vaguely,
at Mother, and went off to put on her hat.

An odd thing about this incident was that she then went to
Park and Tilford's and came carefully back with the soap. It
was always like that. At one moment she'd seem perfectly hopeless and the next she'd be as competent as anyone else. I didn't
believe she was really quite right in the head, but Mother said
she could be quite right enough if she wanted to, and that the
thing to do was to be firm with her. Somehow or other it worked.

Mother began to feel that she could relax, and enjoy her house.
She even made plans to do over the reception room. She had
never been satisfied with the way it looked. Now, as she stood at
the door, her hands parting the portieres, her head a little to one
side, she considered the changes. Every time she did this, her
feeling toward Mrs. Abbott warmed and she wished that she
felt a little less impatient with the poor woman.

"Clare," said Mother one evening, "don't you think I was
right to get Mrs. Abbott?"

Father had just lifted his glass of cognac. He set it down again.
Hard. He also laid down his book.

"If you want to know what I think about that woman, Vinnie—" he began.

"Hush," Mother implored him. "Hush, Clare, she might hear
you."

"Don't care if she does," said Father. "Might do her good. Last night I tried to tell her how I wanted my bacon, and do you know what she did the whole time I was telling her?"

"I don't know what she did, Clare," Mother said indignantly, "but I heard all the noise. And so did my friend Miss Wilkinson. I think she was really quite frightened. If Mrs. Abbott does not satisfy you, it's your own fault for shouting so much."

Father struck his fist on the arm of his chair. "When I can't talk in my own pantry—"

Just at this moment, Mrs. Abbott walked into the room. When she saw Father, her breath came in short gasps.

"Oh, Mrs. Day," she panted, "one of your friends called you up, er—she wants you should phone her but the name has deserted me."

Mother looked at her speechless for a second, then before Father could catch his breath, rushed at Mrs. Abbott, pushing her out of the room, talking all the while. "Now, Mrs. Abbott, that will do, if you have forgotten who called me I don't see what good it does to come rushing in at this time of night."

Mother had some friends, Mr. and Mrs. Robbins, in East Sixty-ninth Street, and she knew another lady, Mrs. Wrenn, who lived on Lexington Avenue. Mrs. Abbott used to get them mixed.

Although Mother had hundreds of friends, she had a feeling that it must have been one of those two that Mrs. Abbott meant. She disapproved so of Mrs. Abbott's mixing them up that she would not mention their names however.

"Now, Mrs. Abbott, you should not give me a long message to call someone and never be able to tell me who it is that I am supposed to call."

"Indeed, Mrs. Day, I do try, but somehow the name never seems to be here when I want to tell you."

"Mrs. Abbott," said Mother severely, "everyone can remember names if they just try. If you can't remember them like any ordinary person, why then keep something in mind about the names that you can remember them by."

For several days things really did seem to go better. Until one day Mrs. Abbott again had trouble with a message.

"What kind of name was it, Mrs. Abbott? I've told you and told you and told you that you simply must remember the name. It wasn't Mrs. Willets, was it?"

"No," Mrs. Abbott said faintly. "No, Mrs. Day, it was one of them birds." Tears came to her eyes and ran down her small earnest face. "And if it was the Wrenns or the Robbins I kinnot recall."

"Now, Mrs. Abbott," Mother said, "you're just being silly about this and you must stop it right now. It's utterly unnecessary to think of people's names in that way. Why, the next thing, you'll be getting all mixed up about Mrs. Crane, too."

Mrs. Abbott hadn't known till then that Mother's friends included Cranes too. She put her hand to her heart in alarm and backed out of the room.

A year later, as it happened, a gentleman from Michigan, Mr. Edward Sparrow, bought the house next door to ours, No. 41, and settled down there to live. Mrs. Abbott then completely gave up. From that time on, Mother said, she didn't even try to keep them straight. When any one of those four names was mentioned, Mrs. Abbott's mind fled.

One day she came stumbling and panting up the stairs so frightened she scarcely could speak. "Oh, Mrs. Day!" she gulped out. "Your friends' house is afire!"

"Whose house?" Mother demanded, getting up in a hurry.

Mrs. Abbott's eyes flickered and that troubled, evasive look appeared in them. "Why, you know who I mean, Mrs. Day. It's them Pidgeons!" she wailed.

Mother was beside herself. She hurriedly put on her hat and coat and went out on the steps. Mrs. Abbott ran out beside her and pointed triumphantly at a fireman coming out of the Sparrows'!

When, not long after this, Mrs. Abbott was called home to look after some sick relative, Mother said it was a mercy, for if she had stayed much longer Mother felt she would never be able again to see her friends as normal human beings.

Not long after Mrs. Abbott left, Mother decided that a well-trained butler and his wife wouldn't need looking after.

It was not easy to find a couple who could satisfy the family requirements. It might have been easier if Mother had not at last seen a use for the empty butler's room off the pantry. As there was space in it for only one narrow cot, this meant that the wife slept alone in her room on the fourth floor. But at length a French couple named Dominique and Henriette arrived at the house. They were a little old, but Henriette's cooking and Dominique's serving were perfect. It looked like a happy arrangement for nearly a month. By that time, however, Dominique had begun to be slack, the quick, careful manner he had had when he came was now gone and he was becoming more languid and weary every day.

Mother said he must be getting old. She had a little talk with Henriette about him. Henriette cried. She said, yes, she herself had seen this change and it frightened her. It was true that he was no longer young, but never had she seen Dominique look this way before.

He certainly looked bad. His face had become gray and he looked like a sick man. Finally he came to Mother and said that they must leave. Very politely, on leaving he explained that his room was of such a heat at night that his suffering had become unbearable.

Mother took this as a kind of impudence. Nevertheless, she went into Dominique's room, off the pantry. It was small and narrow, with a window high up. In the French fashion Dominique had kept this window tightly closed. There was also a large radiator. This feature Dominique had regarded as something mysterious and not to be touched. As we bought the city steam, it had poured liberally and steadily into his radiator night and day. In consequence of his French dislike of drafts and night air and his French distrust of mechanical arrangements, Dominique had spent his nights bathed in perspiration and in an atmosphere of a stoke-hold.

Mother tried to explain to Dominique what had happened, but Dominique felt that he had suffered a great deal and was completely convinced that his health had been permanently injured and that he and Henriette must go.

This discouraged Mother and Father with couples and with the French nation. They settled back into their old routine of cook and waitress.

At the end, even this became too much to contend with and the last waitress, Katherine, finally took charge of Mother and Father and the whole house. The dreams of perfect service were gone, for Katherine was independent and from New England. She spoke her mind on all occasions, particularly if she disapproved.

She browbeat both Mother and Father but served them, in her own way, devotedly. The three of them quarreled but underneath Mother and Father knew they had something on which they could depend.

MOTHER'S LAST HOME

Mother sometimes talked to Father about the advantages of living in an apartment. Father said it was all nonsense. A respectable man owned his own home and didn't go living around in a "hole in the air."

However, as time went on, more and more people they knew lived that way. Many of their conservative friends bought apartments, which Mother felt made things altogether different. She said so to Father one day, adding, "Bessie and Eustis have bought one."

"What the devil did they do that for?" Father asked.

"Why, to live in, Clare," said Mother. "And you'd be a lot more comfortable in an apartment, too," she added.

"I have told you over and over again that I don't want an apartment," said Father.

"But if you buy it, then it is your home just like a house," Mother insisted.

"It's a hole in the air just the same," Father replied, then after a moment added disgustedly, "a damned hole in the air."

Father died in his own house, but a few months afterwards Mother got rid of it, a largish house at 43 East Sixty-eighth Street, and bought herself an apartment at 1170 Fifth Avenue. It was just what she wanted. It was on the fifteenth floor; looking south and west, it was flooded with sunshine, and had a magnificent view all over Central Park and the Reservoir.

All the same, it was hard to leave 43. She had lived there a long time, and memories were strong. Also, as she was always unable to throw things away, when it came time to clear the house, every nook and corner was filled with tightly packed objects. All of these still clamored to be used. However, Mother

will give them something to talk about when they go back to Europe. It'll at least wake them up."

He couldn't take that view of it.

Later in the evening I heard Mother showing everyone the house, in relays. In her excitement she even showed *me* to two of them, Mr. Hunt and Mr. Clyde. Hunt was in a cloudy condition but kept clinging to a phrase he had found helpful—viz.: "No, really I should have thought it more than twenty-five feet wide."

"It's only twenty-five," Mother assured him. And Hunt turned confidentially to me, saying with a fixed smile that really he should have thought it considerably more than that. The—er—halls, you know. He waved his hand. "It's only twenty-five," Mother repeated, and carried him off to the third-floor bathrooms.

"Did you show the rest of the people the house?" I asked Mother the next morning.

"Yes," she said. "You know that horrid old man they dined with last night had shown them his, and I thought they might like to see what a really nice house was like."

The new apartment had a special aspect; it was a kind of toy place that she had ingeniously contrived to make into a home. So it was no wonder that a friend, calling there for the first time, had no sooner got into the living-room and started to make herself comfortable than she found herself hustled right back again to the elevator landing so that Mother could show everything straight from the beginning.

This landing had not seemed very big, but it had managed to absorb several large and elaborate pieces of Empire furniture decorously set off by two oversized steel engravings: one of "Prince Albert's Harriers," the other of a "Meeting of her Majesty's Stag Hounds on Ascot Heath."

Inside, all was rather dark and quiet, except for the loud tick-tick of the grandfather's clock. The hall and the living-room were papered in soft dark green. However the dining-room, opening off one end of the hall, had a strong rich, crimson-flowered, damask-like paper. It somehow was appropriate with the black heavily carved Jacobean furniture and dark woodwork to match. Taking up one whole side of the room were two glass-front china closets, rather like bookcases, where Mother kept her best gold china and Venetian glass. The sideboard, a massive structure, and the serving table were covered with silver pitchers, dishes, plates and platters, a coffee urn and a tea set.

One special feature of this room was a great mirror taken from 43 before the vandals had started work on the house, and set into the wall opposite the door. Not only was the long hall with its sofas and chairs and tables reflected in it, but also the living-room and a glimpse of the Park outside. Many guests narrowly escaped real injury when they bumped into the glass, thinking the apartment really did extend beyond. Mother was divided in her emotions between impatience at their stupidity, and gratification at the success of the illusion.

Mother had always had a blue room, and the one she had in the new apartment was far from being an exception. She said that she had never had a blue room with walls as blue as she wanted before; this blue was bright and strong and Mother liked it very much. The beds were brass and the furniture white. All the upholstery was of the same blue brocade as the curtains, a little greyish in color and woven with a minute leaf-pattern. Also the coverlet and bolster. The bolsters were hard round cylinders which lay precise and unyielding at the head of each bed, firmly repelling any person who was so badly brought up as to try to rest on a bed when it was made up. On the floor was a rather lightish blue carpet. On various pieces of furniture were blue candlesticks, dishes, boxes; and a blue carafe beside the bed was covered with bluebirds flying around it.

As Mother shepherded her visitor out of the room she always carefully lowered the window shades so that the sun should not fade the walls.

There was a middle room, but for some reason it had no hold on Mother's affections and she hardly showed it, but passed straight on to her bedroom.

She had always loved her bedroom at 43, and her main prob-

the intimate circle in the next, as ably as she did at 43 when the library was on the second floor and the reception room right at the front door. Without really taking her mind off her visitor, she could hear the pink porcelain clock ticking and she knew that it stood underneath the great Venetian glass mirror on the glass cabinet filled with its assortment of bric-à-brac and the porcelain figurines that made up the monkey orchestra. She could see from her armchair the two column-like porcelain lamps; one pink with a landscape painted on it, the other of blue Delft. Both of them had as shades round white porcelain globes. Grandma Day's vase with the doves on it was near the alabaster vase with the doves feeding out of it, a memento from Venice.

There was one great difference in this room from its predecessors. It was used. Mother loved to sit in one of the pink satin and gilt chairs by the window. With her feet on the little mahogany footstool and a book of poems resting in her lap, and her light lavender wool scarf thrown over her shoulders when it was a bit cool, she would watch the changing colors over the Reservoir and the lights begin to come on in Fifty-ninth Street and Central Park West.

However, Mother was usually active, and after she felt settled she sent out word she was again at home on Thursdays—wondering if people would come so far uptown. She need not have given it a thought for every Thursday saw a group sitting around the dining-room table, which had been set with a lace cloth, and at one end the tea-service. Mother poured, as she laughed, and got indignant, and told stories on herself and others with equal prodigality.

Katherine might be grumpy on other days, and set Mother's tray down wrong side to, as a sign of displeasure, or worse still a signal that she was about to retire into what Mother called "her spells" when she didn't speak. But on Thursdays she was always jocular and interested as she slipped in and out with hot water or more of her famous doughnut balls.

The dark side of life in the apartment consisted mainly in a kind of warfare with the people who lived on the roof. They seemed to Mother, who could hear them sing and jump, rather noisy. But their great sin came from their efforts to beautify their roof, where they made a garden which was larger than the drainage system could stand. The pink room and the red wallpaper in the dining-room suffered.

There was a great deal of talk but at last all was repaired. And just in time. For Mother was, for the first time in years, giving several big receptions. She had a new and rather young daughter-in-law, that winter. A challenge which Mother met with energy and interest; and solved by treating her as a new granddaughter.

All day long, on the great days, boxes of flowers came every few moments until the apartment was crowded with them. Mother got more and more excited by each arrival. Imported maids and Katherine got under one another's feet as they washed and stacked silver.

A little after four commenced the stream of ladies in black and purple satin, jangly with jet and jeweled lorgnettes. Around their necks were ermine tippets and their hats were of shining velvet and they nearly all wore ostrich plumes. Their husbands, when there were any, wore morning coats and striped trousers. An occasional daughter slipped unsubstantially in and then out again.

Mother sat enthroned in the living-room wearing a new royal purple velvet gown and carrying orchids in her left hand. By her side stood the new daughter-in-law in pale beige lace carrying an old fashioned bouquet of tea roses and forget-me-nots. There was punch, tea, coffee and chocolate, layer cakes, doughnuts, sandwiches, hot biscuits and brownies—in the dining-room.

Mother was in high feather, her voice carrying above the chatter as she sat there completely in her element greeting one old friend after another, until by seven-thirty at each reception, triumphant if exhausted, she had greeted, steered around, introduced and poked up more than a hundred persons.

It was the beginning of a gay and busy winter for Mother until one Thursday, late in January 1929. On that day there were fourteen people around the dining-room table, and Mother was gayer than ever, but afterwards felt a queer pain on her left side. On Friday she lay quiet and unlike herself in her room attended by Katherine. By Saturday, however, she was joking and nudging her doctor while telling him some mischievous story. Ten minutes later without ever having known she had the dreaded angina pectoris she died.

The following Monday, dressed again in her new velvet gown and surrounded by orchids, she seemed to receive for the last time the friends who crowded in to bid her farewell.